STUDYING PUBLIC POLICY:

Policy Cycles and Policy Subsystems

Michael Howlett
and
M. Ramesh

TORONTO NEW YORK OXFORD
OXFORD UNIVERSITY PRESS
1995

Oxford University Press
70 Wynford Drive, Don Mills, Ontario M3C 1J9

Oxford New York
Athens Auckland Bangkok Bombay
Calcutta Cape Town Dar es Salaam Delhi
Florence Hong Kong Istanbul Karachi
Kuala Lumpur Madras Madrid Melbourne
Mexico City Nairobi Paris Singapore
Taipei Tokyo Toronto

and associated companies in
Berlin Ibadan

Oxford is a trade mark of Oxford University Press

Canadian Cataloguing in Publication Data
Howlett, Michael Patrick. 1955–
    Studying public policy : policy cycles and policy subsystems

Includes bibliographical references and index.
ISBN 0-19-540976-0

1. Policy sciences. I. Ramesh, M., 1960–
II. Title.

H97.H69 1995   320'.6   C95-930959-4

Design: Brett Miller

■ Table of Contents

▌ List of Figures

▋ Acknowledgement

We benefited tremendously from the comments of the two reviewers nominated by the publisher. Their comments were detailed, extremely constructive, and set a high standard for us to follow.

The book also benefited from collaborative work done over the years with many colleagues who deserve credit for many of the ideas and insights developed in the book. Special thanks go to Colin Bennett of the University of Victoria, Evert Lindquist of the University of Toronto, Jim Bruton of Simon Fraser University, Jeremy Rayner of Malaspina University-College, and Alex Netherton of the University of British Columbia. Members of the Governance Research Group at Simon Fraser University—especially Paddy Smith, David Laycock, Laurent Dobuzinskis, and Steve McBride—also contributed to the book in many varied ways. Don Blake of the University of British Columbia, Keith Banting of Queen's University, and John Warhurst of the Australian National University have been a source of much inspiration—thank you. Thanks also go out to Bruce Doern, Vince Wilson, Richard Simeon, Richard Phidd, and Paul Pross who broke the ground this volume covers.

Funding for research upon which the book is based was provided from many sources. The B.C. Work Study Program provided funding which allowed us to employ Research Assistants on the project. Grants from the Dean of Arts at Simon Fraser University and funds from the SSHRC, NSERC, IDRC, NSF and CONACyT Tri-National Institute on Innovation, Competitiveness and Sustainability in the North American Region allowed us to work together at conferences in Wellington, New Zealand and Whistler, British Columbia.

Pat MacLean at SFU laboured mightily in proofing the bibliography and citations. At Oxford University Press, Brian Henderson started the project and supported us to the end. Phyllis Wilson ably managed the production process while Euan White and Ric Kitowski saw the book through to completion. And Olive Koyama did a great job at copy-editing.

A special note of thanks goes out to our students over the years in Vancouver, Victoria, Kingston, Singapore, Wellington and Armidale, all of whom provided a very critical audience without which the concepts in this book would not have emerged in the form that they did.

We would also like to thank the folks who wrote MacTCP, InterSLIP, NCSA Telnet, Eudora, Fetch, and the many other software programs that formed an intrinsic part of jointly authoring this book from opposite ends of the earth. It couldn't have been done without them.

On the family front, Alex, Anna Anamika, Becky, and Mandy have been a source of much joy and support over the years. The book is dedicated to them.

Part 1

INTRODUCTION

Chapter 1

Policy Science and Political Science

THE AMBITIONS OF POLICY SCIENCE

Policy Science is a relatively recent discipline, emerging in North America and Europe in the post-World War II era as students of politics searched for new understandings of the relationship between governments and citizens. Before that time, studies of political life tended to focus on the normative or moral dimensions of government or on the minutiae of the operation of specific political institutions. Scholars concerned with the normative or moral dimensions of government studied the great texts of western political philosophy, seeking insights into the purpose of government and the activities governments should undertake if their citizens were to attain the good life. These inquiries generated a rich discussion of the nature of society, the role of the state, and the rights and responsibilities of citizens and governments. However, the increasingly apparent gap between prescriptive political theory and the political practices of modern states led many to search for another method of examining politics, one which would reconcile political theory and practice through empirical analysis of existing polities.

Similarly, scholars interested in the institutions of government had been conducting detailed empirical examination of legislatures, courts, and bureaucracies while generally ignoring the normative aspects of these institutions. These studies of the formal structures of political institutions excelled in attention to detail and procedure but for the most part remained descriptive, failing to generate the basis for evaluating the strengths, weaknesses, or purposes of such structures. In the post-War era of de-colonization, the reconstruction of war-torn states, and the establishment of new institutions of international governance, students of politics sought an approach that would blend their studies with questions of justice, equity, and the pursuit of social, economic, and political development.[1]

In this context of change and reassessment, several new approaches to the study of political phenomena appeared. Some focused on the micro-level of human behaviour and the psychology of citizens, electors, leaders, and led.

Others concentrated on the characteristics of national societies and cultures; still others focused on the nature of national and global political systems. Most of these approaches—behaviourism, élite studies, political cybernetics, and studies of political culture—have come and gone as scholars experimented with each before grasping its limitations and abandoning it to search for something better.[2]

One approach, however, is still with us. Its focus is not so much on the structure of governments or the behaviour of political actors, or on what governments should or ought to do, but on what governments actually do. This is an approach which focuses on public policies and public policy-making, or, as its originators deemed it, *policy science*. Pioneered by Harold Lasswell and others in the United States and the United Kingdom, policy science was expected to replace traditional political studies, integrating the study of political theory and political practice without falling into the sterility of formal, legal studies.[3] Lasswell proposed that the policy science had three distinct characteristics which would set it apart from earlier approaches: it would be multi-disciplinary, problem-solving, and explicitly normative.

By multi-disciplinary, Lasswell meant that a policy science should break away from the narrow study of political institutions and structures and embrace the work and findings of such fields as sociology and economics, law and politics. By problem-solving, he envisioned a policy science adhering strictly to the canon of relevance, orienting itself towards the solution of real world problems and not engaging in purely academic and often sterile debates that, for example, characterized interpretation of classical and sometimes obscure political texts. By explicitly normative, Lasswell meant a policy science should not be cloaked in the guise of 'scientific objectivity', but should recognize the impossibility of separating goals and means, or values and techniques, in the study of government actions.

The general orientation toward the activities of governments suggested by Lasswell remains with us, and forms the subject matter of this book. However, the passage of time has led to some changes in the three specific components of the policy orientation he identified.[4] First, while the emphasis on multi-disciplinarity remains, there is now a large body of literature focused on public policy in general. Policy science is now very much in itself a 'discipline' with a unique set of concepts, concerns, and a vocabulary and terminology all its own. Although many of these concepts have been borrowed from other disciplines, when used in the context of studies of public policy they now have a somewhat particular meaning. Furthermore, the concept of multi-disciplinarity itself has now changed in the sense that the scholars are usually not concerned with whether they must borrow from other disciplines, but rather that they must be experts in at least two fields: the concepts and concerns of policy science, and the history and issues present in the substantive area of policy under examination.[5]

Second, over the past forty years the virtually exclusive concern of many policy scholars with concrete problem-solving has waned. At the outset it was hoped that studies of public policy-making and its outcomes would yield conclusions and recommendations directly applicable to existing social problems. Although laudable, this maxim foundered on the complexity of the policy process itself, in which governments often proved intractable and resistant to 'expert' advice on subjects with which they were dealing.[6] In the real world of public policy, technical superiority of analysis was often subordinated to political necessity.

Finally, the calls for the policy sciences to remain explicitly normative also changed over time, although rather less than have the other founding principles. For the most part, policy scholars have refused to exclude values from their analyses, and have insisted upon evaluating both the goals and the means of policy, as well as the process of policy-making itself. However, analysts' desire to prescribe specific goals and norms declined with increasing realization of the intractability of many public problems. Some investigators therefore now either evaluate policies in terms of efficiency or effectiveness, or use the record of policy efforts in an effort to establish whether governments have in practice been directing their activities towards the achievement of their stated goals.[7]

Some observers have been led to castigate the notion of a policy 'science' and to equate its promotion with an era of unrealized hopes and expectations for social engineering and government planning. Although sometimes justified by the inflated claims of individual studies, this criticism should serve as a warning against premature or ill-founded prescriptions or excessive conceptual sophistry, rather than as a rejection of the need to undertake systematic study of government actions. To the extent that the policy sciences have developed a significant body of empirical and theoretical studies into the activities of numerous governments around the globe, the early efforts and dicta of Lasswell and his followers remain valuable and continue to provide the foundation upon which the study of public policy is based.

DEFINITION OF PUBLIC POLICY

Among the many competing definitions of 'public policy', some are very complex, while others are quite simple. Despite their variations, they all agree on certain key aspects. They agree that public policies result from decisions made by governments and that decisions by governments to do nothing are just as much policy as are decisions to do something. In other respects, however, the competing definitions differ considerably. Three examples of widely-used definitions will suffice to convey the complex meaning of the term.

Thomas Dye offers a particularly succinct definition of public policy, describing it as 'Anything a government chooses to do or not to do'.[8] This formulation is perhaps too simple and fails to provide the means for conceptualizing public policy. It would include as public policy every aspect of governmental behaviour from purchasing or failing to purchase paper clips to waging or failing to wage nuclear war, and thus provides no means of separating the trivial from the significant aspects of government activities. Nevertheless, Dye's definition is not without merits.

First, Dye specifies clearly that the agent of public policy-making is a government. This means that private business decisions, decisions by charitable organizations, interest groups, individuals or other social groups are not public policies. When we talk about public policies we speak of actions of governments. Although the activities of non-governmental actors may and certainly do influence what governments do, the decisions or activities of such groups do not in themselves constitute public policy. How the medical profession interprets the causes of lung cancer and the solutions it proposes for reducing its incidence may have a bearing on what the government eventually does about the problem. However, the profession's proposed solution to the problem is not itself a public policy; public policy is the measure that a government actually takes.

Second, Dye highlights the fact that public policies involve a fundamental choice on the part of governments to do something or to do nothing. This decision is made by individuals staffing the state and its agencies. Public policy is, at its most simple, a choice made by government to undertake some course of action. A slightly more difficult concept to grasp is that of a 'non-decision': that is, the government's decisions to do nothing, or not to create a new program, or simply to maintain the *status quo*. These should be deliberate decisions, however, such as when a government decides not to increase taxes to make additional funds available for arts or health care. The fact we have the freedom to paint the interiors of our homes in colours of our choice, for example, does not mean that this is a public policy, because the government never deliberately decided not to restrict our options in this area.

William Jenkins' conceptualization of public policy is a bit more precise than the one offered by Dye. He defines public policy as 'a set of interrelated decisions taken by a political actor or group of actors concerning the selection of goals and the means of achieving them within a specified situation where those decisions should, in principle, be within the power of those actors to achieve'.[9] Jenkins views public policy-making as a process, unlike Dye who defines it as a choice (which presumes the existence of an underlying process but does not state that explicitly). Jenkins also explicitly acknowledges that public policy is 'a set of interrelated decisions'. Rarely does the government address a problem with a single decision; most policies involve a series of decisions, some of which may be inadvertent rather than deliberate. Thus a health policy really consists of a series of decisions related to addressing citizens' health problems. Often various decisions are made by different individuals and agencies within government, such as Departments of Health as well as Finance or Welfare and the various divisions and sections within them. To fully understand a government's health policy we need to take into account all the decisions of all the governmental actors involved in the financing and administering of health-related decisions.

Jenkins also improves upon Dye by suggesting that the question of a government's capacity to implement its decisions is also a significant consideration in the types of decisions it takes. He recognizes that there are limitations on governments which constrain the range of options they can choose from in a policy area. Internal and external constraints on government make public policy-making, and efforts to understand it, difficult indeed. The government's choice of a policy may be limited by, for instance, lack of resources or international and domestic resistance to certain options. Thus, for example, we will not understand health policy in many countries without recognizing the powerful, self-serving opposition that the medical profession is able to mount against any government's effort to cut health care costs by reducing the profession's income.

Jenkins also introduces the idea of public policy-making as goal-oriented behaviour on the part of governments, an idea which provides a standard by which to evaluate public policies. In this definition, public policies are decisions taken by governments which define a goal and set out the means to achieve it. Although this says nothing about the nature of the goals or the means involved, it provides several avenues for evaluating policies which are missing from Dye's definition. These include the relevance of the goal, the congruence of goal and means, and the degree to which the means ultimately succeed or fail to achieve the initial goal.

James Anderson offers a more generic definition, describing a policy as 'a purposive course of action followed by an actor or a set of actors in dealing with a problem or matter of concern'.[10] Anderson's definition adds two additional elements to those noted by Dye and Jenkins. First, it notes that policy decisions are often taken by sets of actors, rather than a sole set or actor, within a government. Policies are often the result of not only multiple decisions, but of multiple decisions taken by multiple decision-makers, often scattered throughout complex government organizations. Second, Anderson's definition highlights the link between government action and the perception, real or otherwise, of the existence of a problem or concern requiring action.

Within their limitations, any or all of these definitions serve to outline in a general sense what is a public policy. All illustrate that studying public policy in a particular area is a difficult task. It cannot be accomplished simply by going through the official records of government decision-making found in such forms as laws, acts, regulations, and promulgations. Although these are a vital source of information, public policies extend beyond the record of concrete choices to encompass the realm of potential choices, or choices not made.[11] Records of decisions do not reflect the unencumbered will of government decision-makers so much as the record of the interaction of that will with the constraints upon it at given historical, political, and social conjunctures.[12]

Simply describing a government's policy is nevertheless a relatively simple task compared to knowing why the state did what it did and assessing the consequences of its actions. Sometimes it may announce the reasons for making a decision, and that may indeed be the truth. However, often the government does not give any reason for making a decision; or when it does, the publicly avowed reason may not be the actual reason. In such situations it is left to analysts to determine why a particular alternative was chosen and, very often, why some other seemingly more attractive option was not selected. The tasks of understanding why a policy was not implemented as intended or evaluating the outcomes of a policy are no simpler. How analysts explain public policy and the aspects they emphasize depends on their frames of reference,[13] which in turn depends on their interests, ideologies, and experiences.

UNDERSTANDING PUBLIC POLICY

Public policy is a complex phenomenon consisting of numerous decisions made by numerous individuals and organizations. It is often shaped by earlier policies and is frequently linked closely with other seemingly unrelated decisions. As such, it poses grave difficulties for analysts, who, not surprisingly, have developed numerous ways of approaching the public policy process. Given the complexity of the task, most emphasize only a limited range of factors, even if they recognize the general need for a holistic approach encompassing the entire range of possible variables affecting governmental decision-making. In order to get a flavour of the many approaches to the subject that have been employed by various scholars, let us briefly survey some of the significant bodies of literature.

Examining the nature of the political regime—defined loosely as the organization of the political system—is one way of understanding the public policy-making process.[14] It is argued that public policies vary according to the nature of the political system and its links with the society. Some analysts in this view have even a narrower focus and concentrate only on the organization of the state itself in attempting to understand public policy-making.[15] However, classifying regime types can only be a starting point in public policy analysis because it tells us little about how the characteristics of the regime manifest themselves in individual policies. It merely tells us where to look for influences on government decision-making and what general relationships we can expect to find while studying a government's activities.

Another direction which many theorists have taken is to search for causal variables in public policy-making, or for what are sometimes referred to as policy determinants.[16] Analyses in this tradition concentrate on the question of whether public policies are determined by macro-level socio-economic factors or by micro-level behavioural elements, and a great deal of competing evidence has been gathered about the relationship between public policies and these and other characteristics of domestic societies and the international system.[17] Such studies are largely empirical and often quantitative in orientation. While their empirical focus has enhanced our understanding of public policies by dispelling common myths and assumptions about the nature of policy processes, they tend to lean towards general macro-level explanations and often fail to develop their arguments in the sectoral and temporal contexts in which most policies develop.

Yet another literature focuses on policy content. The approach is associated closely with scholars such as Theodore Lowi, who argued that the nature of the policy problem and the solutions devised to address it often determine how it will be processed by the political system. Thus whether the policy is primarily regulatory, distributive, redistributive, or constitutive in character determines how it will be dealt with. As Lowi put it, ultimately 'policy may determine politics' and not the other way around, as most analysts commonly suppose.[18] In a similar vein, James Q. Wilson has argued that the degree of concentration of costs and benefits of a policy shapes the type of political processes that will accompany it.[19] Lester Salamon has similarly argued that focusing on the nature of the policy tools or instruments governments have at their disposal to implement public policies is the best mode of analysis for understanding public policy.[20] While there is no denying that the nature of the problem has an effect on what can be done about it, it is often difficult to comprehend the nature of a policy problem and the patterns of costs and benefits that various solutions to it involve.

The fourth tradition concentrates on policy impact or outcomes. This literature assesses the direct and indirect effects of specific policies and tends to ignore both causal factors and the nature of the tools at the disposal of governments.[21] Their analyses focus on quantitative analyses of links between specific government programs and use techniques of statistical inference to attribute causal relations between different types of government activities. Among economists, such studies have examined a wide range of topics in the easily quantifiable realms of fiscal and industrial policy-making and topics such as the relations between government expenditures and corporate investment activity or labour migration. Since this approach focuses only on policy outputs, however, it can say very little about the policy process which led to those outputs.

These different literatures and traditions have existed, in part, due to the nature of the different communities of analysts working on public policy. Governments themselves have always been involved in the study of public policies, both their own[22] and those of other countries.[23] However, most of the literature on public policy has been generated by analysts working for non-governmental organizations. Some of these analysts work directly for groups affected by public policies, while others work for corporations, churches, labour unions, or whoever else employs them. There are also analysts who work for private 'think tanks' or research institutes, some of which have close ties with government agencies and pressure groups. Finally, some analysts work independently, many of them being associated with the university system.[24]

Analysts working in different organizations tend to have different interests in pursuing policy analysis. Analysts working for governments, groups, and corporations affected by public policies tend to focus their research on policy outcomes. They often have a direct interest in condemning or condoning specific policies on the basis of projected or actual impact on their client organization. Private think tanks and research institutes usually enjoy a fair amount of autonomy from governments, though some may be influenced by the preferences of their funding organizations. Nevertheless, they remain interested in the 'practical' side of policy issues and tend to concentrate either on policy outcomes or upon the instruments and techniques which generate those outcomes. Academics, on the other hand, have a great deal of independence and usually have no direct personal stake in the outcome of specific policies. They can therefore examine public policies much more abstractly than can members of the other two groups and, as such, tend to grapple with the theoretical, conceptual, and methodological issues surrounding public policy-making. Academic studies tend to look at the entire policy process and take into account a wide range of factors including policy regimes, policy determinants, policy instruments, and policy content.[25]

These differing degrees of neutrality and political interests have evolved into distinctions between 'policy study' and 'policy analysis' in the literature.[26] The former refers to study 'of' policy and the latter to study 'for' policy. Policy studies, conducted mainly by academics, relate to meta-policy and are concerned with understanding public policy processes. Policy analyses are, in comparison, pursued by government officials or think tanks and are generally directed at designing actual policies. The former are assumed to be descriptive and explanatory compared to the prescriptive orientation of the latter. While this distinction is worth keeping in mind, it should not be overstated. We cannot understand what the government ought to be doing (or not doing), as emphasized by the 'analysis' literature, unless we know what it can or cannot do, the concern of the 'studies' literature.

The existence of very separate traditions and literatures of inquiry into public policy has led to a plethora of studies suggesting sometimes conflicting conclusions about the public policy-making process. This fragmentation has burdened public policy analysis with an apparent complexity which can be bewildering to anyone approaching the discipline for the first time. This has resulted in efforts to reduce the complexity by synthesizing the diverse literatures on the subject.[27]

An Applied Problem-Solving Model of the Policy Process

One of the most popular means of simplifying public policy making has been to disaggregate the process into a series of discrete stages and sub-stages. The resulting sequence of stages is referred to as the 'policy cycle'. This simplification has its origins in the earliest works on public policy analysis, but has received somewhat different treatment in the hands of different authors. The different descriptions of the policy cycle put forward by several different authors and the common logic their models possess will be presented below. Later in the chapter, we will expand the simple model of the public policy cycle to include a wider range of factors affecting the overall policy process.

The idea of simplifying the complexity of public policy-making by breaking the policy-making process down into a number of discrete stages was first broached in the early work of Harold Lasswell.[28] Lasswell divided the policy process into seven stages: 1) Intelligence, 2) Promotion, 3) Prescription, 4) Invocation, 5) Application, 6) Termination, and 7) Appraisal.[29] In his view, the seven stages described not only how public policies were actually made, but how they should be made. The policy process began with intelligence gathering, that is, the collection, processing, and dissemination of information for those who participate in the decision process. It then moved to the promotion of particular options by those involved in making the decision. In the third stage the decision-makers actually prescribed a course of action. In the fourth stage the prescribed course of action was invoked; a set of sanctions was developed to penalize those who failed to comply with the prescriptions of the decision-makers. The policy was then applied by the courts and the bureaucracy and ran its course until it was terminated or cancelled. Finally, the results of the policy were appraised or evaluated against the aims and goals of the original decision-makers.

Lasswell's analysis of the policy-making process focused on the decision-making process within government and had little to say about external or environmental influences on government behaviour. It simply assumed that decision-making was limited to a presumably small number of participants staffing official positions in government. Another shortcoming of this model was its lack of internal logic, especially with reference to placing appraisal or evaluation after termination, since policies should be evaluated prior to being wound down rather than afterwards. Nevertheless, this model was highly influential in the development of a policy science. Although not entirely accurate, it did reduce the complexity of studying public policy by allowing each stage to be isolated and examined before putting the whole picture of the process back together.

Lasswell's formulation formed the basis for a model developed by Gary Brewer in the early 1970s. According to Brewer, the policy process was composed of six stages: 1) Invention/Initiation, 2) Estimation, 3) Selection, 4) Implementation, 5) Evaluation, and 6) Termination.[30] In Brewer's view, invention or initiation referred to the earliest stage in the sequence when a problem would be initially sensed. This stage, he argued, would be characterized by ill-conceived definition of the problem and suggested solutions to it. The second stage of estimation concerned calculation of the risks, costs, and benefits associated with each of the various solutions raised in the earlier stage. This would involve both technical evaluation and normative choices. The object of this stage is to narrow the range of plausible choices by excluding the unfeasible ones, and to somehow rank the remaining options in terms of desirability. The third stage consists of adopting one, or none, or some combination of the solutions remaining at the end of the estimation stage. The remaining three stages are those of implementing the selected option, evaluating the results of the entire process, and terminating the policy according to the conclusions reached by its evaluation.

Brewer's version of the policy process improved on Lasswell's pioneering work. It expanded the policy process beyond the confines of government in discussing the process of problem-recognition and clarified the terminology in use to describe the various stages of the process. Moreover, it introduced the notion of the policy process as an ongoing cycle. It recognized that most policies did not have a definite life cycle—moving from birth to death—but rather seemed to recur, in slightly different guises, as one policy succeeded another with only minor or major modification.[31] Brewer's insights inspired several other versions of the policy cycle to be developed in the 1970s and 1980s, the most well known of which were set out in popular textbooks by Charles O. Jones[32] and James Anderson.[33]

If a plethora of models of policy stages and their variants is to be avoided, however, it is necessary to clarify the logic behind the cycle model. In the works of Brewer, Jones, and others the operative principle behind the notion of the policy cycle is the logic of applied problem-solving, even though they themselves often do not state this logic clearly. The stages in applied problem-solving and its corresponding stages in the policy process are depicted in Figure 1.

 Figure 1.
Five Stages of the Policy Cycle and their Relationship to Applied Problem-Solving

Phases of Applied Problem-Solving	Stages in Policy Cycle
1. Problem Recognition	1. Agenda-Setting
2. Proposal of Solution	2. Policy Formulation
3. Choice of Solution	3. Decision-Making
4. Putting Solution into Effect	4. Policy Implementation
5. Monitoring Results	5. Policy Evaluation

In this model, *Agenda-Setting* refers to the process by which problems come to the attention of governments; *Policy Formulation* refers to the process by which policy options are formulated within government; *Decision-Making* refers to the process by which governments adopt a particular course of action or non-action; *Policy Implementation* refers to the process by which governments put policies into effect; *Policy Evaluation* refers to the processes by which the results of policies are monitored by both state and societal actors, the result of which may be re-conceptualization of policy problems and solutions.

The most important advantage of the policy cycle model as set out above is that it facilitates the understanding of public policy-making by breaking the complexity of the process into a limited number of stages and sub-stages, each of which can be investigated alone, or in terms of its relationship to any or all the other stages of the cycle. This aids theory-building by allowing numerous case studies and comparative studies of different stages to be undertaken. Another advantage of the model is that it permits examination of the role of all actors and institutions dealing with a policy, not just those governmental agencies formally charged with the task.

The principal disadvantage of this model is that it can be misinterpreted as suggesting that policy-makers go about solving public problems in a very systematic and more or less linear fashion.[34] This is obviously not the case in reality, as the identification of problems and the development and implementation of solutions is often an *ad hoc* and idiosyncratic process. Decision-makers often simply react to circumstances, and do so in terms of their interests and preset ideological dispositions.[35] Another problem with the model is that while the logic of the policy cycle may be fine in the abstract, in practice the stages are often compressed or skipped, or followed in an order unlike that specified by the logic of applied problem-solving. Thus the cycle may not be a single iterative loop, but rather a series of smaller loops in which, for example, the results of past implementation decisions have a major impact on future policy formulation, regardless of the specifics of the agenda-setting process in the case concerned. In short, there is often no linear progression of a policy as conceived by the model. Third, and perhaps most importantly, the model lacks any notion of causation. It offers no pointers as to what or who drives a policy from one stage to another, a matter of crucial interest to scholars working on the subject.

The weaknesses of the model underscore the complexity of the policy process as well as the need to develop better intellectual devices to facilitate its understanding. While the five-stage cycle model helps disaggregate the policy process, it does not well illustrate the nuances and complexities of public policy-making. A model is needed that delineates in greater detail the actors and institutions involved in the policy process, helps identify the instruments available to policy-makers, and points out the factors that may underlie the process and lead to certain policy outcomes. In the following sub-section we examine the aspects of public policy-making that an improved model of a policy cycle must take account of at the conceptual level.

Towards an Improved Model of the Policy Cycle

Over the past four decades scholars and analysts working towards developing a policy science have addressed a series of related questions about the policy process raised in numerous case studies, comparative studies, and conceptual and theoretical critiques. At a very general level, these questions are related to the roles of policy actors, the interests they pursue and the impact of the ideas that they hold on their actions; the nature of the instruments used to implement policies; and the impact of past experiences on the present and future behaviour of governments.

An improved model of public policy-making must be capable of identifying the actors involved in the policy process and the interests they pursue. Policy-making involves a multitude of actors, who may or may not have similar interests. They interact with each other in a countless number of ways in pursuit of their self-interest, and the result of their interaction is what public policy is about. But they are not completely independent and self-determining actors, since they operate within a set of existing social relations which serve to constrain their behaviour.

The context of societal, state, and international institutions and the values these institutions embody condition how a problem is defined, facilitate the adoption of certain solutions to it, and prohibit or inhibit the choice of other solutions. Similarly, the set of ideas and beliefs or the 'discourse' surrounding a policy problem also serves to constrain policy actors. While there will always be conflicting interpretations of problems, almost every problem is characterized by a surprising degree of agreement on its gravity and the limited number of options open for solving it. Finally, the range of instruments available to policy-makers also serves to constrain or limit their choices. Different problems permit the use of different instruments, not all of which are completely substitutable. Until we know the instruments that are available for each task, we will have difficulty knowing why a certain instrument was chosen to implement a policy.

While their activity is conditioned by the nature of the problem under consideration and the larger political, economic, institutional, and ideological context in which they operate, policy actors are not entirely without options. Various contingencies and tactical alliances among policy actors enable them to overcome or at least mitigate the limitations they work under. But even here, the alliances and choices before policy-makers may be constrained by past choices and decisions. It is often the case that in the past policy-makers have discussed the problem and done something about it, or decided deliberately not to do anything about it. The lessons that policy-makers draw from past experiences with addressing problems can shape what views they hold and the actions they take in the present.

An improved model of the policy process must be able to deal with these complexities. Our text retains the basic elements of the policy cycle model in order to simplify the subject matter, and structure its analysis. But it seeks to capture the complexities by building deeper questions into the model and draws upon the terms and concepts of contemporary political science in answering them. Analysing each of the five stages in the public policy process involves addressing a distinct set of questions about actors, institutions, instruments, and discourses along the lines outlined above. In this way, an improved model of the policy process can emerge in which each stage will contain not simply a description of the activities which occur at that point in the process, but also an outline of a set of variables affecting activity at that stage and hypotheses about the relationships existing among the variables. The framework draws upon many strands in the literature and enables students to cover a broad range of material, while maintaining coherence in the analysis. It is not intended to predispose students towards particular conclusions, but to help identify the key variables which affect each stage of the public policy-making process.

Such a line of analysis would help explain why governments tend to develop policies in particular sectors or deal with particular types of issues in a characteristic fashion or 'policy style' related to the context within which they work. Significant aspects of this style are related to the nature of the actors involved in each decision and the state of knowledge or belief about the policy problem in question found among the state and societal actors in the policy process.

By examining each stage of the policy cycle with care and elaborating upon the variables which affect it, it is possible to develop a taxonomy of typical policy styles with relevance to multiple areas of government activity. Such a model contributes to the development of a policy science by providing a much better understanding of why governments choose to do what they do or do not do.

The purpose of this book is to develop an analytical framework that will assist students in studying public policy. It seeks to achieve this objective by providing an examination of the broad approaches to the subject matter, and inventories of the relevant policy actors, institutions, and instruments which are involved in public policy-making. It then moves on to break down the policy process into sub-processes or sub-stages and answer the types of questions posed above. It concludes with a general commentary on studying public policy.

Part 1 provides a general introduction to the discipline. Chapter One has briefly charted the development of public policy as an academic discipline and explained what is generally meant by the term. It has proposed a five-stage model of the policy process and framed research questions for each stage. Chapter Two will examine in more detail the commonly-used approaches to public policy, emphasizing those employed by economists, political scientists, sociologists and others who emphasize interests in the public policy process. The potential and limitations of each approach are discussed briefly.

Part 2 describes the institutional parameters within which policies are made, the nature of the actors who make the policies, and the instruments the actors have at their disposal for implementing policies. Chapter Three discusses the various state and societal actors and institutions that play a salient role in public policy-making. It utilizes the concept of a policy subsystem to capture the complex links between state and societal actors involved in public policy-making. Chapter Four describes the characteristics of the instruments available to the government for implementing policies. It develops a scale of instruments based on the range of possible means by which goods and services of any kind can be delivered, from the use of voluntary or community services to direct delivery by state employees. Each chapter not only inventories the range of institutions, actors and instruments which can affect policy making, but also establishes the difficulties of assessing and predicting which institutions, actors, and instruments will actually be involved in specific policy-making instances.

Part 3 sets out a schema for conceptualizing the policy process in order to allow finer levels of analysis. Each of Chapters Five to Nine examines a critical component or sub-stage of the public policy process, including how and why public concerns make their way onto the government's agenda; how and why some individuals and groups enjoy special input into the formulation of governmental policy options; how and why governments typically decide on a specific course of action; why governments utilize the types of policy instruments that they do; and how their actions and choices are evaluated.

Finally, Part 4 discusses the conclusions from the study in the context of the relationships between ideas, interests, and institutions in public policy-making. Chapter Ten sets out the general pattern of evolution of policies in many policy sectors, establishes a taxonomy of typical policy styles, and establishes the reasons why policies tend to develop and change through a process of 'punctuated equilibria' or 'paradigm shifts'. Chapter Eleven points out the need to continue developing and testing policy theory if the aims of the policy science are to be realized.

NOTES

1   Lawrence M. Mead, 'Policy Studies and Political Science', *Policy Studies Review* 5 (1985): 319-35.
2   Alan C. Cairns, 'Alternative Styles in the Study of Canadian Politics,' *Canadian Journal of Political Science* 7 (1974): 101-34.
3   Harold D. Lasswell, 'The Policy Orientation' in D. Lerner and H. D. Lasswell (eds), *The Policy Sciences: Recent Developments in Scope and Method* (Stanford: Stanford University Press, 1951): 3-15.
4   Peter DeLeon, 'Trends in Policy Sciences Research: Determinants and Developments', *European Journal of Political Research* 14 (1986): 3-22; Peter DeLeon, *Advice and Consent: The Development of the Policy Sciences* (New York: Russell Sage Foundation, 1988); Susan B. Hansen, 'Public Policy Analysis: Some Recent Developments and Current Problems', *Policy Studies Journal* 12 (1983): 14-42.
5   Charles W. Anderson, 'The Place of Principles in Policy Analysis', *American Political Science Review* 73 (1979): 711-23.
6   Aaron B. Wildavsky, *Speaking Truth to Power: The Art and Craft of Policy Analysis* (Boston: Little Brown, 1979).
7   On the difficulties encountered by a policy science see George D. Greenberg et al., 'Developing Public Policy Theory: Perspectives from Empirical Research', *American Political Science Review* 71 (1977): 1532-43, and Peter DeLeon, 'Reinventing the Policy Sciences: Three Steps Back to the Future', *Policy Sciences* 27 (1994): 77-95.
8   Thomas R. Dye, *Understanding Public Policy* (Englewood Cliffs, NJ: Prentice-Hall, 1972): 2.
9   William I. Jenkins, *Policy Analysis: A Political and Organizational Perspective* (London: Martin Robertson, 1978).

10   James E. Anderson, *Public Policy Making: An Introduction*, 3rd ed. (Boston: Houghton Mifflin Company, 1984): 3.

11   Michael Howlett, 'Acts of Commission and Acts of Omission: Legal-Historical Research and the Intentions of Government in a Federal State', *Canadian Journal of Political Science* 19 (1986): 363-71.

12   Ira Sharkansky, 'Constraints on Innovation in Policy Making: Economic Development and Political Routines' in Frank Marini (ed.), *Toward a New Public Administration: The Minnowbrook Perspective* (Scranton: Chandler, 1971): 261-79.

13   Davis B. Bobrow and John S. Dryzek, *Policy Analysis by Design* (Pittsburgh: University of Pittsburgh Press, 1987).

14   See, for example, B. Guy Peters, John C. Doughtie, and M. Kathleen McCulloch, 'Types of Democratic Systems and Types of Public Policy', *Comparative Politics* 9, (1977): 327-55; Joel D. Wolfe, 'Democracy and Economic Adjustment: A Comparative Analysis of Political Change' in Richard E. Foglesong and Joel D. Wolfe (eds), *The Politics of Economic Adjustment* (New York: Greenwood Press, 1989): 153-86; Peter A. Hall, *Governing the Economy: the Politics of State Intervention in Britain and France* (Cambridge: Polity Press, 1986).

15   See Theda Skocpol, 'Bringing the State Back In: Strategies of Analysis in Current Research' in Peter B. Evans, Dietrich Rueschemeyer, and Theda Skocpol (eds), *Bringing the State Back In* (New York: Cambridge University Press, 1985): 3-43.

16   Joyce M. Munns, 'The Environment, Politics, and Policy Literature: A Critique and Reformation', *Western Political Quarterly* 28 (1975): 646-67.

17   Stuart H. Rakoff and Guenther F. Schaefer, 'Politics, Policy, and Political Science: Theoretical Alternatives', *Politics and Society* 1 (1970): 51-77.

18   Theodore J. Lowi, 'Four Systems of Policy, Politics and Choice', *Public Administration Review* 32 (1972): 298-310.

19   James Q. Wilson, 'The Politics of Regulation' in J.W. McKie (ed.), *Social Responsibility and the Business Predicament* (Washington: Brookings Institution, 1974): 135-68.

20   Lester M. Salamon, 'Rethinking Public Management: Third-Party Government and the Changing Forms of Government Action', *Public Policy* 29, 3 (1981): 255-75.

21   For a concise introduction to this approach, see David L. Weimer and Aidan R. Vining, *Policy Analysis: Concepts and Practice* (Englewood Cliffs, NJ: Prentice Hall, 1992).

22   H.G. Rogers, M.A. Ulrick, and K.L. Traversy, 'Evaluation in Practice: The State of the Art in Canadian Governments', *Canadian Public Administration* 24, 3 (1981): 371-86.

23   Richard Rose, 'What is Lesson-Drawing?', *Journal of Public Policy* 11 (1991): 3-30.

24   Leslie A. Pal, *Public Policy Analysis: An Introduction* (Scarborough: Nelson, 1992).

25   I. Gordon, J. Lewis, and K. Young, 'Perspectives on Policy Analysis', *Public Administration Bulletin* 25 (1977): 26-30.

26   On this distinction see Stephen Brooks and Alain-G. Gagnon (eds), *Social Scientists, Policy, and the State* (New York: Praeger, 1990).

27   William N. Dunn, 'Methods of the Second Type: Coping with the Wilderness of Conventional Policy Analysis', *Policy Studies Review* 7 (1988): 720-37.

28   Harold D. Lasswell, *The Decision Process: Seven Categories of Functional Analysis* (College Park: University of Maryland, 1956).

29   Harold D. Lasswell, *A Pre-View of Policy Sciences* (New York: American Elsevier, 1971).

30   Garry D. Brewer, 'The Policy Sciences Emerge: To Nurture and Structure a Discipline', *Policy Sciences* 5 (1974): 239-44.

31 Garry Brewer and Peter DeLeon, *The Foundations of Policy Analysis* (Homewood: Dorsey, 1983).

32 Charles O. Jones, *An Introduction to the Study of Public Policy* (Monterey, CA: Brooks/Cole, 1984).

33 Anderson, *Public Policy Making*.

34 For a critical evaluation of the policy cycle model, see Hank C. Jenkins-Smith and Paul A. Sabatier, 'The Study of the Public Policy Processes' in Paul A. Sabatier and Hank C. Jenkins-Smith (eds), *Policy Change and Learning: An Advocacy Coalition Approach* (Boulder: Westview, 1993): 1-9.

35 Deborah A. Stone, *Policy Paradox and Political Reason* (Glenview: Scott, Foresman, 1988); Laurence H. Tribe, 'Policy Science: Analysis or Ideology?', *Philosophy and Public Affairs* 2 (1972): 66-110.

FURTHER READING

Charles W. Anderson, 'The Place of Principles in Policy Analysis', *American Political Science Review* 73, 3 (1979): 711-23.

Peter DeLeon, *Advice and Consent: The Development of the Policy Sciences*, New York: Russell Sage Foundation, 1988.

Hank C. Jenkins-Smith and Paul A. Sabatier, 'The Study of the Public Policy Processes', pp. 1-9 in Paul A. Sabatier and Hank C. Jenkins-Smith (eds), *Policy Change and Learning: An Advocacy Coalition Approach*, Boulder: Westview, 1993.

Harold D. Lasswell, 'The Policy Orientation', pp. 3-15 in D. Lerner and H.D. Lasswell (eds), *The Policy Sciences: Recent Developments in Scope and Method*, Stanford: Stanford University Press, 1951.

Theodore J. Lowi, 'Four Systems of Policy, Politics and Choice', *Public Administration Review* 32, 4 (1972): 298-310.

Lawrence M. Mead, 'Policy Studies and Political Science', *Policy Studies Review* 5, 2 (1985): 319-35.

Deborah A. Stone, *Policy Paradox and Political Reason*, Glenview: Scott, Foresman, 1988.

Douglas Torgerson, 'Between Knowledge and Politics: Three Faces Of Policy Analysis', *Policy Sciences* 19, 1 (1986): 33-59.

Laurence H. Tribe, 'Policy Science: Analysis or Ideology?', *Philosophy and Public Affairs* 2, 1 (1972): 66-110.

Aaron B. Wildavsky, *Speaking Truth to Power: The Art and Craft of Policy Analysis*, Boston: Little-Brown, 1979.

Chapter 2

Approaches to Public Policy

CONCEPTUAL ISSUES

As Peter DeLeon has noted, policy studies have a long history and a short past; that is, government policies have been a concern of numerous studies over the past millennia, even though their systematic examination dates back only several decades.[1] Indeed, one of the difficulties encountered in studying public policy-making is the range of various approaches, originating in various schools of academic thought, that have been brought to bear on the subject. In this chapter we will outline the main economic and political approaches to the study of public policy, point out their strengths and weaknesses, and suggest ways in which public policy study can profit from the insights they offer while avoiding unnecessary conceptual or theoretical complexity.

First, we should note that there are different types or orders of theory that attempt to explain different things, and we must ensure that we are comparing comparable categories—apples with apples rather than apples with oranges, so to speak—in our theoretical discussion. Second, if all the nuanced variations are considered, there is an almost infinite variety of theories, and the examination of each in one chapter is clearly an impossible task. We will therefore restrict our comments to comparisons with several representative samples, chosen on the basis of their characteristic basic unit of analysis and their general approach to theory construction.

According to these criteria, there are six categories of theories. These theories differ according to whether they develop their insights in a deductive or an inductive manner, and whether they focus their attention on individuals, groups, or institutions. Deductive theories begin from a relatively small number of basic postulates or assumptions accorded universal status and then apply these assumptions to the study of specific phenomena. Inductive theories, on the other hand, begin with observations of specific phenomena and attempt to derive generalizations from these observations which can be combined into more general theory. Theories focusing on individuals interpret all political phenomena in terms of the interests and actions of individuals. Group theories explain the same in terms of interaction among and between social groups. Finally, there are theories that focus on organizations or institutions in their explanation of political phenomena. Representatives of the basic types of general theory classified according to units of analysis and method are set out in Figure 2.

Figure 2.
A Taxonomy of General Approaches to Political Phenomena

		Method of Theory Construction	
		Deductive	Inductive
Fundamental Unit of Analysis	Individual	*Public Choice*	*Welfare Economics*
	Group	*Marxism*	*Pluralism/Corporatism*
	Institutions	*Neo-Institutionalism*	*Statism*

DEDUCTIVE THEORIES

There are many adherents to the deductive approach, and many nuanced versions of its application to specific political phenomena. With respect to understanding public policy-making, however, three general sub-types of this approach are discernible, depending on the unit of analysis utilized: public choice, class analysis, and neo-institutionalism.

Public Choice

One approach to public policy utilizing individuals as the basic unit of analysis that has received a great deal of attention in recent years is the 'Public Choice' theory, named after the Institute for the Study of Public Choice at Virginia Polytechnic University where many scholars who developed the approach worked.[2] It is an application of the principles of neo-classical economics to political behaviour. The chief such assumption is that political actors, like economic ones, act rationally to maximize their utility (satisfaction) and that the only political actor that counts is the individual. As James Buchanan, one of the founders of the theory and the first among them to win a Nobel Prize (for Economics), puts it: 'In one sense, all public choice or the economic theory of politics may be summarized as the "discovering" or "re-discovering" that people should be treated as rational utility maximizers, in all of their behavioural capacities.'[3]

In the public choice approach it is assumed that individual political actors (be they policy-makers or voters) are guided by self-interest in choosing the course of action which is to their best advantage.[4] This simple assumption about the basis of human behaviour leads public choice theorists to a complex series of related propositions which they use to explain various aspects of politics and public policy-making. It has been applied to studies of voting behaviour,[5] the relationship between political and economic systems,[6] the nature of individual and collective decision-making behaviour,[7] and the structure and institutions of government, including bureaucracies,[8] legislatures,[9] political parties,[10] and constitutions.[11]

Voters are deemed to vote for parties and candidates that will best serve their interest. Politicians are seen as constantly vying for election in order to promote their interests in the income, power, and prestige derived from being in office, and offer policies that will win voters' support. Political parties are seen to operate in much the same way as politicians, devising policy packages that will appeal to voters. Bureaucrats' self-interest leads them to maximize their bureau's budget because larger budgets are a source of power, prestige, perks, and higher salaries. The bureaucrats are largely successful in realizing their interest because, as monopoly suppliers of unpriced goods and services, they face no competition and because of the fact that citizens and elected officials lack the expertise to monitor their activities. Peter Self succinctly summarizes the theory as follows:

> Following this approach, voters can be likened to consumers; pressure groups can be seen as political consumer associations or sometimes as co-operatives; political parties become entrepreneurs who offer competing packages of services and taxes in exchange for votes; political propaganda equates with commercial advertising; and government agencies are public firms dependent upon receiving or drumming up adequate political support to cover their costs.[12]

The public choice conception of the role of voters, parties, politicians, and bureaucrats leads to the conclusion that voters constantly seek more programs from the government, constrained only by their willingness to pay taxes, and that the politicians, parties, and bureaucrats are willing to supply the programs because of their own self-interest in power, prestige, and popularity. The result is a constant increase in the level of state intervention in the economy and society, often in the form of a 'political-business cycle'. That is, democratic governments operate in a form of perpetual electoral campaign in which the types of decisions they take will vary according to the timing of the electoral cycle, with popular decisions taken before election and unpopular ones after.[13]

Public policy-making in this view is thus simply a process of the gradual extension of state provision of goods and services to the public. The general conclusion public choice theorists draw from their analysis is that there is a need to develop institutions that will curb the sort of utility maximization that serves the interests of particular individuals while adversely affecting the society as a whole. According to Buchanan, public choice theory does not lead to the conclusion that all collective action, all government action, is necessarily undesirable. It leads, instead, to the conclusion that because people will tend to maximize their own utilities, institutions must be designed so that individual behavior will further the interests of the group, small or large, local or national. The challenge to us is one of constructing, or re-constructing, a political order that will channel the self-serving behavior of participants towards the common good in a manner that comes as close as possible to that described for us by Adam Smith with respect to the economic order.[14]

In this view, the mechanism of utility maximization that promotes general good in the market assumes a decidedly harmful form in the political arena. This leads public choice theorists to reject most of the policy analyses and pre-scriptions generated by other economists which take a more sanguine view of government activity.[15] They tend to argue that government intervention in the affairs of society should be limited to supplementing the market by enforcing and creating property rights where these are weak or non-existent so that mar-ket forces can operate and allocate resources in a manner beneficial to the whole society.

The simplicity and logical elegance of the theory, along with the mathe-matics and the impressive tables that accompany studies within this frame-work, mask its holes.[16] First of all, the theory is a simplification which does not accord with empirical reality. Many political activities are undertaken for sym-bolic or ritualistic reasons; to treat them as goal-oriented behaviour directed at utility-maximization is to underestimate the complexity of politics that sur-rounds public policy-making. Second, because of its over-simplification of the subject matter it describes, the theory has poor predictive capacity. There is no empirical proof for its prediction that governments functions will grow inex-orably because of the competitive dynamics of democracy. If anything, in most industrialized countries in recent times government expenditure has been cut back, or at least not expanded: how and why this occurs is virtually inexplica-ble within a public choice framework of analysis.[17] Third, and again related to its faulty empirical dimension, the theory conceives of party politics as if the contest was always between two parties, thus allowing voters to choose between two clearly definable alternatives. In reality, many democracies are multi-party systems in which parties have to form legislative coalitions, a prac-tice which does not permit a neat dichotomy of choices for voters since elec-toral promises may be over-ridden by post-election legislative deal-making. Fourth, the theory has little to say about policy-making in non-democratic sys-tems that do not rely on free elections, a central assumption of the model. Fifth, the theory, despite its pretensions towards institutional design, disregards or underestimates the effects of institutional factors in shaping actors' preferences. While some recent public choice theorists recognize the constraining effects of institutions on actors' behaviour,[18] most tend to regard the institutions themselves as changeable according to the actors' preferences. The theorists in this tradition are unwilling to recognize fully the durability of institutions and the pervasive impact they have on public policy. Sixth, regardless of the Public Choice theorists' insistence that their analysis is 'positive' and 'value-free', the theory is explicitly normative and seeks to promote a particular vision of orthodox liberalism (also called neo-conservatism or neo-liberalism) which would promote markets wherever possible and severely restrict the scope for government activity.

Class Theories

Class theories are essentially group theories in that they accord primacy to collective entities in their analyses, but unlike inductive group theory they tend to define their units of analysis in 'objective' terms. That is, class theories ascribe group membership on the basis of certain observable characteristics of individuals, whether or not the individuals involved see themselves in those terms. Class membership is usually determined by the presence or absence of certain characteristics, usually (but not always) related to the economy. According to Stanislaw Ossowski, 'class' refers to: 'Groups differentiated in various ways within a more inclusive category, such as the category of social groups with common economic interests, or the category of groups whose members share economic conditions which are identical in a certain respect.'[19] While there are several types of class analysis,[20] we shall concentrate on the 'marxist' variety, which is by far the most well known and theoretically developed.

The various writings of Karl Marx exhibited somewhat different notions of class. However, the one developed in *Manifesto of the Communist Party* is the best known. Here Marx argued that each society has a dichotomous class structure with two classes contesting political and economic power. In his material conception of history, human society has passed through a number of distinct stages ('modes of production'), each of which has a distinct set of technological conditions of production ('means of production') and a distinct manner in which the various actors in the production process relate with each other ('class structure' or 'relations of production').[21] Each mode of production entails a particular class system, which is ultimately determined by ownership (or non-ownership) of the means of production.

In the logic of this model, each mode of production develops a dichotomous class system consisting of those who own the means of production and those who must work for the owners, and the relationship between the two groups is inherently conflictual. Slaves battled slave-owners in slave societies; serfs struggled with landlords in feudal society, and workers struggle with owners in capitalist society. The continued class struggle leads to eventual collapse of the mode of production and its replacement with another mode, which is itself eventually replaced by yet another system. However, in practice, Marx expected that a dichotomous class system would occur only for a brief period at the tail-end of a mode of production, although it would be possible to see its gradual evolution over time as a mode of production matured and developed. At other points in time, modes of production would have more complex class structures in which multiple classes would exist.[22] The term often utilized to capture the complexities of actual multiple class structures as found in practice is 'social formation'.[23]

Class theories interpret public policies in capitalist societies as reflecting the interests of the capitalist class. The capitalists' dominance of the base—that is, the economy—affords them control over the state and what it does. Indeed according to Marx the state is merely an instrument in the hands of the capitalists which is used for the purposes of maintaining the capitalist system and increasing profits ('surplus value'), necessarily at the expense of labour.

Given its deductive nature, analysis of public policy from a marxist perspective usually takes the form of demonstrating how a particular policy serves the interests of capital, which is assumed as a proof that the latter used the state to further its interest (described as *instrumental view of the state* in the marxist literature). Such an instrumentalist line of analysis is problematic on two counts. First, even if it were true that a policy serves the interest of capital, it cannot be concluded *ipso facto* that the policy was enacted at the behest of capital. To show this, one would have to demonstrate that capitalists issued instructions which were faithfully carried out by state officials. Second, and more importantly, this approach cannot explain policies which are adopted over the opposition of capitalists. In most capitalist states, for instance, the adoption of social welfare policies was vehemently opposed by many capitalists, something that cannot be explained from this perspective. The recognition of this theoretical problem forced a re-appraisal of the role of the state in marxist theory.[24]

To account for the state's devising of policies opposed by capital, the notion of 'relative autonomy' of the state was developed by Neo-Marxists. While numerous Neo-Marxists are associated with this line of reinterpretation, the view offered by Nicos Poulantzas in the early 1970s has been perhaps the most prominent.[25] Poulantzas argued that conflicts among the various fractions of capital, coupled with the existence of a bureaucracy staffed by individuals drawn from non-capitalist classes, permit the state some level of autonomy from capital. This autonomy, in turn, allows the state to adopt measures favourable to the subordinate classes if that is found to be politically unavoidable or necessary for promoting the long-term interests of capital in social stability.

While such measures may adversely affect the short-term interests of capital, and may even be vehemently opposed by capitalists, they are always in their long-term interest. This is because the structure of capitalism requires that certain essential functions be performed by the state if capitalism is to survive. Such functions include enforcing property rights, maintaining peace and order, and promoting conditions favourable to continued accumulation of profits. In this 'structural' version of Neo-Marxism, policy-making is still viewed as serving the interest of capital, but not in the same instrumental sense as conceived by early Marxists.

Although this structural form of Neo-Marxism is a significant advance on the earlier class theories of the state and its policies, its reliance on functional determinism—that the state performs functions necessary to perpetuate capitalism—has led to criticisms that it is too simplistic.[26] To say that whatever the state does must be, *a priori*, in the long-term interest of capital is overly deductive. Under similar circumstances, different capitalist states adopt different measures, indicating that there must be factors other than functional imperatives determining state action.

To overcome the problems noted by critics, some Neo-Marxists explicitly recognize the importance of political factors in determining policies, while still adhering to the fundamentals of marxist class analysis. The role of working-class parties operating through normal political channels and trade unions is especially emphasized as a key factor in shaping public policies. The rise of the welfare state, for example, is explained not as a direct response to the needs of capital, but as the result of political pressures exerted by the working class.[27] The structural imperatives of capitalism are not ignored, however, because they are said to impose limits on what the state can do in response to working-class demands. The welfare state that was established by capitalist states in response to working-class demands was designed, it is argued, in a manner that did not undermine fundamental property rights or profits. This is by far the most sophisticated example of class analysis of public policy-making.

Nevertheless, class analysis continues to suffer from severe problems. The first problem concerns the difficulty of determining what exactly is a class and what is not.[28] Marxists sometimes talk in terms of bourgeoisie and proletariat, which is clear enough, but they also refer to categories such as petty (or *petite*) bourgeoisie, nationalist and internationalist fractions of the bourgeoisie, and productive and unproductive labour, categories which are conceptually imprecise. Neo-Marxists' recognition of the importance of intermediate classes between capitalists and workers is no doubt an improvement, but it has also rendered class analysis more difficult. In this view, the capitalist mode of production does not generate a dichotomous class structure as anticipated by Marx. Instead, it fosters a middle class between the bourgeoisie and proletariat and a set of de-commodified groups which no longer rely on the labour market for their incomes and whose politics, therefore, exist outside those related to the material conditions of production. The exact membership in these two additional groups is contested, but the former would include at minimum the old traditional petty bourgeoisie as well as the 'new' petty bourgeois elements of managers and scientific and technological workers.[29] The latter group would include students, retirees, the disabled, and those reliant upon welfare or unemployment payments.[30] In this view, political and ideological factors must also enter into the analysis of social relations, and the tendency to reduce political life to an economic 'base' must be resisted.[31] While this conceptualization is clearly superior to the simple dichotomy proposed by Marx, it threatens to undermine the notion of class upon which marxist theory was built.

The second problem with marxist class analysis centres around the question of the relationship between social 'superstructure' and economic 'base'. In the traditional marxist view, the mode of production and the associated relations of production constituted the basic structure which shaped superstructures such as the state, law, and ideology. This conceptualization is problematic, however, because the state, for instance, has played a crucial role in organizing the economy and shaping the mode of production.[32] The Canadian state's nineteenth-century promotion of natural resource sector production and its protection of inefficient domestic import-competing industries, for example, had a decisive impact on the country's economic structure and class relations and continues to shape the various classes' interests and the policy responses they elicit. Similarly, the proliferation of Keynesian policies in the 1950s and 1960s and of policies promoting privatization and deregulation in the 1980s cannot be understood without reference to ideological factors that cannot be traced entirely to the mode of production or class conflict. Some Neo-Marxists therefore had to ascribe considerable autonomy to the other spheres of social life, yet at the same time arguing that their links with the material base of society should not be forgotten.[33]

Finally, the problem of economic determinism continues to haunt the theory, notwithstanding efforts to avoid it.[34] No matter how hard Neo-Marxists try to overcome the problem by devising concepts such as 'relative autonomy of the state' or 'ideological hegemony' to take non-economic factors into account, they cannot entirely avoid reducing social and political phenomena to an economic base. This is because of the nature of the theory whose fundamental unit of analysis is the largely economically-based 'class'. To remain marxist, no theory can dispense totally with these assumptions, even if it is recognized that policy-makers are affected by factors other than economic imperatives.

The difficulties with marxist analysis have led some recent theorists to attempt to rid the concept of class analysis of economic determinism and use it merely 'to refer to a subject (ontology) rather than a method (epistemology)'. As Goldthorpe and Marshall have argued:

> Class analysis, in our sense, has as its central concern the study of relationships among class structures, class mobility, class-based inequalities, and class-based action. . . . Understood in this way, class analysis does not entail a commitment to any particular theory of class but, rather, to a *research program* . . . within which different, and indeed rival, theories may be formulated and then assessed in terms of their heuristic and explanatory performance.[35]

In such an approach, 'No assumption of the pre-eminence of class is involved.' Thus while classes are treated as analytical units, no *a priori* claim is made about their behaviour. This conception is, however, far removed from the fundamentals of what is usually recognized as class theory.

Neo-Institutionalism

A third deductive approach recognizes the limits of individual and group-based theory to deal with political phenomena. In order to distinguish it from earlier legal-historical studies merely describing political institutions, this approach has been termed 'Neo-Institutionalism'.[36] It grew directly out of expressed concerns about the ability of existing deductive theories to deal with the question of why political, economic, and social institutions like governments, firms, or churches existed at all.[37]

Neo-Institutionalism (also referred to as New Economics of Organization[38]) acknowledges the crucial role of institutions in political life, and argues that these exist in society in order to overcome impediments of information and exchange in social organizations. The basic unit of analysis in this analysis is related to the 'transaction' among individuals within the confines of institutions.[39] Institutions of various kinds are significant to the extent that they increase or lower the costs of transactions. In this perspective institutions themselves are 'the products of human design, the outcomes of purposive actions by instrumentally oriented individuals'.[40]

In the Neo-Institutional perspective, the two types of social organizations which are effective in minimizing transaction costs are the market and the hierarchy or 'bureaucracy'. In the market form, the costs of overcoming information and other needs are largely externalized as multiple producers and consumers share the costs of acquiring and disseminating information and other goods and services. In a hierarchy these costs are internalized, as occurs for example in most corporations and bureaucracies in the modern era.[41]

In the political realm, in the Neo-Institutional perspective, institutions are significant because they 'constitute and legitimize political actors and provide them with consistent behavioural rules, conceptions of reality, standards of assessment, affective ties, and endowments, and thereby with a capacity for purposeful action'.[42] While the Neo-Institutional perspective acknowledges the role of individuals and groups in the policy process, policy preferences and capacities are usually understood in the context of the society in which the state is embedded.[43]

A useful definition of institutions in the political science-inspired version of Neo-Institutionalism was put forward by Robert Keohane who described them as 'persistent and connected sets of rules (formal or informal) that prescribe behavioural roles, constrain activity, and shape expectations'.[44] Thus institutions not only increase or decrease transaction costs, but also shape preferences and the extent to which they can be realized. In his path-breaking work, Peter Hall described an 'institutionalist' analysis as one which 'emphasizes the institutional relationships, both formal and conventional, that bind the components of the state together and structure its relations with society'.[45] He elaborates:

> The concept of institutions . . . refer[s] to the formal rules, compliance procedures, and standard operating practices that structure the relationship between individuals in various units of the polity and economy. As such, they have a

more formal status than cultural norms but one that does not necessarily derive from legal, as opposed to conventional, standing. Throughout the emphasis is on the relational character of institutions; that is to say, on the way in which they structure the interactions of individuals. In this sense it is the organizational qualities of institutions that are being emphasized.

According to James March and Johan Olsen, Neo-Institutionalism emphasizes the autonomy of political institutions from the society in which they exist; the organization of governmental institutions and its effects on what the state does; the rules, norms, and symbols governing political behaviour; and the unique patterns of historical development and the constraints they impose on future choices. These ideas

> deemphasize the dependence of the polity on society in favor of an interdependence between relatively autonomous social and political institutions; they deemphasize the simple primacy of micro processes and efficient histories in favor of relatively complex processes and historical inefficiency; they deemphasize metaphors of choice and allocate outcomes in favor of other logics of action and the centrality of meaning and symbolic action.[46]

Within a policy-making perspective, the neo-institutionalist position has been summarized by Stephen Krasner as follows:

> An institutionalist perspective regards enduring institutional structures as the building blocks of social and political life. The preferences, capabilities, and basic self-identities of individuals are conditioned by these institutional structures. Historical developments are path dependent; once certain choices are made, they constrain future possibilities. The range of options available to policymakers at any given time is a function of institutional capabilities that were put in place at some earlier period, possibly in response to very different environmental pressures.[47]

The argument is not that institutions cause an action. It is rather that they affect actions by shaping the interpretation of problems and possible solutions and by constraining the choice of solutions and the way and extent to which they can be implemented. While individuals, groups, classes, and states have their specific interests, they pursue them in the context of existing formal organizations and rules and norms that shape expectations and affect the possibilities of their realization.

Neo-Institutionalism directs attention to a range of international and domestic factors that may be relevant to explaining policies without presuming in advance that any one set of factors is more important, leaving that to be revealed through empirical research.[48] Here lies the theory's main attraction. Its main problems, however, are its inability to provide a plausible coherent explanation of the origin of institutions without resorting to functionalism.[49] Moreover, while it provides an excellent discussion of the constraints placed on policy-makers, it says very little about what causes them to move in any particular direction. That is, it is at once both limited and vague in its application to public policy-making.

INDUCTIVE THEORIES

Unlike the deductive theories that attempt to apply universal maxims to the study of political phenomena, inductive theories are constructed not from the 'top down' but from the 'bottom up'. That is, they depend on the accumulation of multiple empirical studies of any phenomena for their raw data, from which they attempt to extract generalizable propositions. By their very nature these theories are less elegant and parsimonious than deductive theories; they often do not have a fully integrated or unified set of theoretical propositions that can be applied to any case under consideration, since they are, by definition, always 'under construction'.

Like deductive theories, several sub-types of inductive political theories exist. These too can be usefully distinguished according to whether they focus on individuals, groups, or institutions in their efforts to explain the political world and public policy-making.

Welfare Economics

Welfare economics is perhaps the most widely used approach to the study of public policy. Indeed much of what is called policy analysis in the literature is really applied Welfare Economics, even though this is rarely stated explicitly. This approach is based on the notion that individuals, through market mechanisms, should be relied upon to make most social decisions. Welfare economists recognize, however, that markets cannot always distribute resources efficiently or, to put it another way, cannot aggregate individual utility-maximizing behaviour so as to optimize overall social welfare. In such instances, referred to as *market failures*, welfare economists argue that political institutions can act to supplement or replace markets. The principles of welfare economics were first worked out by the British economist Alfred Pigou.[50] Although he himself only identified instances of market failures related to the tendency of some industries to generate monopolies and the inability of both consumers and investors to receive information necessary for decision-making, later analysts argued the existence of many more such market failures.[51] At minimum, these include the following:

- *Natural Monopoly*, which refers to the situation in certain industries with large capital requirements and disproportionate returns to scale that tends to promote a single firm over its competitors. In industries such as telecommunication, electricity, and railways, the first company to establish the necessary infrastructure enjoys, if unregulated, cost advantages which make it difficult for other firms to compete. The lack of competition, when it occurs, leads to loss of the society's economic welfare.

- *Imperfect Information* refers to those instances in which consumers and investors lack adequate information to make rational decisions. Pharmaceutical firms, for instance, have no incentive to reveal adverse side effects of their products, nor do consumers have the expertise required to evaluate such products. Once again, decisions may be taken that do not serve the society as a whole.

- In the presence of *Externalities* too the market is deemed to fail. These involve situations in which production costs are not borne by producers ('internalized') but passed on to others outside (external to) the production process. The most often cited example of an externality relates to the costs of pollution which a company in pursuit of reduced costs and increased profits imposes on the society as a whole.

- *The Tragedy of the Commons* is a market failure relating to circumstances involved in the use of common property resources without regulation, such as fisheries, pastures, forests, or pools of oil. In these circumstances individual users often benefit from increasing their use of the resource in the short term although all users will suffer in the long term from the increased depletion of the resource.

- *Destructive Competition* is a controversial market failure which, it is argued, appears in instances in which aggressive competition between firms causes negative side effects on workers and society.[52] It is argued that excessive competition can drive down profit margins and lead to the unnecessary reduction of wages and a deterioration of living and working conditions, adversely affecting overall social welfare.

These are the core types of market failures; others have sought to broaden the concept by including other types within this schema. Thus education, industrial research and development, art and culture, and social peace and stability are argued by many as instances of activities with 'positive externalities' which the market does not supply adequately despite a social need, indicating the existence of market failure.

Although the exact status and causes of market failures are controversial and largely inductively derived, welfare economists have developed a theory of public policy-making based on this concept. They argue that governments have a responsibility to correct market failures, because optimal social outcomes will not result from purely unco-ordinated individual decision-making. In this view, governments facing a demand for action should first determine if a market failure is causing a social problem; only if one is found should it intervene to correct the problem.[53]

Once it is agreed that a problem requires state intervention, the key public policy question for welfare economists is to find the most efficient way of doing so. The most efficient way, in this perspective, is the least costly one, and the technique used to determine it is cost-benefit analysis. Its objective is to find out how to achieve the same output for less input, or more output for the same input.[54] Conducting the analysis involves evaluating all alternatives and their consequences in terms of their monetary costs and benefits and then choosing the alternative that maximizes benefits while minimizing costs. Costs and benefits in this mode of analysis are determined by:

1. Enumerating all adverse and positive consequences arising from implementation of an option in monetary terms.
2. Estimating the probability of occurrence.
3. Estimating the cost or benefit to society should it occur.
4. Calculating the expected loss or gain related to each consequence by multiplying (2) and (3).
5. Discounting from year to year of occurrence back to present to give a net present value.[55]

Cost-benefit analysis is essentially a technique for making the government replicate market decision-making as closely as possible for the purpose of allocating resources. It is 'an attempt to use economic technique, in place of formal market bargaining or price setting, to locate a Pareto-optimal policy alternative'.[56] The criterion of *Pareto Optimality* requires that an action be undertaken only if it offers the possibility of making at least one person better off without worsening the situation of any other person. While Pareto Optimality may be achievable in a competitive market (though that is disputable as well), it is impossible to apply in the public policy arena because all government actions make some better off at the expense of others. Social security for the poor, financed from income taxes, makes the rich worse off and is therefore not Pareto Optimal; nor is putting criminals in jail, because it makes them worse off.

The difficulties with the principle of Pareto Optimality have resulted in its replacement in contemporary Welfare Economics by the so-called Kaldor criterion, which requires that only policy alternatives maximizing net benefits over cost be chosen. Under this criterion, a policy can be chosen even if some lose as long as the total gains are higher than the sum of losses. A cost-benefit analysis is employed to find out the Kaldor-efficient allocation, and the option offering the highest benefit-to-cost ratio is selected for adoption and implementation.

While not without merits, cost-benefit analysis is often problematic. Despite numerous attempts to refine the model, there is no acceptable way of putting a dollar value on various intangible costs and consequences.[57] There is no way, for instance, to calculate precisely the costs of social security programs in terms of their effects on the recipients' work incentive, or their benefits in terms of the social peace and tolerance they promote. Moreover, the costs and benefits of any policy are often not evenly distributed, for some pay more than others, while some benefit more than others. And there is often a severe problem of aggregating or summing up the various components of an option. Building a new airport involves disparate problems such as increased noise for residents in adjoining areas, decreased travelling time for some and increased time for others, increased pollution, beneficial employment and savings effects and so on, all of which affect different sections of the society differently and so need to be evaluated differently, yet there is no generally acceptable way of so doing.[58] Efforts to improve cost-benefit technique continue; however, so have its criticisms.

Recent critics have argued that market failures are in fact only one side of an equation and that there are also innate limitations—'government failures'—to government's ability to correct market failures. They posit that in several specific instances the state cannot improve upon the market, despite the latter's failings.[59] There are three commonly cited instances of such government failure:

- *Organizational displacement*, understood as the situation in which the administrative agency charged with producing a particular good or service displaces public goals with its own 'private' or 'organizational' ones, is regarded as a government failure by some scholars. These may extend to maximizing its budget or power or whatever else the organization values. In such circumstances, government action to correct market failure may simply increase inefficiency.
- *Rising costs*. Because of the supposed separation between government revenues and costs this is cited as another instance of government failure. Governments receive tax revenues from general sources but have specific program costs. Without a method to match costs to revenues, it is argued, governments often fail to control expenses.
- Instances of *Derived externalities* are the third type of such failure. It is argued that government actions have a broad impact on the society and economy, as a result of which they have the effect of excluding viable market-produced goods and services or otherwise negatively affect overall levels of social welfare.[60]

The conclusion this literature suggests is that not only must governments carefully examine market failures, they must also carefully evaluate their own capacity to correct the failures before attempting to do so.[61]

Sustained criticisms have led many welfare economists to attempt to re-conceptualize the original notion of a market failure. To this end a typology of goods and services has been developed to help determine the possible role of the government and markets in their provision. In this typology, all goods and services in society can be divided into four types according to the criteria of exclusivity and exhaustiveness, that is to say, whether the good or service is limited to a single consumer and whether it is completely consumed after an economic transaction. These criteria of exclusivity and exhaustiveness generate the four types of goods and services listed in Figure 3.

■ Figure 3.
A General Taxonomy of Goods and Services

	Exhaustiveness	
	High	Low
Exclusivity		
High	*Private Good*	*Toll Good*
Low	*Common Pool Good*	*Public Good*

SOURCE: Adapted from: E.S. Savas, *Alternatives for Delivering Public Services: Toward Improved Performance*, Boulder: Westview, 1977.

In this view, pure private goods make up the bulk of goods and services produced in society. These are goods or services, such as food or a hair-cut, that can be divided up for sale and are no longer available to others after their consumption by consumers. At the other extreme are pure public goods or services, such as street lighting or defence, which cannot be parcelled out and can be consumed without diminishing the sum of the good available. Between the two are toll goods and common pool goods. The former include semi-public goods such as bridges or highways which do not diminish in quantity after use but for the use of which it is possible to charge. Common pool goods are those, like fish in the ocean, whose usage cannot be directly charged to individuals but whose quantity is reduced after use.

According to the principles of Welfare Economics, governments should not interfere in transactions and activities related to private goods and services. They should simply enforce basic property rights and prevent criminal behaviours (such as theft) undermining these types of transactions. Public goods, however, should be provided by the government because markets cannot provide goods or services for which businesses cannot charge or profit. Governments should also not allow toll goods to be treated like public goods and so must charge for their usage. From this perspective, the costs of constructing and maintaining roads and bridges should not be charged to all tax-payers and then offered for 'free' to those using the facilities, which encourages the latter to treat these as public goods; rather, those using the facilities must pay for the costs. In the case of common pool goods, the government should establish property regimes through licensing in order to prevent their depletion.[62] The sale of fishing quotas through public auction, which gives the 'right' to a certain quantity of fish to those succeeding at the auction, is often cited as an example of this principle.

The main problem with all the various conceptions of public policy offered by welfare economists, however, is not related to its notions of the general types of goods and services available in society, nor to the elegance of its theoretical assumptions. It is due to the failure of theorists using this approach to recognize that states almost never make their policies in the essentially technical manner assumed by the theory. Even if one could identify the most efficient and effective policy, which is difficult given the limitations innate to the social sciences, the actual choice is a political one, bound by political institutions, and made by political actors, often in response to political pressures. As such, the technical analyses generated by welfare economists are often merely another political resource used by proponents of one or another option for government action or inaction to further their claims.[63] Only in very specific circumstances when welfare economists happen to be policy-makers—as happens at times in some countries in some sectors, such as taxation or fiscal management—would one expect political decisions to be made solely upon the basis of welfare-maximizing criteria as defined by welfare economists.[64] Welfare Economics' neglect of political variables has led its critics to describe it as 'a myth, a theoretical illusion'[65] which promotes 'a false and naïve view of the policy process'.[66]

Pluralism and Corporatism

A second prominent inductive approach to policy-making focuses on groups and not individuals. The most well known of these are 'Pluralism', which originated in the United States and continues to be the dominant perspective within American political science, and 'Corporatism', which is a group theory developed in Europe.

While evidence of pluralist thinking can be found in the works of one of the United States' founding fathers, James Madison,[67] and a French observer of early nineteenth-century America, Alexis de Tocqueville,[68] the doctrine received its first formal expression in the hands of Arthur Bentley in 1908.[69] The theory has been considerably modified and refined over the years, but the fundamental tenets postulated by Bentley remain intact. Some prominent pluralist thinkers, apart from Bentley, include David Truman, Robert Dahl, and Nelson Polsby.[70]

Pluralism is based on the assumption of the primacy of interest groups in the political process. In his book *The Process of Government*, Bentley argued that 'society itself is nothing other than the complex of the groups that compose it.' There were different interests in society which found their concrete manifestation in different groups consisting of individuals with similar interests.[71] Truman modified Bentley's notion of a one-to-one correspondence between interests and groups and argued that there were instead two kinds of interests—latent and manifest—which resulted in the creation of two kinds of groups—potential and organized.[72] For Truman, latent interests in the process of emerging provided the underpinnings for potential groups which over time led to the emergence of organized groups.

Groups in pluralist theory are not only many and free-forming, they are also characterized by overlapping membership and a lack of representational monopoly. The same individual may belong to a number of groups for pursuing his or her different interests; a person, for instance, may belong at the same time to the Consumers' Association of Canada as well as to the Canadian Medical Association. Overlapping membership is said to be a key mechanism for reconciling conflicts and promoting co-operation among groups. In addition, the same interest may be represented by more than one group.[73] Environmental causes, for example, are espoused by a large number of groups in every industrialized country. Politics in the pluralist perspective is the process by which various competing interests are reconciled. Public policies are thus a result of competition and collaboration among groups working to further their members' collective interests.[74]

Contrary to the interpretation presented in many commentaries, pluralists do not believe that all groups are equally influential or that they have equal access to government.[75] In fact they recognize that groups vary in terms of the financial or organizational (personnel, legitimacy, members' loyalty, or internal unity) resources they possess and the access to government they enjoy.[76] Nevertheless, as McLennan has observed, 'It is impossible to read the standard works without getting the sense that resources, information and the means of political communication are openly available to all citizens, that groups form an array of equivalent power centres in society, and that all legitimate voices can and will be heard.'[77] As such, pluralist theories are to some extent justifiably criticized for not having a sufficiently developed notion of groups' varying capacity to affect government decision-making.

A more significant problem with the application of Pluralism to public policy-making, however, is that the role of the government in making public policies is quite unclear. The early Pluralists assumed that the government was a sort of transmission belt registering and implementing demands placed upon it by interest groups. The government was not actually an entity so much as a place, an 'arena' where competing groups met and bargained.[78] The recognition that this view did not accord with the reality of what governments actually did led to its reconceptualization as a 'referee' or 'umpire'. In this view, the state was still ultimately a place where competing groups met to work out their differences, but this time the government was considered a kind of neutral official setting out the rules of group conflict and ensuring that groups did not violate them with impunity.[79] As Earl Latham put it:

> The legislature referees the group struggle, ratifies the victories of the successful coalitions, and records the terms of the surrenders, compromises, and conquests in the form of statutes. Every statute tends to represent compromise because the very process of accommodating conflicts of group interest is one of deliberation and consent. The legislative vote on any issue thus tends to represent the composition of strength, i.e., the balance of power among the contending groups at the moment of voting. What may be called public policy is actually the equilibrium reached in the group struggle at any given moment, and it represents a balance which the contending factions of groups constantly strive to weight in their favor.[80]

This is an overly simplistic view of the government because it assumes that public officials do not have their own interests and ambitions which they seek to realize through their control of the governmental machinery. It also neglects the fact that states often maintain special ties with certain groups and may even sponsor establishment of groups where there are none or if those in existence are found to be difficult to work with.

The pluralist notion of the government responding to groups' pressure is also misconceived because it assumes unity of purpose and action on the part of the government. As some scholars have pointed out, 'bureaucratic politics' is a pervasive phenomenon which has a critical impact on public policies.[81] Different bureaus have different interests and conflicting interpretations of the same problem, and how they are resolved has an impact on what policies are adopted and how they are implemented.

Recognition of these problems with Pluralism[82] led to the emergence of what is described as Neo-Pluralism within the American political science community. The reformulation retains the significance attributed to competition among groups, but modifies the idea of approximate equality among groups and explicitly acknowledges that some groups are more powerful than others. Charles Lindblom, for example, has argued that for two reasons business is more powerful than others. First, governments in a capitalist society need a prosperous economy to serve as the basis for tax revenues to spend on programs and for its own re-election. To promote economic growth, governments must maintain business confidence, which often means paying special heed to the demands of the business community. Second, in capitalist societies there is a division between public and private sectors, the former under the control of the state and the latter dominated by business. The private sector's dominance by business gives it a privileged position in comparison to other groups in that much employment and associated social and economic activity is ultimately dependent on private-sector investment behaviour.[83] Unlike the classical Pluralists, who seemed only to acknowledge but not incorporate the observation that some groups may be more powerful than others because of their superior organization and resources, Lindblom argued that the strength of business lay in the nature of capitalism and democracy itself. As such, business need not, though it may, exert pressure on the government to realize its interests; the government itself will, in accordance with the imperatives of capitalism, ensure that business interests are not adversely affected by its actions.

The basic problem with pluralist analyses of public policy-making, however, remains their excessive concentration on the role of interest groups and neglect of other equally important factors in the policy-making process. While Neo-Pluralism is a significant improvement on its predecessor, it does not address all the problems innate to a concentrated focus on social groups. The theory continues to overlook the roles of the state and the international system in shaping public policies and their implementation. The state itself may have interests and objectives which have an effect on public policies. Similarly, international economic interdependence makes states' policies increasingly subject to international pressures, regardless of domestic group pressures. It is difficult to understand, for example, the industrial and trade policies of industrialized countries without reference to the international economy and the political pressures it places upon policy-makers. The role of ideology is also unjustifiably neglected in the pluralist explanations of politics and public policy. The liberal tradition pre-eminent in Anglo-Saxon countries (including Canada, the US, Australia, and others), for example, has had a significant impact on their governments' hesitant and often contradictory intervention in the economy.

Pluralism's applicability to countries besides the United States is especially problematic because of differences in political institutions and processes.[84] British parliamentary institutions found in Australia, Canada, or the United Kingdom for example do not lend themselves to the kind of open access that groups enjoy in relation to the Congress in the US.[85] Many countries simply lack the kinds of groups conceived by Pluralists. Even if the groups have the freedom to organize themselves, the numbers actually formed are fewer than in the US and tend to be much more permanent and formalized. This finding led some group theorists like Schmitter to speculate that Pluralism was only one form in which group systems could develop in different countries. Schmitter argued that, depending upon a range of variables and historical factors, a corporatist form of political organization was much more likely than a pluralist one to emerge in countries outside the US.[86]

In the United States, Pluralism has long been the dominant group theory. In Europe theories treating groups as their primary unit of analysis have tended to take a corporatist form. The roots of Corporatism extend back to the middle ages when there were concerns about protecting the 'intermediate strata' of autonomous associations between the state and the family.[87] These included guilds and other forms of trade associations as well as, most significantly, religious organizations and churches. Corporatist theory argues that these intermediate strata have a life of their own above and beyond the constituting individuals, and that their existence is part of the 'organic' or natural order of society. Much of political life and conflict in Europe in the fifteenth and sixteenth centuries concerned efforts by emerging national states to control the operations of these 'autonomous strata' and the latter's efforts to resist state control.[88]

Corporatism can be best understood, as Schmitter has observed, in contrast to Pluralism. The latter is a theory in which multiple groups exist to represent their respective members' interests, membership is voluntary, and groups associate freely with each other without state interference in their activities. In contrast, Corporatism is:

> [A] system of interest intermediation in which the constituent units are organized into a limited number of singular, compulsory, non-competitive, hierarchically ordered and functionally differentiated categories, recognized or

licensed (if not created) by the state and granted a deliberate representational monopoly within their respective categories in exchange for observing certain controls on their selection of leaders and articulation of demands and supports.[89]

The groups here are not free-forming, voluntary, or competitive as in Pluralism. Nor are they as autonomous, for they depend on the state for recognition and support in return for a role in policy-making. Corporatism thus explicitly takes into account two problems endemic to Pluralism: its neglect of the role of the state, and of institutionalized patterns of relationships between the state and groups.

In corporatist theory, public policy is shaped by the interaction between the state and the interest group or groups recognized by the state. Interaction among groups is institutionalized within and mediated by the state.[90] Public policy toward a declining industry, for instance, would take the form of bargaining between and among the state and relevant industry associations and trade unions as to how best to rationalize the industry and make it competitive. The making of social welfare policies would similarly involve negotiations with the overall business association (whose members may have to pay higher taxes), social welfare groups, and possibly trade unions—if the proposed policies affect their members. The outcome of these negotiation would depend not only on the organizational characteristics of the groups but upon the closeness of their relationship with the state. The state itself is not seen as a monolith, but as an organization with internal fissures that affect its actions.

Although this conception accords fairly well with political practices in many European countries, there are problems with Corporatism as an approach to politics or the study of public policy. First, it is a descriptive category of a particular kind of political arrangement between states and societies (such as in Sweden or Austria), not a general explanation of what governments do, especially those in non-corporatist countries. Thus it has little to say about why countries such as Australia, Canada, or the United States have the particular public policies that they do, except to point out that the lack of institutionalized co-operation between the state and groups in these countries often leads to fragmented and incoherent policies.[91] Second, the theory does little to further our understanding of public policy processes, even in the so-called corporatist countries. While it is significant to know that not all countries have open-ended competition among groups as suggested by Pluralism, this in itself does not say anything about why a policy is adopted or why it is implemented in a particular manner. The close links between governments and certain groups is certainly only one among many factors shaping policies. Third, the theory does not contain a clear notion of even its own fundamental unit of analysis, the interest group. Contemporary societies contain myriad interests, and it is not clear which are or should be represented by the state. In some cases, the relevant groups are defined in terms of ethnicity, language, or religion, while in others they are defined with reference to their economic activities. The bulk of corporatist literature concentrates somewhat arbitrarily upon producer groups, such as industry associations and trade unions. Fourth, the theory is vague about the relative significance of groups in politics. Are we to treat all groups as equally influential? If not, then what determines their influence? The corporatist literature is silent on such questions. Finally, the theory has no clear conception of the nature of the state, its interests, and why it recognizes some groups and not others as representatives of corporate interests. The answers to these questions vary dramatically among scholars working in the corporatist framework. Some argue that Corporatism is a manifestation of an autonomous state desiring to manage social change or ensure social stability.[92] Others suggest that it is a system which is desired by the major corporate actors themselves and simply put into place by the state at their behest.[93]

Despite its shortcomings, Corporatism has played a significant role in the analysis of public policy. By highlighting the autonomous role of the state in politics, it paved the way for more sophisticated explanations of public policy-making than those provided by group theory. More significantly, by emphasizing the importance of institutionalized patterns of relationship between states and societies, it fostered the emergence of new explanations which offer a more comprehensive explanation of public policies.

Statism

A third general type of inductive political theory has taken to heart the insights of critics of Pluralism and Corporatism and has focused on organized social structures or political institutions as its basic unit of analysis. Many analyses in this mould focus solely on the state, seeing it as the leading institution in society and the key agent in the political process. Others, however, attribute explanatory significance to other social forms, such as business or labour, in addition to the state.

Both interpretations have their origin in the works of late-nineteenth-century German historical sociologists and legal theorists who highlighted the effects of the development of modern state institutions on the development of society. Rather than argue that the state reflected the nature of a nation's populace or social structure, theorists such as Max Weber and Otto Hintze noted how its monopoly on the use of force allowed it to re-order and structure social relations and institutions.[94]

Such a line of analysis yielded, to use Theda Skocpol's terms, a 'state-centric' as opposed to 'society-centric' explanation of political life.[95] In the strong version of the statist approach,

> states create, organize and regulate societies. States dominate other organizations within a particular territory, they mould the culture and shape the economy. Thus the problem of the autonomy of the state with regard to society has no sense within this perspective. It should not even appear. The concept of

'autonomy' is a useful instrument of analysis only if the domination by the state over society is a contingent situation, that is, if the state derives its efficacy from private property, societal values, or some other sources located outside it. Within a true 'state-centric' approach this concept has nothing to contribute.[96]

The state is viewed as an autonomous actor with the capacity to devise and implement its own objectives, not necessarily just to respond to pressure imposed upon it by dominant social groups or classes. Its autonomy and capacity are based on its staffing by officials with specialized areas of expertise and the fact that it is a sovereign organization with unparalleled financial, personnel, and—in the final instance—coercive resources. The proponents of this perspective claim that its emphasis on the centrality of the state as an explanatory variable enables it to offer more plausible explanations of long-term patterns of policy development in many countries than do other types of political theory.[97]

It is difficult to accept Statism in the strong form described above, however. For one, it cannot account for the existence of social liberties and freedoms or explain why states cannot always enforce their will, such as in times of rebellion, revolution, or civil disobedience. In fact, even the most autocratic governments make some attempt to respond to what they believe to be the population's preferences. It is, of course, impossible for a democratic state to be entirely autonomous from a society with voting rights. In addition to efforts to maintain and nurture support for the regime among the population, capitalist states, both democratic and autocratic, need to accommodate the imperatives of the market-place in their policies. Second, the statist view suggests implicitly that all 'strong' states respond to the same problem in the same manner because of their similar organizational features. This is obviously not the case, as different states (both 'strong' and 'weak') often have different policies dealing with the same problem. To explain the difference, we need to take factors other than the features of the state into account.[98]

To be fair, however, few subscribe to Statism in the 'strong' form described above. Instead of replacing the pluralist notion of the societal direction of the state with the statist notion of the state's direction of society, most statist theorists merely want to point out the need to take both sets of factors into consideration in their analyses of political phenomenon.[99] As Skocpol herself concedes:

> In this perspective, the state certainly does not become everything. Other organizations and agents also pattern social relationships and politics, and the analyst must explore the state's structure in relation to them. But this Weberian view of the state does require us to see it as much more than a mere arena in which social groups make demands and engage in political struggles or compromises.[100]

The milder version of Statism concentrates on the links between the state and society in the context of the former's pre-eminence. To that extent, Statism complements rather than replaces society-centredness.[101]

Conclusion

The first conclusion to emerge from our brief discussion of the manner in which broad approaches to the study of political phenomena apply to public policy-making is that there are significant problems with each of the approaches mentioned above.

Not surprisingly, in the deductive literature there is an overwhelming tendency to apply deductively derived theoretical insights to actual instances of public policy-making. In so doing, researchers often seem to forget the contingent nature of the hypotheses generated by various approaches and the need to test them. Consequently, instead of using the study of public policy to test the hypotheses and assess the explanatory capacity of their theories, analysts often simply read public policy-making in terms of the theoretical framework, models, or metaphors they are using.[102]

As for the inductive theories, their application to the study of public policy-making has revealed that although built on empirical observations, the claim of any of these approaches to the status of 'general theory' is suspect. Neither Welfare Economics, nor Pluralism, Corporatism, or Statism effectively deal with the multi-faceted empirical reality of public policy-making.

Second, both deductive and inductive approaches tend to explain the phenomena under consideration in mono-causal terms. This is a temptation that must be resisted if we are to attain a comprehensive understanding of public policy. Analysts working in different theoretical frameworks study the same case differently and, not surprisingly, arrive at different conclusions. While bringing different points of view to bear on a question furthers our understanding of a phenomenon, the exercise also involves the danger of turning into a dialogue among the deaf, serving no useful purpose.

Third, the most widely used approaches, whether they are inductive or deductive in nature, tend to view human activity as part of the struggle to survive in a world in which the resources available to satisfy human wants are limited while the wants themselves are limitless. This view extends to all political phenomena, including public policy-making. In recent times, however, the policy sciences have begun to abandon this notion of all-pervasive conflict, and have suggested that the lessons actors learn from their own and others' experiences are significant determinants of their behaviour in the policy process. That is, the objectives actors seek depend on what they believe to be desirable and achievable, which in turn depends on their previous achievements and disappointments. Discussion, arguments, and persuasion among actors are viewed as an integral part of the policy process conceived of as a process of learning by trial, error, and example.[103]

What this overview reveals, then, is that the policy sciences cannot be furthered simply through the utilization of any existing general theoretical construct, be it deductive or inductive in nature. What is needed, as was suggested in Chapter One, is an analytical framework that permits consideration of the entire range of factors affecting public policy, and allows hypotheses to be tested through the empirical analysis of the reality analysts are attempting to describe and understand.

This also means that the development of theory in the policy sciences must remain rooted at the 'middle level'. That is, policy theory cannot and should not claim to be more than a part of the development of some general theory of political phenomena whose contours remain to be discerned at some point in the future. Careful study of empirical cases and careful generalization will perhaps lead to tentative conclusions that may appear inelegant, but as the discussion of the six general theories presented above reveals, in policy analysis, precision and adequacy should be more important objectives than parsimony and aesthetics.

The present book is strongly influenced by emerging trends towards broadening the analytical framework of policy studies to include both conflict and learning and towards a greater emphasis on incorporating the results of empirical analyses of many policy domains into the process of theory-building in policy science. The framework it proposes for analysing public policy takes into consideration the characteristics of policy actors, institutions, and instruments. In order to begin the process of middle-range theory construction, these elements will be considered in greater detail in Part 2.

NOTES

1 Peter DeLeon, 'Reinventing the Policy Sciences: Three Steps Back to the Future', *Policy Sciences* 27 (1994): 77-95.

2 John S. Dryzek, 'How Far Is It from Virginia and Rochester to Frankfurt? Public Choice as Global Theory', *British Journal of Political Science* 22, 4 (1992): 397-418.

3 James M. Buchanan et al., *The Economics of Politics* (London: Institute of Economic Affairs, 1978): 17.

4 Iain McLean, *Public Choice: An Introduction* (Oxford: Basil Blackwell, 1987).

5 Anthony Downs, *An Economic Theory of Democracy* (New York: Harper, 1957).

6 Gary S. Becker, 'Competition and Democracy', *Journal of Law and Economics* 1 (1958): 105-09.

7 R.H. Coase, 'The Problem of Social Cost', *Journal of Law and Economics* 3 (1960): 1-44.

8 Anthony Downs, *Inside Bureaucracy* (New York: Harper and Row, 1967).

9 William A. Niskanen, *Bureaucracy and Representative Government* (Chicago: University of Chicago Press, 1971).

10 W. Riker, *The Theory of Political Coalitions* (New Haven: Yale University Press, 1962).

11 James M. Buchanan, *The Limits of Liberty* (Chicago: University of Chicago Press, 1975).

12 Peter Self, *Political Theories of Modern Government: Its Role and Reform* (London: Allen and Unwin, 1985): 51.

13 Raford Boddy and James Crotty, 'Class Conflict and Macro-Policy: The Political

Business Cycle', *Review of Radical Political Economics* 7 (1975): 1-19; David K. Foot, 'Political Cycles, Economic Cycles and the Trend in Public Employment in Canada' in Meyer W. Bucovetsky (ed.), *Studies in Public Employment and Compensation in Canada* (Toronto: Butterworths, for Institute for Research on Public Policy, 1979): 65-80; Bruno S. Frey, 'Politico-Economic Models and Cycles', *Journal of Public Economics* 9 (1978): 203-20; Gareth Locksley, 'The Political Business Cycle: Alternative Interpretations' in Paul Whiteley (ed.), *Models of Political Economy* (London: Sage Publications, 1980); Edward R. Tufte, *Political Control of the Economy* (Princeton, NJ: Princeton University Press, 1978).

14   Buchanan et al., *The Economics of Politics*: 17.

15   See C.K. Rowley, 'The Political Economy of the Public Sector' in R.J.B. Jones (ed.), *Perspectives on Political Economy* (London: Pinter, 1983).

16   See Frans A.A.M. Van Winden for a sympathetic critique of the theory, 'The Economic Theory of Political Decision-Making' in Julien van den Broeck (ed.), *Public Choice* (Dordrecht: Kluwer, 1988): 9-57.

17   Patrick Dunleavy, 'Explaining the Privatization Boom: Public Choice versus Radical Approaches', *Public Administration* 64, 1 (1986): 13-34.

18   Elinor Ostrom, 'An Agenda for the Study of Institutions', *Public Choice* 48 (1986): 3-25; Elinor Ostrom, 'A Method of Institutional Analysis' in F.X. Kaufman, Giandomenico Majone, and Vincent Ostrom (eds), *Guidance, Control and Evaluation in the Public Sector* (Berlin: deGruyter, 1986).

19   Stanislaw Ossowski, *Class Structure in the Social Consciousness* (New York: Free Press of Glencoe, 1963): 71.

20   Ossowski (1963) has argued that over the course of history there have been four different types of class analysis used to explain political phenomena: dichotomous class systems; gradation schemes; functional conceptions; and the 'Marxian' synthesis of those other models.

21   G.A. Cohen, *Karl Marx's Theory of History: A Defense* (Oxford: Clarendon Press, 1978).

22   Martin Nicolaus, 'Proletariat and Middle Class in Marx: Hegelian Choreography and the Capitalist Dialectic', *Studies on the Left* 7, 1 (1967): 22-49.

23   Nicos Poulantzas, 'On Social Classes', *New Left Review* 78 (1973): 27-54.

24   Fred Block, 'Beyond Relative Autonomy: State Managers as Historical Subjects', *Socialist Register* (London: Merlin Press, 1980): 227-42; Duncan K. Foley, 'State Expenditure From a Marxist Perspective', *Journal of Public Economics* 9 (1978): 221-38; Ian Gough, 'State Expenditure in Advanced Capitalism', *New Left Review* (1975): 53-92; Nicos Poulantzas, *State, Power, Socialism* (London: New Left Books, 1978); Goran Therborn, 'The Rule of Capital and the Rise of Democracy', *New Left Review* 103 (1977): 3-41; Goran Therborn, 'Neo-Marxist, Pluralist, Corporatist, Statist Theories and the Welfare State' in Ali Kazancigil (ed.), *The State in Global Perspective* (UK: Gower, 1986): 204-31.

25   Nicos Poulantzas, *Political Power and Social Classes* (London: New Left Books, 1973). See also the roots of this analysis in L. Althusser and E. Balibar, *Reading 'Capital'* (London: New Left Books, 1977).

26   E.P. Thompson, *The Poverty of Theory and Other Essays* (London: Merlin Press, 1978).

27   Gosta Esping-Andersen, 'From Welfare State to Democratic Socialism: The Politics of Economic Democracy in Denmark and Sweden' in Maurice Zeitlin (ed.), *Political Power and Social Theory* (1981): 111-40; Gosta Esping-Andersen, *Politics Against*

Markets: The Social Democratic Road to Power (Princeton: Princeton University Press, 1985); Gosta Esping-Anderson and Walter Korpi, 'Social Policy as Class Politics in Post-war Capitalism: Scandinavia, Austria and Germany' in J.H. Goldthorpe (ed.), *Order and Conflict in Contemporary Capitalism* (Oxford: Clarendon Press, 1984): 179-208.

28 Adam Przeworski, 'Proletariat into a Class: The Process of Class Formation' in Adam Przeworski (ed.), *Capitalism and Social Democracy* (Cambridge: Cambridge University Press, 1985): 47-97; Erik Olin Wright, *Classes* (London: Verso, 1985); Erik Olin Wright (ed.), *The Debate on Classes* (London: Verso, 1989).

29 Nicos A. Poulantzas, *Political Power and Social Classes* (London: New Left Books, 1973); Nicos Poulantzas, *State, Power, Socialism* (London: New Left Books, 1978).

30 James R. O'Connor, *The Fiscal Crisis of the State* (New York: St. Martin's Press, 1973); Claus Offe, 'Political Authority and Class Structures–An Analysis of Late Capitalist Societies', *International Journal of Sociology* 2 (1972): 73-108; Claus Offe, 'Social Policy and the Theory of the State' in John Keane (ed.), *Contradictions of the Welfare State* (London: Hutchinson, 1984): 88-118.

31 A. Gramsci, *Selections from the Prison Notebooks* (New York: International Publishers, 1972); Gwyn A. Williams, 'The Concept of "Egemonia" in the Thought of Antonio Gramsci: Some Notes on Interpretation', *Journal of the History of Ideas* 21 (1960): 586-99.

32 Robert Cox, *Production, Power and World Order: Social Forces in the Making of History* (New York: Columbia University Press, 1987).

33 Jack L. Amariglio, Stephen A. Resnick, and Richard D. Wolff, 'Class, Power, and Culture' in Cary Nelson and Lawrence Grossberg (eds), *Marxism and the Interpretation of Culture* (Urbana: University of Illinois Press, 1988): 487-501.

34 Gregor McLennan, *Marxism, Pluralism and Beyond: Classic Debates and New Departures* (Cambridge: Polity Press, 1989): 117-19.

35 John H. Goldthorpe and Gordon Marshall, 'The Promising Future of Class Analysis: A Response to Recent Critiques', *Sociology* 26, 3 (1992): 382.

36 See Kathleen Thelan and Sven Steinmo, 'Historical Institutionalism in Comparative Perspective' in S. Steinmo, K. Thelen, and F. Longstreth (eds), *Structuring Politics: Historical Institutionalism in Comparative Analysis* (Cambridge: Cambridge University Press, 1992).

37 Paul Cammack, 'The New Institutionalism: Predatory Rule, Institutional Persistence, and Macro-Social Change', *Economy and Society* 21, 4 (1992): 398. John A. Hall and G. John Ikenberry, *The State* (Minneapolis: University of Minnesota Press, 1989); Bert A. Rockman, 'Minding the State–Or a State of Mind? Issues in the Comparative Conceptualization of the State', *Comparative Political Studies* 23, 1 (1990): 25-55.

38 Beth V. Yarbrough and Robert M. Yarbrough, 'International Institutions and the New Economics of Organization', *International Organization* 44, 2 (1990): 235-59.

39 R.H. Coase, 'The Problem of Social Cost', *Journal of Law and Economics* 3 (1960): 1-44.

40 Walter W. Powell and Paul J. DiMaggio (eds), *The New Institutionalism in Organizational Analysis* (Chicago: University of Chicago Press, 1991): 8.

41 For example, see Douglas C. North, *Institutions, Institutional Change and Economic Performance* (Cambridge: Cambridge University Press, 1990); Oliver Williamson, *The Economic Institutions of Capitalism* (New York: Free Press, 1985). For a concise summary of this literature, see Larry Kiser and Elinor Ostrom, 'The Three Worlds of Action' in Elinor Ostrom (ed.), *Strategies of Political Inquiry* (Beverly Hills: Sage, 1982): 179-222; M. Levi, *Of Rule and Revenue* (Berkeley: University of California Press, 1988).

42   James G. March and Johan P. Olsen. 'Institutional Perspectives on Political Institutions', paper presented at the meeting of the International Political Science Association, Berlin (1994): 5

43   J.P. Nettl, 'The State as a Conceptual Variable', World Politics 20 (1968): 559-92; Adam Przeworski, *The State and the Economy Under Capitalism* (Chur, Switzerland: Harwood Academic Publishers, 1990); Goran Therborn, 'Neo-Marxist, Pluralist, Corporatist, Statist Theories and the Welfare State' in Ali Kazancigil (ed.), *The State in Global Perspective* (UK: Gower, 1986): 204-31.

44   Robert O. Keohane, *International Institutions and State Power: Essays in International Relations Theory* (Boulder: Westview Press, 1989): 163.

45   Peter A. Hall, *Governing the Economy: the Politics of State Intervention in Britain and France* (Cambridge: Polity Press, 1986): 19.

46   James G. March and Johan P. Olsen, 'The New Institutionalism: Organizational Factors in Political Life', *American Political Science Review* 78, 3 (1984): 738.

47   Stephen D. Krasner, 'Sovereignty: An Institutional Perspective', *Comparative Political Studies* 21, 1 (1988): 67.

48   Michael M. Atkinson, 'Public Policy and the New Institutionalism' in M.M. Atkinson (ed.), *Institutions and Public Policy* (Toronto: Harcourt Brace Jovanovich, 1993).

49   For a discussion of this critique, see Paul Cammack, 'The New Institutionalism: Predatory Rule, Institutional Persistence, and Macro-Social Change', *Economy and Society* 21, 4 (1992): 397-429.

50   A.C. Pigou, *The Economics of Welfare* (London: Macmillan, 1932).

51   Francis M. Bator, 'The Anatomy of Market Failure', *Quarterly Journal of Economics* 72, 3 (1958): 351-79.

52   M.A. Utton, *The Economics of Regulating Industry* (Oxford: Basil Blackwell, 1986).

53   Edith Stokey and Richard Zeckhauser, *A Primer for Policy Analysis* (New York: W.W. Norton, 1978).

54   Michael Carley, *Rational Techniques in Policy Analysis* (London: Heinemann, 1980): 51.

55   Baruch Fischoff, 'Cost-Benefit Analysis and the Art of Motorcycle Maintenance', *Policy Sciences* 8, 2 (1977): 177-202.

56   John Martin Gillroy and Maurice Wade, 'Introduction' in John Martin Gillroy and Maurice Wade (eds), *The Moral Dimensions Of Policy Choice: Beyond The Market Paradigm* (Pittsburgh: University of Pittsburgh Press, 1992): 7.

57   Richard Zeckhauser, 'Procedures for Valuing Lives', *Public Policy* 23, 4 (1975): 419-64.

58   For examples of some proposals for overcoming the problem, see Michael Carley, *Rational Techniques in Policy Analysis* (London: Heinemann, 1980): 51-5.

59   Julian Le Grand and Roy Robinson (eds), *Privatization and the Welfare State* (London: George, Allen and Unwin, 1984). See also Renate Mayntz, 'Governing Failures and the Problem of Governability: Some Comments on a Theoretical Paradigm' in J. Kooiman (ed.), *Modern Governance: New Government-Society Interactions* (London: Sage, 1993).

60   Charles Wolf Jr, 'A Theory of Nonmarket Failure', *Journal of Law and Economics* 22, 1 (1979): 107-39.

61   Aidan R. Vining and David L. Weimer, 'Government Supply and Government Production Failure: A Framework Based on Contestability', *Journal of Public Policy* 10, 1 (1990): 1-22; David L. Weimer and Aidan R. Vining, *Policy Analysis: Concepts and Practice* (Englewood Cliffs: Prentice Hall, 1992).

62 E.S. Savas, *Alternatives for Delivering Public Services: Toward Improved Performance* (Boulder: Westview, 1977); E.S. Savas, *Privatization: The Key to Better Government* (Chatham: Chatham House Publishers, 1987).

63 Carol Weiss, 'Research for Policy's Sake: The Enlightenment Function of Social Research', *Policy Analysis* 3, 4 (1977): 531-45.

64 John Markoff and Veronica Montecinos, 'The Ubiquitous Rise of Economists', *Journal of Public Policy* 13, 1 (1993): 37-68.

65 Robert Formaini, *The Myth of Scientific Public Policy* (New Brunswick: Transaction Publishers, 1990): 1.

66 Martin Minogue, 'Theory and Practice in Public Policy and Administration', *Policy and Politics* 1, 1 (1983): 76. See also Brian W. Hogwood and Lewis A. Gunn, *Policy Analysis for the Real World* (New York : Oxford University Press, 1984): 50-1.

67 James Madison and Jay Hamilton, *The Federalist Papers: A Collection of Essays Written in Support of the Constitution of the United States* (Garden City, NY: Anchor Books, 1961).

68 Alexis de Tocqueville, *Democracy in America* (New York: New American Library, 1956).

69 Arthur F. Bentley, *The Process of Government* (Chicago: University of Chicago Press, 1908).

70 David R. Truman, *The Government Process: Political Interests and Public Opinion* (New York: Knopf, 1964); Robert A. Dahl, *A Preface to Democratic Theory* (Chicago: University of Chicago Press, 1956); Robert A. Dahl, *Who Governs?: Democracy and Power in an American City* (New Haven: Yale University Press, 1961): Nelson Polsby, *Community Power and Political Theory* (New Haven: Yale University Press, 1963).

71 Bentley, *The Process of Government*: 211.

72 Truman, *The Governmental Process*.

73 Phillipe C. Schmitter, 'Modes of Interest Intermediation and Models of Societal Change in Western Europe', *Comparative Political Studies* 10, 1 (1977): 7-38.

74 Peter Self, *Political Theories of Modern Government: Its Role and Reform* (London: Allen and Unwin, 1985).

75 Martin J. Smith, 'Pluralism, Reformed Pluralism and Neopluralism: The Role of Pressure Groups in Policy-Making', *Political Studies* 38 (1990): 303-4.

76 Charles E. Lindblom, *The Policy-Making Process* (Englewood Cliffs: Prentice-Hall, 1968); Theodore Lowi, *The End of Liberalism: Ideology, Policy and the Crisis of Public Authority* (New York: Norton, 1969); Grant McConnell, *Private Power and American Democracy* (New York: Knopf, 1966); E.E. Schattschnieder, *The Semisovereign People: A Realist's View of Democracy in America* (New York: Holt, Rinehart and Winston, 1960).

77 Gregor McLennan, *Marxism, Pluralism and Beyond*: 25.

78 Robert A. Dahl, *Pluralist Democracy in the United States: Conflict and Consent* (Chicago: Rand McNally, 1967).

79 Adolf Berle, *Power Without Property* (New York: Harcourt Brace, 1959).

80 Earl Latham, 'The Group Basis of Politics: Notes for a Theory', *American Political Science Review* 46, 2 (1952): 376-97, 390.

81 Graham T. Allison and Morton H. Halperin, 'Bureaucratic Politics: A Paradigm and Some Policy Implications', *World Politics* 24 (1972): 40-79.

82 William E. Connolly, 'The Challenge to Pluralist Theory' in W.E. Connolly (ed.), *The Bias of Pluralism* (New York: Atherton Press, 1969): 3-34.

83 Charles Lindblom, *Politics and Markets: The World's Political Economic Systems* (New York: Basic Books, 1977).

84   L. Harmon Zeigler, *Interest Groups in American Society* (Englewood Cliffs: Prentice Hall, 1964).

85   See Robert V. Presthus, *Elite Accommodation in Canadian Politics* (Cambridge: Cambridge University Press, 1973). However, the use of a pluralist analysis in the examination of socialist one-party states proved much more beneficial than earlier analysis based on notions of 'totalitarianism'. See, for example, Jerry F. Hough, 'The Soviet System: Petrification or Pluralism', *Problems of Communism* 21 (1972): 25-45; H.G. Skilling, 'Interest Groups and Communist Politics', *World Politics* 18, 3 (1966): 435-51.

86   Phillipe C. Schmitter, 'Modes of Interest Intermediation and Models of Societal Change in Western Europe', *Comparative Political Studies* 10, 1 (1977): 7-38.

87   Otto von Gierke, *Natural Law and the Theory of Society, 1500-1800* (Cambridge: Cambridge University Press, 1958); Otto von Gierke, *Political Theories of the Middle Age* (Cambridge: Cambridge University Press, 1958). The term 'Neo-Corporatism' is often used simply to distance contemporary corporatist theory from the authoritarian practices of fascist governments throughout Europe and Latin America in the 1930s and 1940s which claimed to be corporatist. Neo-Corporatism is thought to be less likely to conjure up images of militarism, nationalism, or totalitarianism associated with fascism, but is otherwise identical to 'Corporatism'. We will, however, use the terms 'Corporatism' and 'neo-Corporatism' interchangeably. James M. Malloy, 'Statecraft, Social Policy, and Governance in Latin America', *Governance* 6, 2 (1993): 220-74; P.C. Schmitter, 'Reflections on Where the Theory of Neo-Corporatism Has Gone and Where the Praxis of Neo-Corporatism May be Going' in G. Lehmbruch and P.C. Schmitter (eds), *Patterns of Corporatist Policy-Making* (London: Sage, 1982): 259-79; Klaus von Beyme, 'Neo-Corporatism: A New Nut in an Old Shell?', *International Political Science Review* 4, 2 (1983): 173-96.

88   See Alan Cawson, *Corporatism and Political Theory* (Oxford: Basil Blackwell, 1986); Michael Mann, 'The Autonomous Power of the State: Its Origins, Mechanisms and Results' *European Journal of Sociology* 25, 2 (1984): 185-213 and J.T. Winkler, 'Corporatism', *European Journal of Sociology* 17, 1 (1976): 100-36.

89   Phillipe C. Schmitter, 'Modes of Interest Intermediation': 9.

90   Gregor McLennan, *Marxism, Pluralism and Beyond*: 245.

91   Leo Panitch, 'The Development of Corporatism in Liberal Democracies', *Comparative Political Studies* 10, 1 (1977): 61-90 and Leo Panitch, 'Corporatism in Canada', *Studies in Political Economy* 1 (1979): 43-92.

92   Alan Cawson, 'Pluralism, Corporatism and the Role of the State', *Government and Opposition* 13, 2 (1978): 178-98.

93   Phillipe C. Schmitter, 'Neo-Corporatism and the State' in Wyn Grant (ed.), *The Political Economy of Corporatism* (London: Macmillan, 1985): 32-62.

94   Otto Hintze, *The Historical Essays of Otto Hintze* (New York: Oxford University Press, 1975); J.P. Nettl, 'The State as a Conceptual Variable', *World Politics* 20, 4 (1968): 559-92; Max Weber, *Economy and Society: An Outline of Interpretive Sociology* (Berkeley: University of California Press, 1978).

95   Theda Skocpol, 'Bringing the State Back In: Strategies of Analysis in Current Research' in Peter B. Evans, Dietrich Rueschemeyer, and Theda Skocpol (eds), *Bringing the State Back In* (New York: Cambridge University Press, 1985): 3-43.

96   Adam Przeworski, *The State and the Economy Under Capitalism* (Chur, Switzerland: Harwood Academic Publishers, 1990): 47-8

97   Stephen D. Krasner, 'Approaches to the State: Alternative Conceptions and Histor-
     ical Dynamics', *Comparative Politics* 16, 2 (1984): 223-46; Theda Skocpol, 'Bringing
     the State Back In': 3-43.
98   Przeworski, *The State and the Economy Under Capitalism.*
99   John A. Hall and G. John Ikenberry, *The State* (Minneapolis: University of
     Minnesota Press, 1989); Gregor McLennan, *Marxism, Pluralism and Beyond.*
100 Theda Skocpol, 'Bringing the State Back In': 7-8.
101 Gregor McLennan, *Marxism, Pluralism and Beyond.*
102 Laurent Dobuzinskis, 'Modernist and Postmodernist Metaphors of the Policy
     Process: Control and Stability vs Chaos and Reflexive Understanding', *Policy Sciences*
     25 (1992): 355-80.
103 While the learning theories represent a major departure for policy analysis from
     political, economic, or sociological theorization, only recently have they started
     taking insights revealed by the actor- and institution-centred theories into account
     See for example, Jenny Stewart, 'Corporatism, Pluralism and Political Learning: A
     Systems Approach', *Journal of Public Policy* 12, 3 (1992): 243-56 and Steven G. Liv-
     ingston, 'Knowledge Hierarchies and the Politics of Ideas in American International
     Commodity Production', *Journal of Public Policy* 12, 3 (1992): 223-42.

FURTHER READING

Jenkins-Smith, Hank, 'Continuing Controversies in Policy Analysis', pp. 23-43 in David
     L. Weimer (ed.), *Policy Analysis and Economics: Developments, Tensions, Prospects*, Boston:
     Kluwer, 1991.

Kiser, Larry and Elinor Ostrom, 'The Three Worlds of Action', pp. 179-222 in Elinor
     Ostrom (ed.), *Strategies of Political Inquiry*, Beverly Hills: Sage, 1982.

Krasner, Stephen, 'Sovereignty: An Institutional Perspective', *Comparative Political Studies*
     21 (1988): 66-94.

March, James G. and Johan P. Olsen, 'The New Institutionalism: Organizational Factors
     in Political Life', *American Political Science Review* 78 (1984): 734-49.

McLennan, Gregor, *Marxism, Pluralism and Beyond: Classic Debates and New Departures*,
     Cambridge: Polity Press, 1989.

Self, Peter, *Political Theories of Modern Government: Its Role and Reform*, London: Allen and
     Unwin, 1985.

Skocpol, Theda, 'Bringing the State Back In: Strategies of Analysis in Current Research',
     pp. 3-43 in Peter B. Evans, Dietrich Rueschemeyer, and Theda Skocpol (eds), *Bringing
     the State Back In*, New York: Cambridge University Press, 1985.

Smith, Martin J., 'Pluralism, Reformed Pluralism and Neopluralism: The Role of
     Pressure Groups in Policy-Making', *Political Studies* 38 (June 1990): 302-22.

Winden, Frans A.A.M. Van, 'The Economic Theory of Political Decision-Making', pp.
     9-57 in Julien van den Broeck (ed.), *Public Choice*, Dordrecht: Kluwer, 1988.

Part 2

ACTORS, INSTITUTIONS, AND INSTRUMENTS

Chapter 3

Actors and Institutions: Assessing the Policy Capabilities of States

CONCEPTUAL ISSUES

There is a vibrant, though ultimately inconclusive, debate in the literature on the role of actors and institutions in the public policy process. The dispute hinges on the causal significance of the actors' interests and capabilities compared to the institutional context in which they operate. Some analysts regard actors as the only relevant category of analysis; others maintain that what the actors seek and do depends on the political, economic, and social institutions that surround them.

Most of the approaches to public policy discussed in the preceding chapter treat actors as the key explanatory variables. Thus the Welfare Economics and Public Choice theories regard individuals as the agents that shape policy, whereas the theories built on Pluralism and Corporatism attribute primacy to organized groups. Similarly, Statism and Neo-Institutionalism treat the state itself as an actor and explain public policy in terms of its objectives and capabilities. While some of the more nuanced of these analyses do consider the institutional context within which these actors operate, their theoretical predisposition prevents them from dealing adequately with the institutional factors affecting public policy. In contrast, theories based on class treat actors as creatures of economic structures, explaining all their actions in terms of structural imperatives or functional necessity. Again, while the more sophisticated of these analyses do recognize the importance of actors, there are limits to the extent to which actors can be incorporated into these analyses given the theories' emphasis on the economic base and the class conflicts it generates. The more empirical bent of policy science requires analysts to include both actors and institutions in their analysis, and this is the orientation we intend to follow here.

In our view both actors and institutions play a crucial role in the policy process, even though one may be more important than the other in specific instances. Individuals, groups, classes, and states participating in the policy process no doubt have their own interests, but the manner in which they interpret and pursue their interests, and the outcomes of their efforts, are shaped by institutional factors. However, there is no way of predicting in advance which one is more important in a particular instance. We must therefore consider both, leaving it to empirical analysis to reveal the relative significance of each in specific circumstances.

Figure 4 diagrams the relationship between actors and institutions that typically obtains in the policy process.

Figure 4.
Actors and Institutions in the Policy Process

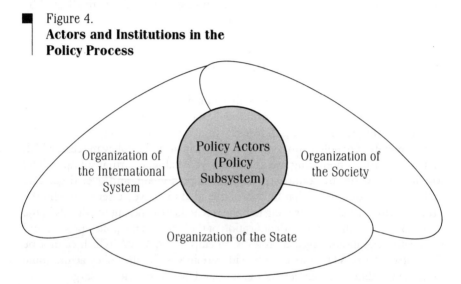

Policies are made by *policy subsystems* consisting of actors dealing with a public problem. The term 'actor' includes both state and societal actors, some of whom are intimately involved in the policy process while other are only marginally so. In Chapter Six, we will discuss the actors who participate directly in the policy process as members of *policy networks* and those involved in a more general sense as belonging to *policy communities*. Policy subsystems are forums where actors discuss policy issues and persuade and bargain in pursuit of their interests. During the course of their interaction with the other actors, they often give up or modify their objectives in return for concessions from other members of the subsystem. These interactions, however, occur in the context of various institutional arrangements surrounding the policy process and affecting how the actors pursue their interests and ideas and the extent to which their efforts succeed.

In this book we define institutions narrowly as the structures and organization of the state, society, and the international system. We are concerned with the way they are organized internally and in relation to each other. In addition to their formal organizational characteristics—membership, rules, and operating procedures—we need to know the principles, norms, and ideas they embody. Institutions shape actors' behaviour by conditioning the latters' perception of their interests and affecting the probability of realizing them by constraining some choices and facilitating others. Even more significantly, some institutional arrangements are believed to be more conducive to effective policy-making and implementation than others.[1] While not monolithic, omnipresent, or immutable, institutions cannot be avoided, modified, or replaced without considerable effort. The purpose of the following discussion is to examine the role of the various actors in policy subsystems and assess how they are affected by the surrounding institutional arrangements.

ACTORS IN THE POLICY PROCESS

Actors in the policy process may be either individuals or groups. As mentioned earlier, the actors involved in a particular policy area can be referred to collectively as a 'policy subsystem'. There is, however, almost an infinite variety of actors who may be members of policy subsystems and participate in the policy process, which makes the task of preparing a comprehensive catalogue virtually impossible. Membership varies by country, policy sector, or domain, and over time. The highly abstract discussion that follows is intended to convey a sense of who the primary actors usually are, leaving it to the researcher to find out the details in the particular area of their study. Identification of the actors in the policy process and the relative significance of their roles is an empirical question which cannot be delineated *a priori*. All that we can say with certainty is that the policy actors come both from within the machinery of the state and from the society at large.

For the sake of simplification, policy actors may be divided into the following five categories: elected officials, appointed officials, interest groups, research organizations, and mass media. The first two reside within the state and the latter three in the society, and together they form the principal elements from which members of specific policy subsystems are drawn. But before we discuss the role of these actors, we need to say something about the role of voters and political parties, two actors straddling the divide between state and society.

Surprising as it may appear, voters play a rather small role in the policy process. On the one hand, in democratic states voting is the most basic means of participating in the political and, by implication, policy processes. It not only affords voters the opportunity to express their choice of government, it also empowers them to pressure the political parties and candidates seeking their votes to offer attractive policy packages. But on the other hand, the voters' policy capacity usually cannot be actualized, at least not directly, for various reasons. In modern democracies policies are made by representatives of voters, who, once elected, are not required to heed the preferences of their voters in their day-to-day functioning. Moreover, most legislators participate very little in the policy process which tends to be dominated by experts in specific sectoral issues rather than legislative generalists.[2] More significantly, candidates and political parties often do not run in elections on the basis of their policy platforms; even when they do, voters usually do not vote on the basis of proposed policies alone. Having said that, it is true that politicians do heed public opinion in some general sense while devising policies, even though they do not always respond to it, much less accommodate it.

Similarly, political parties have a significant impact on public policy, but they do so only indirectly. They are not represented in the policy subsystem, though many of the actors in the subsystem may be influenced by the party to which they are affiliated. Thus empirical studies show significant differences in the policies of governments run by different parties. Governments led by social democratic and Christian democratic parties, for example, have been found to relate positively to the development of welfare state programs.[3] However the significance of parties is challenged by those who argue that government has become too complex for influence by generalists at periodic party conventions, with day-to-day influence stemming more from specialists in government or in the employ of interest groups or specialized policy research institutes.[4] Be that as it may, to the extent political parties do influence public policy, they do so through their members in the executive and, to a lesser degree, in the legislature, rather than directly. Indeed, it is not uncommon for party members in government to ignore their official party platform while designing policies.

Elected Officials

The elected officials participating in the policy process may be divided into two categories—members of the executive and of the legislature—though the latter, as we shall see shortly, often play only a minor role.

The Executive
The executive, also referred to as the cabinet in many countries, is one of the key players in the policy sub-system. Its central role derives from its constitutional authority to govern the country. While there are other actors also involved in the process, the authority to make and implement policies rests ultimately with the executive. There are indeed few checks on the executive in parliamentary systems (such as Japan, Canada, Australia, and Britain) as long as the government enjoys majority support in the legislature. It is somewhat different in Republican or Presidential systems (as in the United States or Brazil) where the executive often has a difficult task convincing the Congress to approve its measures. But even here, the executive has a wide area of discretion beyond legislative control.

In addition to its prerogative in policy matters, the executive possesses a range of other resources that strengthen its position. Control over information is one such critical resource. The executive has unmatched information which it withholds, releases, and manipulates in a manner that bolsters its preference and weaken the case of those opposed to it. Control over fiscal resources is another asset favouring the executive because legislative approval of the budget usually permits wide areas of discretion for the government. The executive also has unparalleled access to mass media in publicizing its positions and undermining those of its opponents. Moreover, it has the bureaucracy at its disposal to provide advice and to carry out its preferences. It can, and often does, use these resources to control and influence societal actors such as interest groups, mass media, and think tanks. In many countries, as well, the government has important powers allowing it to control the timing of the introduction and passage of laws in the legislature. This confers a great deal of control of the political agenda on the executive.[5]

Counteracting the executive's immense constitutional, informational, financial, and personnel resources are conditions that make their task difficult. The tremendous growth in the size, scope, and complexity of government functions over the years prevents generalist politicians from controlling, or often even being aware of, the specific activities of government nominally under their control.[6] Moreover, ministers are constantly bombarded with societal demands, many of which are mutually contradictory but which they often cannot ignore because of the need to maintain voters' support. Finally, and perhaps most importantly, a government may not have the organizational capacity to make coherent policies and implement them effectively—a point discussed in detail later in the chapter.

The Legislature

In parliamentary systems the task of the legislature is to hold governments accountable to the public rather than to make or implement policies. But the performance of this function permits opportunities for influencing policies. Legislatures are crucial forums where social problems are highlighted and policies to address them are demanded. Legislators also get to have their say during the process of approving government bills enacting policies and governmental budgets funding their implementation. In return for their consent, they are sometimes able to demand changes to the policies in question. Legislators may also raise and discuss problems of implementation and request changes. However, a legislature's policy potential may not be realized in practice.[7] This is because of the dominance enjoyed by the executive and its effects upon the internal organization of the legislatures, and upon the role played by legislative committees.

Most laws are proposed by the executive and more often than not subsequently adopted by the legislature. This is especially so in parliamentary systems where the majority party forms the government and therefore is generally expected to support the passage of bills proposed by the executive. In parliamentary democracies, only in situations of minority government can legislatures normally expect to shape executive bills. In Presidential systems, on the other hand, the Congress is autonomous of the government constitutionally as well as in practice, which explains why Presidents, irrespective of whether their party holds a majority in the Congress, must strike bargains with the legislature or risk defeat.

The internal organization of the legislature is also a significant determinant of the legislatures' role in the policy process. Legislatures where the membership is tightly organized along party lines, and marked by a high degree of cohesion and discipline, permit little opportunity for legislators to take an independent stand. This is particularly true in parliamentary systems where the legislators belonging to the governing party are always expected to support the government. Similarly, the role of individual legislators is lower in parliaments in which one party has a clear majority; the existence of several minor parties in coalition governments permits greater opportunity for legislators to express their opinion and force the government to compromise.

In many contemporary legislatures, policy functions are performed not on the floor of the legislature but in the committees established along functional lines to review proposed legislation. Committees often build considerable expertise in the area with which they deal, and the extent to which this happens enables the legislature to exercise influence over making and implementing policies. But to build expertise, the members need to serve on the committees over a relatively long period of time. Committee members must also not necessarily vote along party lines if their autonomy and assertiveness are to be maintained.

The nature of the problem being considered also affects legislative involvement in the policy process. Technical issues are unlikely to involve legislators because they may not fully understand the problems or solutions, or they may see little political benefit in pursuing the matter. National security and foreign policies are usually conducted in a shroud of secrecy and outside the legislature. Similarly, policies dealing with a problem perceived to be a crisis are also unlikely to involve the legislature very much because of the time it takes to introduce, debate, and pass a bill. Policies dealing with allocation or redistribution of resources or income generate the highest degree of passion and debate in legislatures, but usually do not have much effect on the government's policy. However, other policies related to propagation and maintenance of certain symbolic values—such as the choice of a national flag, multiculturalism, prayers in schools, or the elimination of racism and sexism—are often so divisive that the executive may be somewhat more willing to take the legislators' views into account in forming legislation.

As a result of these limitations, legislatures generally play only a small role in the policy process. While some individual legislators may, on the basis of their expertise or special interest in the problem, be included in the policy subsystem, legislatures as a whole are not very significant actors in the making or implementing of public policies.

Appointed Officials

The appointed officials dealing with public policy and administration are often collectively referred to as the 'bureaucracy'. Their function is to assist the executive in the performance of its tasks, as is suggested by the terms 'civil servants' or 'public servants' used to describe them. However, the reality of modern government is such that their role goes well beyond what one would expect of a 'servant'. Indeed bureaucrats are very often the keystone in the policy process and the central figures in many policy subsystems.

Most of the policy-making and implementing functions once performed by legislatures and the political executive are now performed by the bureaucracy. The functions of modern government are too complex and numerous to be performed by the cabinet. The bureaucracy, in contrast, consists of a large number of specialists who have the time and expertise to deal with a policy issue on a continuing basis. It is also sometimes argued that regulation has replaced legislation, and that appointed officials through their specialized knowledge of government regulatory activities have to a large extent replaced the elected politician.[8]

The bureaucracy's power and influence is based on a range of resources.[9] First, the law itself provides for certain crucial functions to be performed by the bureaucracy, and may confer wide discretion on individual bureaucrats to make decisions on behalf of the state. Second, bureaucracies have unmatched access to material resources for pursuing their own organizational, even personal, objectives if they so wish. The government is the largest single spender in most (if not all) countries, a situation that gives its officials a powerful voice in policy areas involving significant government expenditure. Third, the bureaucracy is a repository of a wide range of skills and expertise, resources that make it a premier organization in society. It employs large numbers of just about every kind of professional, hired for their status as experts in their areas of specialization. That they deal with similar issues on a continuing basis endows them with unique insights into many problems. Fourth, modern bureaucracies have access to vast quantities of information on the different aspects of society. At times the information is deliberately gathered, but at others the information comes to the bureaucracy simply as a part of its central location in the government. Fifth, the permanence of the bureaucracy and the long tenure of its members often gives it an edge over its superiors, the elected executive. Finally, the fact that policy deliberations for the most part occur in secret within the bureaucracy denies other policy actors the opportunity to mount opposition to its plans.

However, we must avoid exaggerating the role of the bureaucracy. The executive is ultimately responsible for all policies, an authority it does assert at times. High profile political issues are more likely to involve higher levels of executive control. Executive control is also likely to be higher if the bureaucracy consistently opposes a policy option preferred by the politicians. Moreover, the bureaucracy itself is not a homogeneous organization but rather a collection of organizations, each with its own interests, perspectives, and standard operating procedures which make arriving at a unified position difficult. Even within the same department, there are often divisions along functional, personal, political, and technical lines. Thus it is not uncommon for the executive to intervene to resolve intra- and inter-bureaucratic conflicts, and bureaucrats in democratic countries usually require the support of elected officials if they are to exercise their influence in any meaningful way.[10]

Interest Groups

While policy-making is a preserve of the government, and particularly of the executive and bureaucracy, the realities of modern politics enable interest groups to play a significant role in the process. One of the most important resources of interest groups is knowledge: specifically, information that may be unavailable or less available to others. The members of such a group often know the most about their area of concern. Since policy-making is a highly information-intensive process, those with information may normally expect to play an important role. Politicians and bureaucrats often find the information provided by groups indispensable for performing their tasks. Government and opposition politicians often curry favour with interest groups to secure the information required for effective policy-making or for attacking their opponents. Bureaucrats similarly need the relevant groups for developing and implementing policies.

The other resources interest or pressure groups possess are organizational and political. Groups often make financial contributions to the campaign chests of sympathetic political parties and politicians. They also campaign for and deliver votes to sympathetic candidates who they think would support their cause in the government.

However, interest groups' political impacts on the formulation and implementation of public policies vary considerably according to their varying organizational resources.[11] First, interest groups differ tremendously in terms of size of membership. All other things being equal, larger groups can be expected to be taken more seriously by the government.[12] Second, some groups may form a 'peak association' consisting of groups with similar interest.[13] A coherent peak association may be expected to be more influential than those operating individually. Third, some groups are well funded which enables them to hire permanent specialized staff and make campaign contributions to parties and candidates during election. While the exact impact of financial resources on government policy is contentious,[14] there is no doubt that differences in financial resources matter.

In democratic political systems the information and power resources of interest groups make them key members of policy subsystems. While this does not guarantee that their interests will be accommodated, they are unlikely to be entirely ignored, except in rare circumstances when executives make a high-level and deliberate decision to go ahead with a policy despite opposition from the concerned groups.

Later in the chapter we will discuss how the organization of two particular groups, business and labour, have a critical impact on the policy process and its outcomes.

Research Organizations

Another significant set of societal actors in the policy process is composed of the researchers working at universities and think tanks. University researchers often have theoretical and philosophical interests in public problems that may not lead to research results that can be translated into usable knowledge for policy purposes. To the extent that they do conduct research for the purpose of participating in the policy debate, they often function in a manner similar to their counterparts in think tanks. Indeed in many instances academics undertaking policy-relevant research are often sponsored by think-tank organizations. The following discussion will therefore concentrate on the role of think tanks.

A think tank can be defined as 'an independent organization engaged in multi-disciplinary research intended to influence public policy'.[15] Such organizations maintain an interest in a broad range of policy problems and employ a variety of expertise enabling them to develop a more comprehensive perspective. Their research tends to be directed at proposing practical solutions to public problems or, in the case of some think tanks, finding evidence to support the ideology-driven positions they advocate. This sets them apart from academic researchers at universities whose interests are more specialized and who do not necessarily seek practical solutions to policy problems. Explicitly partisan research is also generally eschewed in academia. While the think tanks are generally more partisan than their purely academic counterparts, they too must maintain an image of intellectual autonomy from the government or political party if policy-makers are to take them seriously. Prominent think tanks in the United States include the Brookings Institution, the American Enterprise Institute, and the Urban Institute. The corresponding organizations in Canada include the C.D. Howe Institute and the Fraser Institute; in Britain, the list would include the Policy Studies Institute, and the National Institute for Economic and Social Research. However there are literally hundreds of such institutes active in each of these countries.[16]

Think tanks target their research and recommendations on those politicians who may be expected to be favourably disposed to the ideas being espoused. They also seek originality in their ideas and, unlike the researchers working in universities or the government, spend efforts on publicizing them. Over the last few decades, much of the work of think tanks has been devoted to promoting economic efficiency, since this has been an important preoccupation of the governments in the industrialized world. Through sustained analysis and critique, they can have a notable impact on public policy.[17]

Mass Media

Opinions on the role of the mass media in the policy process range from those who regard it as pivotal[18] to those who describe it as marginal.[19] There is no denying that the mass media are crucial links between the state and society, a position that permits them to strongly influence the preferences of the government and the society on public problems and solutions to them. Yet at the same time, their role in the policy process is often sporadic and most often quite marginal.

The role of the media in the policy process lies in the fact that in reporting problems they combine the roles of passive reporter with active analyst as well as an advocate of a solution. News programs do not just report on a problem but often go to great lengths in locating a problem not otherwise obvious, defining its nature and scope, and sometimes suggesting solutions. The media's role in agenda setting is thus particularly significant.[20] Media portrayal of public problems and proposed solutions often conditions how they are understood by the public and the government, thereby shutting out some alternatives and making the choice of another more likely. Questions raised in parliaments are often based on stories in the day's newspaper. This is particularly significant considering that news-reporting is not an objective mirror of reality, undistorted by bias or inaccuracy. News reporters and editors are news-makers, in the sense that they define what is worthy of reporting and the aspects of the case that need highlighting. Thus policy issues that may be presented as an interesting story tend to be viewed by the public as more important than would have otherwise been the case. Similarly, groups and individuals able to present problems to the media in a packaged form are more likely than their less succinct counterparts to have their views projected.

We must not, however, exaggerate the mass media's role in the policy process. The other policy actors too have resources to counteract media influence. Policy-makers are for the most part intelligent and resourceful individuals who understand their own interest and have their own ideas about appropriate or feasible policy options and are not easily swayed by media or the mere fact of media attention. Indeed they often use the media to their own advantage. It is not uncommon for public officials and successful interest groups to provide selective information to the media to bolster their case.

ORGANIZATION OF THE STATE

We have argued public policy-making to be the government's prerogative and its officials the key actors in the process. But beyond this there is the issue of the organization of the state. How the state is organized shapes what it, or rather its officials, can do. Two dimensions of the organization of the state affect its ability to make and implement policies: *autonomy* and *capacity*.

Autonomy refers to the extent of the state's independence from self-serving and conflicting social pressures. Observers of politics have long argued that the self-serving motives and actions of groups benefit their members at the expense of the rest of the society.[21] So policy-making institutions responsive to societal demands, as is supposed to be the case in democratic government, are likely to generate policies that benefit some groups but worsen the welfare of the society as a whole. The problem can be overcome, however, if the government is insulated from the need to respond to the societal pressures placed upon it. While this may compromise some of the basic tenets of democracy, the trade-off is that it is often conducive to effective policy-making.[22] For example, it has been argued that corporatist regimes in Europe and some semi-authoritarian regimes in East Asia possess the political institutions necessary to resist group demands, and as a result have produced sound policies that promote economic prosperity as well as equity.[23]

The state must also have the capacity to make and implement effective policies. The capacity of the state, which is a function of its organizational coherence and expertise, determines its success in performing policy functions. Unity within and among various levels, branches, and agencies of the government, and high levels of bureaucratic expertise are regarded as crucial to enhance state capacity. An executive bogged down in constant bargaining with the legislature or government departments in constant conflict among themselves cannot be expected to perform policy functions adequately. Similarly, the society will not be well-served by a bureaucracy without the expertise necessary to tackle the complex problems it is required to address.

States with political institutions that promote autonomy and capacity are sometimes described as *strong states*; those without such institutions as *weak states*.[24] Japan is often cited as a classic example of a strong state in the industrialized world, whereas the United States is described as a weak state; other industrialized countries fall somewhere in between.[25] States such as Singapore, South Korea, and Taiwan in East Asia are often regarded as some of the strongest in the world. The executive-bureaucratic apparatus is the core of strong states; weak states have legislatures at the core and interest groups dominate policy-making. The reasons why some states are strong and others weak are primarily historical.[26]

However, while describing states as strong or weak is intuitively appealing, it is not without its problems in terms of public policy analysis. First, there is no reason to believe that strong states will necessarily make policies that serve the interests of the society as a whole, rather than those of self-serving groups.[27] It is just as possible that such states will make ill-conceived or predatory policies that will benefit state élites and lower the society's general welfare. Indeed, in such a situation, a strong state will be worse than a weak state, as far as the society is concerned, because of its higher capacity to cause damage. The Ferdinand Marcos government in the Philippines or many former communist regimes in Europe are cases in point. Second, the overall characterization of states as strong or weak is too general to be of much analytical use in public policy analysis.[28] No state is strong in all sectors, nor is any state weak in every sector. Thus even the so-called strong states have shown remarkable weakness in some areas—note the Japanese government's handling of agricultural policy—and the supposedly weak states may show remarkable strength in some areas, such as the Reagan Administration's strong military capacity despite the fragmentation of the overall US state apparatus.

Rather than characterizing states as strong or weak, we must devote efforts to examining empirically the role of governmental institutions in reinforcing or weakening states' policy capabilities and their effects on the actors' behaviour in the policy process. But first, we should note several additional points about the effects of institutions. Among the most important is the fact that many of the effects of institutions are contingent rather than pre-determined. Institutions usually do not *cause* action; they are rather intermediate variables that affect policy choices and outcomes in conjunction with other factors and in response to particular situations. It is also the case that the effects of institutions are not unidirectional; what is a constraint in one situation may be an opportunity in another. Thus, the diffuse policy institutions in the United States make it difficult to make and implement contentious policies, but, once made, they have greater chances of survival against attacks. Moreover, the effects of institutions almost always vary across policy sectors; the same institutions may have different consequences depending on the nature of the problem or the surrounding circumstances. And governments generally have ways of bypassing, or even replacing, institutions if there is sufficient political will and support to do so.[29]

Intergovernmental Division of Power—Federalism

One of the most important factors affecting a government's capacity to make policy is whether it has a federal or unitary form of government. The salient feature of federal political systems with respect to public policy is the existence of two autonomous levels of government within the country. The two levels of government found in countries like Australia, Canada, and the US are not bound together in a superordinate/subordinate relationship, but rather enjoy more or less complete discretion in matters under their jurisdiction and guaranteed by the constitution. This is distinct from the unitary systems found in Britain, Japan, New Zealand or other countries where there is only one level of government; the local bodies (for example, municipalities) owe their existence to the national government rather than to the constitution.

The existence of a federal system significantly affects the capacity of state officials to deal with pressing issues in a timely and consistent fashion because public policies are made and implemented by the national/central as well as state/provincial governments. The problem is aggravated in policy areas characterized by jurisdictional overlap. It makes public policy-making a long, drawn-out and often rancorous affair as the different governments wrangle over jurisdictional issues or are involved in extensive intergovernmental negotiations or constitutional litigation. Different governments within the same country may make contradictory decisions which may weaken or nullify the effects of the policy. The existence of courts to adjudicate jurisdictional disputes further complicates policy-making.[30]

Federalism has been cited as a major reason for the weak policy capacity of governments in Australia, Canada, and the United States. It has constrained these states' capacity to develop consistent and coherent policies. In Canada, national policies in most areas require inter-governmental agreement, which involves the federal and provincial governments in complex, extensive, and time-consuming negotiations with no guarantee that negotiations will conclude in the manner envisioned by the initiating government.[31] Similarly, both levels of government are subject to unpredictable judicial review of their measures which further limits options.

Intragovernmental Division of Power—the Executive, Legislature, and Judiciary

Another institutional variable affecting public policy concerns the links between the executive, legislature, and judiciary provided under a country's constitution. In parliamentary systems, the executive is chosen by the legislature from among its members and remains in office only as long as it enjoys majority support from legislators. In presidential systems, the executive is separate from the legislature, is usually elected directly by the voters, and need not enjoy majority support in the legislature. The United States is the archetype of the presidential system, whereas most of the rest of the world has some version of the parliamentary system; other countries like France have a hybrid of the two systems.

The separation between the executive and legislative branches of the government in the presidential system, and the fusion of the two in the parliamentary system, has important consequences for the policy process.[32] The division of powers promotes difficulties for policy-makers in presidential systems. The individual members and committees of the Congress play an active role in designing policies, including those proposed by the President. It matters only marginally if the party of the President's affiliation forms the majority in both houses of the Congress because of the local concerns that often motivate legislators. To ensure majority support for policy measures requiring legislative approval, it is common for the President to bargain with the members of the Congress, offer concessions in return for support, and thereby change the intent of the policy. The active involvement of the members of the Congress in drafting bills promotes multiple points of conflict with the executive; it also opens up greater opportunities for interest groups and voters to influence the policy process, the result of which may be diluted or even conflicting policies.

In parliamentary systems, in contrast, the executive can more often than not take legislative support for its measures for granted, thanks to the strict party discipline enforced upon individual members of the parliament. While there may be some bargaining over a policy within the caucus, there is little chance of changing it in the parliament. The only time when this may not be the case is when the governing party does not have an outright majority in the legislature and governs in coalition with other parties, who often demand modification to the policy in return for their support. In many countries, coalition governments are routine, which complicates policy-making, though not as much as in the presidential system. Generally speaking, however, policy-making in parliamentary systems is centralized in the executive, which usually enables the government to take decisive action if it so chooses. This is not entirely undesirable, insofar as policy capability is concerned, because the adversarial politics that characterize legislatures' functioning reduces the likelihood of generating coherent or effective policies.

The structure and role of the judiciary also affects the policy process. In federal systems, there is typically an autonomous judiciary entrusted with the task of adjudicating jurisdictional disputes. The same is true for countries with entrenched bills of rights which typically give the courts the power to strike down laws inconsistent with the individuals' rights guaranteed under the constitution.[33] In these countries, the judiciary acts as another potential veto point which constrains what the executive can do in policy matters. In countries without federalism or bills of rights, such as Great Britain, the courts play a more limited role, which permits policy-makers greater room for manoeuvre.[34]

The role of the judiciary in the policy process varies according to the nature of the country's political institutions. British practices developed out of efforts on the part of central officials under the monarchy to control local officials. Many of these efforts were, of course, resisted by the local populace, both commoners and nobles. When Parliament replaced the monarchy as the source of central political power, however, the same principles of judicial review which had been a symbol of despotism became a symbol of democratic government. This differs substantially from the judicial practice in the US where, following the American revolution, natural-law principles of sovereignty which had informed British legal thought were replaced by principles of natural rights and constitutional supremacy. One manifestation of this was the division of powers so characteristic of the American system of government. Another, less obvious, manifestation was the refusal of the American judiciary to subordinate itself to either Congress or the executive, and to insist upon its own role in determining the legality of laws and regulations of all kinds, including those enacted or promulgated by the other two branches of government.

Ultimately, the differences in the US and Canadian principles of judicial review stem from this history of institutional development. Canadian justices remain subordinate to Parliament and in so doing feel they are upholding the principles of democratic government. US justices, citing the same reverence for democratic government, do the opposite.[35] Judicial restraint in British parliamentary systems (such as in Australia and Canada) reflects the unwillingness of judges to replace Parliament as a source of law, and their willingness to defer to democratically-elected politicians in setting the framework within which their decisions will be made.[36] Generally speaking, judicial autonomy and assertiveness complicate policy-making and erode the state's policy capacity to a greater or lesser extent.

The Structure of the Bureaucracy

The structure of the bureaucracy has perhaps the strongest effect on public policy processes, especially at the sectoral level.[37] Indeed Atkinson and Coleman measure state strength in terms of the bureaucracy's strength at the sectoral level, and argue that:

> it is critical to determine, first, the degree to which ultimate decision-making power is concentrated in the hands of a relatively small number of officials and, secondly, the degree to which these officials are able to act autonomously. . . . the state is weak in a given sector when authority is dispersed and no one group of officials can take the lead in formulating policy.[38]

Concentration of power in only a few agencies reduces occasions for conflict and permits long-term policy planning. Diffusion of power, in contrast, fosters inter-agency conflicts and lack of co-ordination; decisions may be made on the basis of their acceptability to all concerned agencies rather than intrinsic merit. The bureaucracies' autonomy from politicians and societal groups also contributes to their strength and effectiveness in policy-making. To be strong, a bureaucracy must have a clear mandate, a professional ethos, and enjoy strong support but not interference from politicians in its day-to-day activities. Close ties with client groups are also to be avoided if a bureaucracy is to be effective. An ability to generate and process its own information is also important if reliance on interest groups is to be avoided.

The strong states in countries like France and Japan have bureaucracies that enjoy an exalted status in government and society.[39] They are said to constitute an homogeneous élite grouping which plays the most important role in the policy process. They undergo long professional training and pursue service in the government as a life-long career. In societies with weak-state traditions, bureaucracies enjoy relatively low status and lack the capacity to resist pressures from legislators or social groups, which often promotes incoherence and shortsightedness in policies. Despite the massive expansion in bureaucracies all over the world over the last several decades, weak bureaucracies in the sense understood here are the norm rather than the exception.[40]

The effective mobilization of bureaucratic expertise is more rare than commonly believed. In many countries with corruption, low wages, and poor working conditions, bureaucracies often do not have the capability to deal with the complex problems they are asked to address. If these conditions obtain in a country, then it is quite likely that the state will have difficulty devising effective policies and implementing them in the manner intended. And in many countries bureaucratic expertise in a particular area may well exist but problems of organization and leadership prevent its effective marshalling.[41]

ORGANIZATION OF THE SOCIETY

The capabilities of a state are determined not just by how it is organized internally, but also by how it is linked to the society whose problems it is supposed to resolve through appropriate policies. To be able to make and implement policies effectively, the state needs the support of prominent social groups for its actions. The extent to which these groups are able to offer the necessary level and form of support depends on their own internal organization. Fragmentation within and among groups weakens the state's ability to mobilize them towards the resolution of societal problems. If the societal conflicts are particularly severe, the state may find itself paralysed in performing policy functions.

Unity within and among social groups makes for a stable policy environment which facilitates policy-making and promotes effective implementation. Strong organizations can bargain more effectively and need not make unreasonable demands for the sake of maintaining their members' support. And when they agree to a measure, they can enforce it upon their membership, through sanctions if necessary. Mancur Olson has argued that in societies characterized by 'encompassing' (that is, umbrella groups consisting of a variety of similar interests) rather than 'narrow' interest groups, the groups 'internalize much of the cost of inefficient policies and accordingly have an incentive to redistribute income to themselves with the least possible social cost, and to give some weight to economic growth and to the interests of society as a whole'.[42] The existence of numerous narrow interest groups, in contrast, promotes competition among groups to pressure the state to serve their members' interests only, regardless of the effects on others, the cumulative effect of which is often contradictory and ineffective policies that leave everyone worse off.

The problem of societal fragmentation is particularly severe when the narrow sectional groups are too strong to be ignored or if the state is too weak to ignore societal pressures. However, the best situation, insofar as effective making and implementing of policies is concerned, is for both state and society to be strong, with close partnership between the two. Peter Evans calls this institutional arrangement 'embedded autonomy'.[43] In contrast, policy effectiveness is lowest when the state is weak and the society fragmented. In the former scenario, states in partnership with social groups can be expected to devise cohesive and long-term policies. In the latter, the state can be expected to produce ineffective and short-sighted policies.

As pointed out by both neo-pluralist and corporatist theorists, among societal groups it is the organization of business and labour that is often most significant in determining a state's policy capabilities. This is because of their vital role each plays in the production process, which is in every society a fundamental activity that has effects far beyond the economy.

Business

Among interest groups, business is generally the most powerful, with an unmatched capacity to affect public policy. To understand what is referred to as the 'structural power of capital', we need to comprehend the broader socio-economic context of a capitalist economy. Such an economy, by definition, entails a market form of economic organization in which ownership of the means of production is concentrated in firms or corporations. It is this fact that lies at the root of business's unparalleled power.[44]

The increasing globalization of production and financial activities due to improvements in modern means of communication and transportation and the gradual removal of controls on international economic transactions have contributed tremendously to the power of capital in recent decades. It is possible for investors and managers to respond, if they so wish, to any unwanted government action by removing capital to another location. Although this theoretical mobility is limited by a variety of factors—including the availability of suitable investment opportunities in other countries—the potential loss of employment and revenues is a threat with which the state must contend in making decisions. Because of the negative consequences this entails for state revenues, capitalists—both domestic and foreign—have the ability to 'punish' the state for any action it might take of which they disapprove.

The financial contributions that businesses make to political parties and their ability to fund researchers of their choice also afford them an important resource with which to influence policy-makers. Elections can sometimes turn on relatively short-term issues and personalities, which necessitate large budgets to influence voters through extensive media advertising campaigns. In such situations, political parties supported by contributions from business are in a better position to run such campaigns and thus influence voting behaviour. This can lead political parties and candidates running for office to accommodate business interests more than they would those of other groups. Similarly, the financial contributions that businesses often make to research institutions and individual researchers serves to further entrench their power. The organizations and individuals receiving funds tend to be sympathetic towards business interests and can provide business with the intellectual wherewithal often required to prevail in policy debates.

The structural strength of business has the potential to both promote and erode social welfare. The latter is likely to be the case when business lacks organizational coherence. The ability of individual firms and capitalists to pressure the government to serve their interests can lead, if the latter succumbs to the pressure, to incoherent and short-sighted policies. Endemic conflicts among various business groups only aggravate such situations. The problem may be offset if business has a central cohesive organization able to thrash out differences and come up with coherent policy proposals. If the government does accept such proposals, they are likely to serve the interest of the broader economy (though not all sections of the society equally) rather than the interests of particular firms or economic sectors. A strong business organization is therefore necessary, though not sufficient, for coherent and effective policies.

A strong business organization is one which is able to adopt a bold position if necessary and convey it to the government, without incurring serious opposition from its rank and file. It usually takes the form of a peak association (a sort of federation of associations) with the authority to impose sanctions and discipline among its members, since the state must have confidence that once a commitment has been made by the association, it can expect adherence to it by individual businesses. Moreover, if the state is confident of the strength of the business association, then it can delegate some business-related responsibilities to the business association itself. Generally speaking, the US is regarded as having the weakest business organizations in the industrialized world and Japan the strongest, with countries like Britain or Canada falling closer to the US model and those like France, Germany, Austria, or Sweden closer to the Japanese model.[45]

The strength or weakness of business and the varying patterns of government-industry relations found in a country are usually shaped by a range of historical factors.[46] Although the example of Japan cited above is somewhat atypical, business is often strongly organized if it has been confronted with strong, persistent challenges from trade unions or socialist parties. The stronger the unions, the stronger will be the business influence. The threat does not necessarily have to be continuing, so long as such was the case in the past. Second, countries with strong states often have strong business organizations because in order to pressure strong governments, business itself must be well organized. A strong state may also nurture a strong business association in order to avoid the problems arising from too many groups making conflicting demands on the same issue. The existence of strong business associations simplifies the government's job by aggregating their demands within the organization. Third, the organizational strength of business is affected by the structure of the economy. Economies characterized by low industrial concentration or high levels of foreign ownership make organizing the disparate elements and devising a common position difficult. Fourth, political culture too has an important bearing on the extent and nature of business involvement in politics. In countries such as the US or Canada with cultures highly supportive of business, corporations have seen few reasons to organize. Moreover, the degree to which social norms approve of functional representation affects the strength of business. US, and to a lesser extent British and Canadian, citizens are distrustful of business representing its interests on a regular basis behind closed doors. In the corporatist countries, on the other hand, functional representation is accepted as a part of the political culture and indeed is often encouraged.

Labour

Labour too occupies a powerful position among groups, though not so power-ful as business. Unlike business, which enjoys considerable weight with policy-makers even at the individual level of the firm, labour needs a collective organization, a trade union, to have its voice heard in the policy subsystem. In addition to bargaining with employers on behalf of their members, which is their primary function, trade unions engage in political activities to shape gov-ernment policies affecting them.[47] The origin of the role of the trade unions in the public policy process is rooted in late-nineteenth-century democratization which enabled workers, who form a majority in every industrialized society, to have a say in the functioning of the government. Given the voting clout afforded them by democracy, it was sometimes easier for them to pressure the government to meet their needs than to bargain with their employers. The for-mation of labour or social democratic parties, and eventually forming govern-ments in many countries, further reinforced labour's political clout.

The factors shaping the nature and effectiveness of the trade unions' par-ticipation in the policy process depend on a variety of institutional and contex-tual factors. The structure of the state itself is an important determinant of union participation in the policy process. A weak and fragmented state will not be able to secure effective participation by the unions, because the latter would see little certainty that the government would be able to keep its side of any bar-gain. Weak businesses can also inhibit the emergence of a powerful trade union organization because the need for it is less immediate.

However, the most important determinant of labour's capacity to influence the policy process and its outcomes is its own internal organization. The level of union membership affects the extent to which states seek or even accept unions' participation in the policy process. The same is true for the structure of the bar-gaining units: de-centralized collective bargaining promotes a fragmented sys-tem of articulation of labour demands. Britain, Canada, and the United States are said to have decentralized bargaining structures, whereas in Australia, Aus-tria, and the Scandinavian countries bargaining takes place at the industry or even country-wide level.[48] A union movement fragmented along any or all of possible regional, linguistic, ethnic, religious, or industrial versus craft, foreign versus domestic, or import-competing versus export-oriented lines will also experience difficulties in influencing the policy process. Fragmentation among labour ranks tends to promote local and sporadic industrial strife, and incoher-ent articulation of labour's interest in the policy process.[49]

Finally, labour needs a central organization (such as the Australian or British Trade Union Congress, the Canadian Labour Congress, and the Amer-ican Federation of Labor-Congress of Industrial Organizations) to realize its policy potential even more than business. Collective action is the only tool labour has to influence the employers' or the government's behaviour, so the more united a front it is able to put up, the more successful it is likely to be.

To be effective, the trade union central needs to enjoy comprehensive membership and have the organizational capacity to deal with conflicts among its members and maintain unity. Trade unions' role in the policy process tends to be the highest in corporatist political systems, such as Scandinavia, Austria, and the Netherlands, and the lowest in pluralist political systems such as the United States or Canada.[50]

ORGANIZATION OF THE INTERNATIONAL SYSTEM

In addition to the domestic institutions discussed above, the public policy process and its outcomes in many countries are shaped increasingly by international institutions. As one would expect, their influence is the strongest in policy sectors that are by their very nature international: trade and defence, for example. But even in sectors with no apparent international connection—such as health or old age pensions—states find themselves affected by forces originating outside the country. Like their domestic counterparts, international institutions affect public policy by shaping actors' preferences and the facility with which they can be realized.

Assessing the effects of international institutions is, however, a lot more difficult than assessing those of institutions in the domestic arena. For one thing, states are sovereign entities with the legal authority to close their borders to any and all foreign influences as and when they choose. However, in reality it is nearly impossible for states to stop foreign influences at the border because of constraints rooted in the international system.[51] The extent to which a state is able to assert its sovereignty depends on the severity of international pressures and the nature of the issue in question, as well as features innate to the state. All these make it difficult to study systematically the effects of international institutions on states' public policies, as evidenced by the paucity of studies on the subject, and the contradictory conclusions drawn by the few that do exist. Let us briefly discuss the sources and character of international pressures before studying their effects.

To conceptualize the disparate international factors affecting states' behaviour, scholars have developed the notion of 'international regimes' to describe the institutionalized arrangements in a given policy area.[52] Regimes have been defined by Robert Keohane and Joseph Nye as 'sets of governing arrangements' or 'networks of rules, norms, and procedures that regularize behaviour and control its effects'.[53] Regimes define what constitutes appropriate behaviour and thus introduce a modicum of certainty in an otherwise anarchic system. In doing so, they affect not only the international behaviour of states but also what they can do domestically. Thus a government willing, under pressure from interest groups or at its own initiative, to assist domestic producers by offering export subsidies may not be able to do so because of formal and informal international constraints. Regimes of varying scope and depth can be found in most, though not all, prominent policy areas.

The origin and the extent of the effects of regimes are highly contentious. Some view the origin of regimes as a creation of the hegemonic power (such as the United States in the post-war period) seeking to establish order in the international system for its own as well as other countries' benefit.[54] Others view regimes' emergence as responding to the common needs of states seeking prosperity and security, goals that can be best achieved through co-operation with other states.[55] There is, of course, no reason why both cannot be true. Indeed, it is our contention that both factors have played a significant role in the establishment of the prominent international regimes governing relations among states.

International regimes vary considerably according to their form, scope of coverage, level of adherence, and the instruments through which they are put into practice.[56] Some regimes are based on explicit treaties whereas others are based simply on conventions that develop as a result of repeated behaviour. Some cover a variety of related issues while others are quite narrow in coverage. Some are closely adhered to and others just as often flouted, and some are enforced through formal or informal penalties whereas others make no such provision. Besides, some regimes are administered by formal organizations with large budgets and staffs, while some are more akin to moral codes.[57]

Mapping all the effects of all international regimes is clearly beyond the scope of this book; we will only indicate areas that need to be considered in the analysis of public policy. International regimes in the areas of trade and finance are clearly the most important in this respect, and to them we now turn.

International Trade Regime

In the area of international trade, the edifice on which the contemporary international trade regime is based is the General Agreement on Tariffs and Trade, or GATT. The agreement was signed in 1947 among twenty-three members, but has over the years expanded to include over one hundred members, with many more maintaining *de facto* adherence to it. The overwhelming majority of world exports is governed by its provisions. As a result of the Uruguay Round of GATT bargaining, completed in 1994, a new entity—the World Trade Organization (WTO)—will come into existence in 1995 and succeed the GATT.

The GATT/WTO establishes reciprocal rights and obligations among the signatories to reduce barriers to international trade. The main provisions of the GATT/WTO regime include maintaining non-discrimination in trade practices, constant pressure to reduce tariffs, general prohibition against quantitative restrictions on imports, and regulation of other practices that inhibit trade.[58] The provisions are intended to expand opportunities for exporters to sell in other countries' markets, but they also constrain states' ability to maintain barriers against imports, except under circumstances provided for in the agreement.

The main outcome of the obligation incurred as a result of acceding to the GATT/WTO is that nations lose their autonomy with respect to assisting domestic producers. By joining GATT/WTO, a country agrees to lower its trade barriers, to not subsidize exports, and to accord 'national treatment' to imports from other members. Accession to GATT/WTO is especially problematic for small economies which are under constant pressure to adjust and readjust to international economic pressures. For producers that do succeed in becoming internationally competitive, the economic rewards are high because of the larger markets they can sell to as a result of the lowering of trade barriers. Producing countries which fail to maintain international competitiveness bear the costs in terms of reduced profits and loss of jobs. Of course, there are ways of getting around the constraints of the GATT/WTO, such as by pressuring the exporter to 'voluntarily' reduce their exports (euphemistically called Voluntary Export Restraint Agreements), but these options are not generally open to smaller countries because of their weak bargaining power.

In addition to economic benefits and costs, liberalized trade also has political benefits and costs. Trade relations reinforce diplomatic and security relations. It is no coincidence that the world's largest trading partners are also bound together by security alliances: the North Atlantic Treaty Organization (NATO), for example. However, trade relations also make nations vulnerable to international diplomatic and political pressures. A high degree of dependence on just one country is especially constraining because of the leverage enjoyed by the larger trading partner. It is for this reason, for example, that Canada's dependence on the US for the vast majority of its exports and imports is regarded as a matter of concern by many Canadians.

International Financial Regime

To facilitate international trade in conjunction with the GATT, a liberal monetary system—called the Bretton Woods system, named after the place in New Hampshire where it was signed—was established in 1944. It provided for fixed exchange rates for national currencies against the US dollar, which was believed to promote greater predictability in international economic transactions.[59] For various reasons (the discussion of which would be a diversion from our concerns here) which were causing problems to both the US and other countries, in 1976 the fixed exchange system was replaced with a flexible exchange rate system, a system that continues to this day. Exchange rates under this regime are not fixed, but rather determined by financial markets according to the demand and supply of a country's currency. Since the financial markets are highly volatile and depend as they do on the dealers' interpretation of a country's present economic conditions and their expectations in the future, this system often results in unpredictable but sizeable fluctuations in the value of national currencies.

Even more important than the flexible exchange rate system are the effects of financial deregulation and technological improvements that enable the transfer of money around the globe at astonishing speed. As a result, international financial markets are now so integrated that they impose severe constraints on policy-makers. For example, in April 1989, foreign exchange trading in the world's financial markets averaged US$ 650 billion a day, about forty times the amount of world trade.[60] With such huge volumes at stake, international money markets have the ability to cause havoc for a country whose economic policies are viewed unfavourably by international capital. States must now be extremely careful about the effects of their policies, as these affect exchange rates, which in turn affect interest rates and export competitiveness, the repercussions of which are felt by the entire economy. A government's decision to increase expenditure on social welfare, for instance, may be viewed unfavourably by money traders, who may sell off the currency, thereby depreciating it, which may in turn necessitate an increase in interest rates by the government, the result of which will be a slow-down in the economy and higher unemployment. The net result of all these would be negation of the original decision to increase spending.

The vulnerability of industrialized countries to international monetary pressures pales in comparison to those faced by poor countries suffering from chronic balance-of-payment problems. Unlike rich countries that can cover their payment deficits by borrowing from private sources, the poor countries are regarded as high risks by banks, which are therefore generally unwilling to extend loans to them. This leaves the poor countries little option but to obtain loans from the International Monetary Fund (IMF), which was established as a part of the Bretton Woods system for dealing with such problems. But if the IMF believes a country's payment problems are chronic and long-term, it usually insists on a *structural adjustment program*—involving cut-backs in public expenditure, reduction of import barriers, and depreciation of currency—as a condition for receiving loans. Countries accepting these loans have faced severe economic hardships and grave political repercussions as a result. The acceptance of the IMF's conditions for structural adjustment represents perhaps the most dramatic instance next to outright military conquest of international constraints on a state's policy options.

Foreign Direct Investment (FDI) is another aspect of international finance which affects states' policy options. FDI involves direct ownership and control of a firm by residents of another country. Since the owners' interests lie only in profits they can repatriate, their actions may contradict the interests of the host country. To appreciate the role of FDI, one needs to note that while the book value of the worldwide stock of FDI amounted to US$ 1.7 trillion in 1990, the market value is estimated to have been in excess of US$ 20 trillion.[61] Transnational corporations (TNCs), the organizational manifestations of FDI, are now found in all sectors of the economy, and the largest ones have turnovers that exceed the GDP of all but the largest countries. They not only control large pools of capital, they are also major players in international trade, and control much of the leading technology and management skills.

Given their size and strength, TNCs are major players in the world economy and, by implication, politics and public policy. They can cause serious damage to a country's economy by withholding investment or deciding to take their investment elsewhere, possibilities that policy-makers can ignore only at great economic peril. There is also now a competition among countries to attract TNCs by offering conditions the latter would find appealing. This often takes the form of a state commitment to controlling labour costs, maintaining tax levels that are comparable to those in other similar nations, and setting minimal restrictions on international trade and investment. All these pressures represent severe restrictions on states' policy options, not just in economic matters but in non-economic matters as well. Thus, reduction in taxes affects not only the overall level of economic activity in the economy but also the state's ability to fund its programs.

Assessing the Effects of International Institutions

There is a tendency in the literature on the subject to exaggerate the effects of international economic forces on nations along the lines of the authors' personal theoretical and/or ideological predilections. Liberals (who are also referred to as 'free marketeers' or 'economic rationalists') celebrate the strengthening of global economic forces because they curb political interference in the economy. Most Neo-marxists and nationalists, in contrast, go to the other extreme and highlight only the ill effects of economic globalization. We need to be more cautious if we are to understand this very complex phenomenon. The effects of international institutions vary by country and policy sector, and studies of the phenomenon should take these nuances into account.[62]

The extent to which states are able to control international pressures depends on a host of factors, including military and economic might, as well as the state's domestic strength. Thus, militarily powerful states such as the United States, Russia, and China have high capabilities to protect their citizens from foreign pressures, as do large economies such as the US, Japan, and the European Union. Openness to foreign trade and investment—as is the case for most industrialized and many industrializing countries—generally has a weakening effect on states' policy capabilities. But even this weakness can be offset, and indeed turned into a strength, by states with the domestic capacity to rationalize their economies through strategic intervention in a manner that enables their producers to compete on the world market.

International economic institutions do not lead to a general erosion of states' policy capabilities, as is often suggested in the literature. The effects, rather, vary by policy sector. They are strongest at the macro-economic level, where states find their ability to engage in demand management severely limited by international forces.[63] Since the market for goods, services, and capital is increasingly outside the national borders, the familiar fiscal and monetary tools to boost or slow the economy are no longer as effective as they used to be. The effects of domestic demand-management measures can be offset quickly by extraneously determined interest and exchange rate changes by international market forces working in the opposite direction.

In contrast to macro-economic policies, states continue to enjoy broad room to manoeuvre in micro-economic matters. Different states have resorted to different strategies, for instance, in promoting industrial adjustment and international competitiveness, some of which involve very high levels of intervention. However, the extent to which states can successfully undertake micro-economic intervention depends on their domestic strength. Countries with strong states possessing considerable autonomy and capacity are in the best position to undertake micro-economic intervention to take advantage of the opportunities offered by the global economy. In contrast, weak states which in the past could employ broad macro-economic levers find themselves especially handicapped because of their inability to use micro-economic intervention as an alternative. The extraordinary level of autonomy and capacity of the states in East Asia is said to be at the root of their ability to target industries (even individual firms) for special assistance, and this is said to be the secret of their industrial success. States in most industrialized countries (with the exception of 'corporatist' polities) do not usually have the autonomy or the capacity to mount such detailed, yet coherent, micro-economic interventions.

CONCLUSION

The chapter began by noting that the policy process involves both state and societal actors, the most important of which are referred to as constituting a policy subsystem. The membership in a subsystem is determined by constitutional and legal provisions, as well as by the power and knowledge resources of the actors involved. The minister(s) and bureaucrats in charge of a policy area are the key governmental actors in the policy process involving the area, with the legislators playing a secondary role. Their societal counterparts are drawn mainly from amongst interest groups and research organizations, with the media being involved only in the agenda-setting process. All these actors have their own objectives which they seek to achieve through participation in the policy process.

But what objectives they pursue, the manner in which they carry out their pursuit, and the extent to which they succeed in their efforts depends to a large extent on the domestic and international institutional context in which they operate. At the domestic level, it is the political institutions affecting the autonomy and capacity of the executive and bureaucracy that have the most decisive effect on the actors' interests and behaviour, and the outcomes of the policy process. The concept of state strength, however, makes sense only at the sectoral level, and even then must allow for contingencies, because of the difficulties of generalization across sectors, countries, and all possible situations. At the international level, trade and financial regimes have a critical impact on what the policy-makers can or cannot do, and the policy choices they finally make. Again, we need to exercise caution when generalizing about the effects of international institutional constraints, for a lot depends on the organization of the particular state and society, not to mention a range of contingencies. We cannot therefore sufficiently emphasize the need for thorough empirical research in the study of public policy.

NOTES

1   See, for example, Joel D. Wolfe, 'Democracy and Economic Adjustment: A Comparative Analysis of Political Change' in Richard E. Foglesong and Joel D. Wolfe (eds), *The Politics of Economic Adjustment* (New York: Greenwood Press, 1989): 153-86; John R. Freeman, *Democracy and Markets: The Politics of Mixed Economies* (Ithaca: Cornell University Press, 1989); Harold L. Wilensky and Lowell Turner, *Democratic Corporatism and Policy Linkages: The Interdependence of Industrial, Labor-Market, Incomes, and Social Policies in Eight Countries* (Berkeley: Institute of International Studies, 1987); Peter J. Katzenstein, 'Conclusion: Domestic Structures and Strategies of Foreign Economic Policy', *International Organization* 31, 4 (1977): 879-920.

2   George C. Edwards III and Ira Sharkansky, *The Policy Predicament: Making and Implementing Public Policy* (San Francisco: Freeman, 1978): 23.

3   Francis Castles et al. (eds), *The Future of Party Government: Vol. 3: Managing Mixed Economies* (New York: DeGruyter, 1987); Francis G. Castles, 'The Impact of Parties on Public Expenditure' in Francis G. Castles (ed.), *The Impact of Parties: Politics and Policies in Democratic Capitalist States* (London: Sage Publications, 1982): 21-96; Douglas A. Hibbs Jr, 'Political Parties and Macroeconomic Policy', *American Political Science Review* 71, 4 (1977): 1467-87; Klaus von Beyme, 'Do Parties Matter? The Impact of Parties on the Key Decisions in the Political System', *Government and Opposition* 19, 1 (1984): 5-29.

4   Anthony King, 'Ideas, Institutions and the Policies of Governments: A Comparative Analysis: Part III', *British Journal of Political Science* 3, 4 (1973): 409-23; Anthony King, 'What Do Elections Decide?' David Butler, Howard R. Penniman, and Austin Ranney (eds), *Democracy at the Polls: A Comparative Study of Competitive National Elections* (Washington, DC: American Enterprise Institute for Public Policy Research, 1981).

5   Herman Bakvis and David MacDonald, 'The Canadian Cabinet: Organization, Decision-Rules, and Policy Impact' in M. Michael Atkinson (ed.) *Governing Canada: Institutions and Public Policy* (Toronto: Harcourt Brace Jovanovich, 1993).

6   R.F. Adie and P.G. Thomas, *Canadian Public Administration: Problematical Perspectives* (Scarborough: Prentice Hall, 1987); K. Kernaghan, 'Power, Parliament and Public Servants in Canada: Ministerial Responsibility Reexamined', *Canadian Public Policy* 5, 3 (1979): 383-96; K. Kernaghan, 'The Public and Public Servant in Canada' in K. Kernaghan (ed.), *Public Administration in Canada: Selected Readings* (Toronto: Methuen, 1985): 323-30.

7   See David M. Olson and Michael L. Mezey, 'Parliaments and Public Policy' in David M. Olson and Michael L. Mezey (eds), *Legislatures in the Policy Process: The Dilemmas of Economic Policy* (Cambridge: Cambridge University Press, 1991): 1-24.

8   Stephen Breyer, *Regulation and Its Reform* (Cambridge: Harvard University Press, 1982); Alan Cairns, 'The Past and Future of the Canadian Administrative State',

University of Toronto Law Journal 40 (1990): 319-61; Richard A. Posner, 'Theories of Economic Regulation,' *Bell Journal of Economics and Management Science* 5, 2 (1974): 335-58; Margot Priest and Aron Wohl, 'The Growth of Federal and Provincial Regulation of Economic Activity 1867-1978' in W.T. Stanbury (ed.), *Government Regulation: Scope, Growth, Process* (Montreal: Institute for Research on Public Policy, 1980): 69-150; George J. Stigler, *The Citizen and the State: Essays on Regulation* (Chicago: University of Chicago Press, 1975).

9   See Larry B. Hill, 'Introduction' in Larry B. Hill (ed.), *The State of Public Bureaucracy* (Armonk, NY: M.E. Sharpe, 1992): 1-11.

10   Sharon L. Sutherland, 'The Public Service and Policy Development' in M. Michael Atkinson (ed.), *Governing Canada: Institutions and Public Policy* (Toronto: Harcourt Brace Jovanovich, 1993).

11   A. Paul Pross, *Group Politics and Public Policy* (Toronto: Oxford University Press, 1992): 101.

12   The relative strength provided by ideological and organizational resources is a subject of some debate. See for example Sandra Burt, 'Canadian Women's Groups in the 1980s: Organizational Development and Policy Influence', *Canadian Public Policy* 16, 1 (1990): 17-28.

13   William D. Coleman, *Business and Politics: A Study of Collective Action* (Kingston: McGill-Queen's University Press, 1988).

14   Sandra Burt, 'Canadian Women's Groups in the 1980s': 17-28.

15   Simon James, 'The Idea Brokers: The Impact of Think Tanks on British Government', *Public Administration* 71 (1993): 492.

16   Evert A. Lindquist, 'Think Tanks or Clubs? Assessing the Influence and Roles of Canadian Policy Institutes', *Canadian Public Administration* 36, 4 (1993): 547-79.

17   Alan Bryman, *Quantity and Quality in Social Research* (London: Unwin Hyman, 1988); Carol Weiss, 'Research for Policy's Sake: The Enlightenment Function of Social Research', *Policy Analysis* 3, 4 (1977): 531-45; Carol H. Weiss, *Using Social Research in Public Policy Making* (Lexington: Lexington Books, 1977).

18   Edward S. Herman and Noam Chomsky, *Manufacturing Consent* (New York: Pantheon, 1988); Michael Parenti, *Inventing Reality* (New York: St Martin's, 1986). For review see F.L. Cook et al., 'Media and Agenda Setting: Effects of the Public, Interest Group Leaders, Policy Makers, and Policy', *Public Opinion Quarterly* 47, 1 (1983): 16-35; Doris A. Graber, *Mass Media and American Politics* (Washington: C.Q. Press, 1989).

19   John W. Kingdon, *Agendas, Alternatives and Public Policies* (Boston: Little, Brown and Company, 1984).

20   See Robert J. Spitzer (ed.), *Media and Public Policy* (Westport: Praeger, 1993) and David Pritchard, 'The News Media and Public Policy Agendas' in David Kennamer (ed.), *Public Opinion, the Press, and Public Policy* (Westport: Praeger, 1992): 103-12.

21   See Mancur Olson, *The Logic of Collective Action: Public Goods and the Theory of Groups* (Cambridge: Harvard University Press, 1965); Mancur Olson, *The Rise and Decline of Nations: Economic Growth, Stagflation, and Social Rigidities* (New Haven: Yale University Press, 1982).

22   Stephen Haggard and Chung-In Moon, 'Institutions and Economic Policy: Theory and a Korean Case Study', *World Politics* XLII, 2 (1990): 212.

23   Mancur Olson, 'A Theory of the Incentives Facing Political Organizations: Neo-Corporatism and the Hegemonic State', *International Political Science Review* 7, 2 (1986): 165-89.

24 See Michael Atkinson and William Coleman, 'Strong States and Weak States: Sectoral Policy Networks in Advanced Capitalist Economies', *British Journal of Political Science* 19, 1 (1989): 47-67; Peter J. Katzenstein, 'Conclusion: Domestic Structures and Strategies of Foreign Economic Policy', *International Organization* 31, 4 (1974): 879-920; Eric A. Nordlinger, 'Taking the State Seriously' in Myron Weiner and Samuel P. Huntington (eds), *Understanding Political Development* (Boston: Little, Brown and Company, 1987): 353-91.

25 Peter J. Katzenstein, 'Conclusion: Domestic Structures and Strategies of Foreign Economic Policy', *International Organization* 31, 4 (1977): 879-920.

26 Kenneth H.F. Dyson, *The State Tradition in Western Europe: A Study of an Idea and Institution* (Oxford: Martin Robertson, 1980).

27 Haggard and Moon, 'Institutions and Economic Policy: Theory and a Korean Case Study': 215.

28 Atkinson and Coleman, 'Strong States and Weak States': 47-67.

29 R. Kent Weaver and Bert A. Rockman, 'When and How Do Institutions Matter' in R. Kent Weaver and Bert A. Rockman (eds), *Do Institutions Matter? Government Capabilities in the United States and Abroad* (Washington, D.C.: Brookings Institution, 1993): 445-61.

30 Kenneth McRoberts, 'Federal Structures and the Policy Process' in M. Michael Atkinson (ed.), *Governing Canada: Institutions and Public Policy* (Toronto: Harcourt Brace Jovanovich, 1993).

31 Keith G. Banting, *The Welfare State and Canadian Federalism*, (Kingston: Queen's University Institute of Intergovernmental Relations, 1982); Richard Schultz and Alan Alexandroff, *Economic Regulation and the Federal System* (Toronto: University of Toronto Press, 1985); Michael Atkinson and William Coleman, *The State, Business, and Industrial Change in Canada* (Toronto: University of Toronto Press, 1989).

32 For a detailed comparison of the policy consequences of parliamentary and presidential systems, see R. Kent Weaver and Bert A. Rockman (eds), *Do Institutions Matter? Government Capabilities in the United States and Abroad* (Washington, DC: Brookings Institution, 1993).

33 Peter H. Russell, 'The Effect of a Charter of Rights on the Policy-making Role of Canadian Courts', *Canadian Public Administration* 25 (1982): 1-33.

34 S.A. de Smith, *Judicial Review of Administrative Action* (London: Stevens and Son, 1973); Louis L. Jaffe, *Judicial Control of Administrative Action* (Boston: Little Brown, 1965); Louis L. Jaffe, *English and American Judges as Lawmakers* (Oxford: Clarendon, 1969); H.W.R. Wade, 'Anglo-American Administrative Law: Some Reflections', *Law Quarterly Review* 81 (1965): 357-79; H.W.R. Wade, 'Anglo-American Administrative Law: More Reflections', *Law Quarterly Review* 82 (1966): 226-52.

35 Louis L. Jaffe, *Judicial Control of Administrative Action* (Boston: Little Brown, 1965).

36 William H. Angus, 'Judicial Review: Do We Need It?' in Daniel J. Baum (ed.), *The Individual and the Bureaucracy* (Toronto: Carswell, 1974): 101-35; R. Dussault and L. Borgeat, *Administrative Law: A Treatise* (Toronto: Carswell, 1990); N. Finkelstein and B.M. Rogers (eds), *Recent Developments in Administrative Law* (Agincourt, ON: Carswell, 1987); P.W. Hogg, 'The Supreme Court of Canada and Administrative Law, 1949-1971', *Osgoode Hall Law Journal* 11, 2 (1973): 187-223; Kenneth Kernaghan, 'Judicial Review of Administration Action' in Kenneth Kernaghan (ed.), *Public Administration in Canada: Selected Readings* (Toronto: Methuen, 1985): 358-73.

37 Atkinson and Coleman, 'Strong States and Weak States': 50.

38   Atkinson and Coleman, 'Strong States and Weak States': 51.

39   Peter J. Katzenstein, 'Conclusion: Domestic Structures and Strategies of Foreign Economic Policy', *International Organization* 31, 4 (1977): 879-920.

40   Peter Evans, 'State as Problem and Solution: Predation, Embedded Autonomy, and Structural Change' in Stephen Haggard and Robert R. Kaufman (eds), *The Politics of Economic Adjustment: International Constraints, Distributive Conflicts, and the State* (Princeton: Princeton University Press, 1992): 139-81.

41   James A. Desveaux, Evert Lindquist, and Glen Toner, 'Organizing for Innovation in Public Buraucracy: AIDS, Energy and Environment Policy in Canada', *Canadian Journal of Political Science* 27, 3 (1994): 493-528.

42   Mancur Olson, *The Rise and Decline of Nations: Economic Growth, Stagflation, and Social Rigidities* (New Haven: Yale University Press, 1982): 92.

43   Peter Evans, 'State as Problem and Solution': 139-81.

44   Charles Lindblom, *Politics and Markets: The World's Political Economic Systems* (New York: Basic Books, 1977).

45   Peter J. Katzenstein, 'Conclusion: Domestic Structures and Strategies of Foreign Economic Policy', *International Organization* 31, 4 (1977): 879-920.

46   Graham K. Wilson, *Business And Politics: A Comparative Introduction* (London: Macmillan, 1990).

47   Andrew J. Taylor, *Trade Unions and Politics* (Basingstoke: Macmillan, 1989): 1.

48   G. Esping-Andersen and Walter Korpi, 'Social Policy as Class Politics in Post-War Capitalism: Scandinavia, Austria, and Germany' in J.H. Goldthorpe (ed.), *Order and Conflict in Contemporary Capitalism* (Oxford: Oxford University Press, 1984); Douglas A. Hibbs Jr, *The Political Economy of Industrial Democracies* (Cambridge, Mass.: Harvard University Press, 1987).

49   Douglas A. Hibbs Jr, 'On the Political Economy of Long-run Trends in Strike Activity', *British Journal of Political Science* 8, 2 (1978): 153-75; R. Lacroix, 'Strike Activity in Canada' in W.C. Riddell (ed.), *Canadian Labour Relations* (Toronto: University of Toronto Press, 1986).

50   Australia is an exception where trade unions play a significant role in the policy process, despite the generally pluralist character of the political system, because of their close links with the Labour Party.

51   David Held and Anthony McGrew, 'Globalization and the Liberal Democratic State', *Government and Opposition* 28, 2 (1993): 261-85.

52   For a comprehensive review of the literature on international regimes, see S.D. Krasner, 'Structural Causes and Regime Consequences: Regimes as Intervening Variables', *International Organization* 36, 2 (1982): 185-205; Stephen Haggard and Beth A. Simmons, 'Theories of International Regimes', *International Organization* 41, 3 (1987): 491-517.

53   Robert O. Keohane and Joseph S. Nye, *Power and Interdependence*, (Glenview, IL: Scott Foresman, 1989): 19.

54   Robert Gilpin, *The Political Economy of International Relations* (Princeton: Princeton University Press, 1987).

55   Keohane and Nye, *Power and Interdependence*.

56   Haggard and Simmons, 'Theories of International Regimes': 491-517.

57   For a discussion on these points, see various articles in Volker Rittberger and Peter Mayer (eds), *Regime Theory and International Relations* (Oxford: Clarendon Press, 1993).

58   For detailed discussion of the provisions of GATT, see Jock A. Finlayson and Mark
      W. Zacher, 'The GATT and the Regulation of Trade Barriers: Regime Dynamics and
      Functions', *International Organization* 35, 4 (1981): 561-602; M.A.G. Van Meerhaeghe,
      International Economic Institutions (Dordrecht: Kluwer, 1992).
59   For a discussion on the topic, see Robert Gilpin, *The Political Economy of International
      Relations* (Princeton: Princeton University Press, 1987).
60   Jeffry Frieden, 'Invested Interests: the Politics of National Economic Policies in a
      World of Global Finance', *International Organization* 45, 4 (1991): 428.
61   Gilpin, *The Political Economy of International Relations, The Economist*, 'Special Survey of
      Multinationals' (27 March 1993): 6.
62   The following discussion drews heavily on M. Ramesh, 'Economic Globalization
      and Policy Choices: Singapore', *Governance* 8, 2 (1995): 243-60.
63   See Geoffrey Garrett and Peter Lange, 'Political Responses to Interdependence:
      What's "Left" for the Left?', *International Organization* 45, 4 (1991): 539, 564.

FURTHER READING

Atkinson, M. and W. Coleman, *The State, Business and Industrial Change in Canada*,
    Toronto: University of Toronto Press, 1989.

Gourevitch, Peter, *Politics in Hard Times: Comparative Responses to International Economic Crises*,
    Ithaca: Cornell University Press, 1986.

Hall, Peter A., *Governing the Economy*, Cambridge: Polity Press, 1986.

Held, David, 'Democracy, the Nation-State and the Global System', pp. 197-235 in David
    Held (ed.), *Political Theory Today*, Oxford: Polity, 1991.

James, Simon, 'The Idea Brokers: The Impact of Think Tanks on British Government',
    Public Administration 71 (1993): 471-90.

Katzenstein, Peter, *Small States in World Markets*, Ithaca: Cornell University Press, 1985.

Offe, Claus, 'Competitive Party Democracy and the Keynesian Welfare State: Factors of
    Stability and Disorganization', *Policy Sciences* 15 (1983): 225-46.

Olson, David M. and Michael L. Mezey (eds), *Legislatures in the Policy Process: The Dilemmas
    of Economic Policy*, Cambridge: Cambridge University Press, 1991.

Page, E.C., *Political Authority and Bureaucratic Power*, Brighton: Wheatsheaf, 1985.

Peters, B. Guy, *The Politics Of Bureaucracy: A Comparative Perspective*, New York: Longman,
    1984.

Spitzer, Robert J. (ed.), *Media and Public Policy*, Westport: Praeger, 1993.

Wilensky, Harold L. and Lowell Turner, *Democratic Corporatism and Policy Linkages: The
    Interdependence of Industrial, Labor-Market, Incomes, and Social Policies in Eight Countries*,
    Berkeley: Institute of International Studies, 1987.

Wilson, Graham K., *Business And Politics: A Comparative Introduction*, London: Macmillan,
    1987.

Wilson, Graham K., *Interest Groups*, Oxford: Basil Blackwell, 1990.

Chapter 4

Policy Instruments

In the preceding chapter we discussed the key actors and institutions which determine and comprise membership in policy subsystems affecting the public policy process. Now we turn to discussing the policy instruments—also called policy tools or governing instruments—by which governments attempt to put policies into effect. These are the actual means or devices which governments have at their disposal for implementing policies, and from among which they must select. Thus a government not only decides whether or not to do something about deteriorating water quality, for example, but also whether it should implement its decision through mass campaigns urging people to refrain from polluting activities, regulation prohibiting all activities causing the pollution, or the provision of a subsidy to the polluting firms encouraging them to switch to safer production technologies. The choice of instrument is often no less contentious than the choice of the policy itself.

In this chapter we will set out a classification of the policy instruments available to policy-makers. We will then describe the main features of the key instruments and note the extent of their substitutability. Our intent at this stage is descriptive rather than prescriptive, because contextual factors affect the appropriateness of various instruments. The question of why governments tend to select a particular instrument and not some other, technically equal or even more appealing, instrument is addressed in Chapter Eight.

CLASSIFICATION OF POLICY INSTRUMENTS

The variety of instruments available to policy-makers to address a policy problem is limited only by their imagination. Scholars have made numerous attempts to identify the policy instruments used by policy-makers and classify them into meaningful categories.[1] Unfortunately, no two schemes share much in common. They are either pitched at a very high level of abstraction or dwell on the idiosyncrasies of particular tools. We favour a scheme that is sufficiently abstract to encompass the various possibilities, yet concrete enough to correspond with the way policy-makers actually interpret their choices.

The first attempt to develop a catalogue of policy instruments was set out by the Dutch economist E.S. Kirschen and his colleagues in the early 1960s. Kirschen investigated whether there was a set of instruments for implementing economic policies that would generate optimal results.[2] He concluded that there were 64 general types of instruments; no systematic effort was made to classify them or to theorize about their origin or effects. Political scientists like Cushman, Lowi, and Dahl and Lindblom, made similar studies but their taxonomies all tended to compress multiple instruments into very general categories such as those which involved government regulation and those which did not.[3] Lester Salamon marginally furthered the discussion by adding categories for expenditure and non-expenditure instruments.[4]

A more systematic taxonomy was offered by Christopher Hood who proposed that all policy tools utilize one of four broad categories of 'governing resources'.[5] He argued that governments confront public problems through the use of the information in their possession ('Nodality'), their legal powers ('Authority'), their money ('Treasure'), or the formal organizations available to them ('Organization'). McDonnell and Elmore also used a four-fold classification of instruments, although they classified instruments according not to the resources used, but to the end desired. For these latter two authors instruments could be categorized as 'Mandates', 'Inducements', 'Capacity-building', and 'System-changing'.[6] Schneider and Ingram proposed a similar list of categories, which they called 'Incentives', 'Capacity-building', 'Symbolic and Hortatory', and 'Learning'.[7]

All of these taxonomies are problematic. They offer overly broad categories which can include a variety of unrelated instruments or, as in the case of Hood's categorization scheme, are mutually exclusive. It is unclear, for example, where in Hood's scheme government expenditure on advertising should appear. Is this activity an instance of the use of organization, authority, treasure, or nodality? The terms used to describe the categories also appear too far removed from political reality to be useful for students of public policy. It is difficult to imagine a cabinet deliberating upon whether to use Nodality or Treasure, or Capacity-building, or System-changing instruments.

The Canadian political scientists G. Bruce Doern and Richard Phidd produced a turning point in the classification of policy instruments by arranging them along a scale according to the amount of 'legitimate coercion' they entailed.[8] Their schema considered 'self-regulation' as the least coercive and 'public ownership' the most coercive. Although this taxonomy, too, had difficulties—including troubles encountered in operationalizing coercion, and in arriving at the placement of various instruments along the coercion scale—it provided the basis for future classifications by establishing the need to analyze instruments in the context of the relationship existing between the state and society as embodied in each category of instrument.

Rather than focus on the slippery concept of 'coercion' per se, it is possible to arrive at a more complete yet simpler taxonomy simply by focusing on the level of state presence in the provision of goods and services involved with the use of each instrument.[9] Using the level of state provision as the criterion, we can develop a taxonomy that arranges the various instruments of public policy on a voluntary-compulsory axis. The truly voluntary instruments are totally devoid of state involvement, the totally compulsory ones permit no room for private discretion. Between the two extremes lies a range of instruments involving varying levels of state and private provision.

Combining this scale with the inventories of instruments provided by Kirschen and others yields a list of ten major types of policy instruments. In ascending order of the level of state intervention they are Family and Community, Voluntary Organization, Private Markets, Information and Exhortation, Subsidy, Auction of Property Right, Tax and User Charges, Regulation, Public Enterprise, and Direct Provision. The list is depicted graphically in Figure 5.

■ Figure 5.
A Spectrum of Policy Instruments

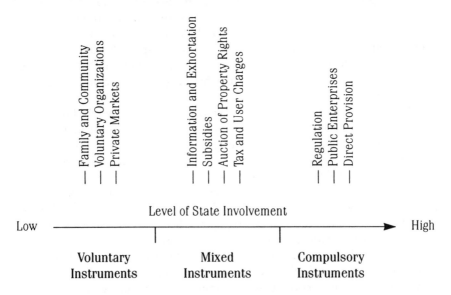

Most policy objectives can, in theory, be accomplished by a number of instruments; in other words, most instruments are to some degree 'substitutable'. Thus, in theory, a government seeking to promote health care for the population could leave it entirely to the family to provide health services, with the competence and availability of family members determining who gets how much and at what cost. Or the government might go to the other extreme and provide health services through its own administrative agency, paid for directly out of its general tax revenues, leaving no room for the market or other private organizations. In between the two extremes lie a range of other instruments, including exhorting the population to keep healthy, subsidizing those who are poor, and regulating doctors and hospitals. The task before the government in public policy-making is to select an instrument or combination of instruments that is most appropriate for the task at hand, taking into account both the limitations and capabilities of each category of instrument, as well as the political consequences of its employment.

Although most instruments are in a technical sense 'substitutable', in practice they differ in a number of ways which makes the choice of instrument a complex matter. Salamon and Lund, for example, suggest that different instruments involve varying degrees of effectiveness, efficiency, equity, legitimacy, and partisan support, which affect their appropriateness for a particular situation.[10] Thus some instruments are more effective in carrying out a policy than others. Some are also more efficient than others in terms of financial and personnel costs, an important consideration in the present climate of budgetary restraint. The ability to attract the support of the population in general and, particularly, of those directly involved in the policy subsystem must also be taken into account. For example, particular government departments or agencies may prefer certain instruments such as subsidies or crown corporations, because they remain under their control.[11] Moreover, cultural norms and institutional arrangements may accord greater legitimacy to some instruments than others. Thus it is possible that in liberal democracies citizens and policy-makers may prefer instruments that are less coercive rather than other equally effective or efficient alternatives. Such societies can be expected to prefer voluntary and mixed instruments to compulsory instruments. Moreover, instruments have varying distributional effects, and so policy-makers may need to select instruments that are, or at least appear to be, equitable. Tax incentives, for example, are inherently inequitable because they offer no benefit to those (the poor) without taxable income.

Voluntary Instruments

The characteristic feature of voluntary instruments is that they entail no or little involvement by the government; the desired task is instead performed on a voluntary basis. Governments often decide deliberately that they will do nothing ('non-decision') about a recognized public problem, because they believe it can be best done by the market, or by family or voluntary organizations. These are non-governmental organizations that operate on a voluntary basis, in that their members are not compelled to perform a task by the government. If they do something that serves public policy goals, it is for reasons of self-interest, ethics, or emotional gratification.

Voluntary instruments are an important tool for implementing both economic and social policies. Indeed many public problems are still addressed through these instruments, despite this century's proliferation of compulsory and mixed instruments accompanying the expansion of the role of the state. And their usage may well be increasing because of the spread of privatization in recent years. They are preferred in many societies because of their cost-efficiency, consistency with the cultural norms of individual freedom, and support for family and community ties.

Family and Community

The first set of voluntary instruments the government can rely upon for implementing policies is family and community. In all societies relatives, friends, and
neighbours provide numerous goods and services, and the government may
take measures to expand their role in ways that serves its policy goals. It may do
so either indirectly by cutting back on government services in the hope that the
family or community will step in to fill the gap, or directly by promoting their
involvement.

All societies regard looking after the needs of family members and others
close to them as an essential responsibility of the individual. Children, the aged,
and the sick are ordinarily looked after in this manner, mainly in terms of care,
but financial assistance if necessary is also common. It has been calculated that
in 1978 the total cost of the transfer of cash, food, and housing within families
in the US amounted to US$ 86 billion.[12] Non-monetary transfers are almost
impossible to estimate because families provide a range of services whose value
cannot be measured in monetary terms. It is estimated for example that about
80 per cent of home health care services for the elderly are provided by family
members.[13] Normally, for the care provided in this manner no financial reward
is expected, but there is emotional gratification and the expectation that the
effort would be reciprocated.

The primary advantage of promoting the family and community as an instrument of public policy is that it does not cost the government anything, unless
it chooses to provide grants or subsidies for these efforts. In many circumstances,
as in the case of family or community care for the long-term disabled compared to
their care in public institutions, alternatives to this instrument are difficult to imagine. Moreover, their function enjoys widespread political support in most societies. But pitted against these advantages are some serious disadvantages. Family-
and community-based instruments, for example, are generally weak instruments
for addressing complex economic problems. Efficiency of scale may also warrant
centralized provision by the government rather than decentralized provision by
the family or community. Reliance on these types of instruments for solving public problems may also be inequitable because many individuals do not have anyone, or anyone with the financial resources or emotional commitment, to look
after them. It is similarly inequitable for the care-givers. In most societies women
tend to be the main care providers, a role increasingly difficult to perform because
of increasing female participation in the labour force. As such, family and community instruments can often only be relied upon as adjuncts to other instruments needed to address the pressing social problems of our times.

Voluntary Organizations

Voluntary organizations involve 'activities that are indeed voluntary in the dual
sense of being free of [state] coercion and being free of the economic constraints

of profitability and the distribution of profits'.[14] Charitable bodies providing health services, education, and food to the poor and temporary shelter for battered women and runaway children are prime examples of such organizations. Voluntary groups that form to clean up beaches and river banks are other examples. Although these functions could well be provided by the market or the government, they may also be left wholly or partially to voluntary organizations.

Charitable, not-for-profit groups used to be the primary means of fulfilling the basic needs of those who could not do so on their own, but over the last century the expansion of the welfare state has gradually diminished their importance. Even so, they are a widely used means of addressing social problems today. In fact, in the US, often seen as the archetype of an individualist and materialistic society, the non-profit voluntary sector delivers more services than the government itself.[15] In recent years, because of the budgetary crises faced by governments, many countries have pressed to expand the role of the voluntary sector.

Voluntary organizations are, in theory, an efficient means of delivering most economic and social services. If that were feasible it would be obviously cost-efficient to provide social security or health and education services, or build dams and roads on the basis of voluntary efforts of individuals. They also offer flexibility and speed of response and the opportunity for experimentation that would be difficult in governmental organizations.[16] They are often quicker than the government in providing relief to victims of natural disaster, for instance. Moreover, meeting social needs in this manner decreases the need for government action, which appeals to those who believe that state intervention is inherently inimical to political freedom. Not-for-profit groups are also an equitable instrument because they are usually directed at only those in need. Another beneficial spill-over is their positive contribution to promoting community spirit, social solidarity, and political participation.

However, most practical circumstances severely limit the usefulness of voluntary organizations. Their efforts are largely inapplicable to many economic and social problems. Their efficiency and effectiveness is compromised by the fact that large voluntary groups may become bureaucratic and may in practice be no different from government organizations. If they depend on the government for funds they may not also be cost-efficient; it might be cheaper for the state to perform the task directly. In the US, the government provides 40 per cent of total expenditure by voluntary organizations; it is a larger source of funds than private contributions.[17] And the proportion of private contributions would have been even lower without the tax deductibility that is allowed for such contributions. Contemporary economic and social problems are simply too vast to be adequately addressed on the basis of voluntary efforts alone; most people have neither the time nor the resources required to contribute to such activities, even if they wished to do so. They are therefore unlikely to work outside areas in which their members find satisfaction in their deeds for religious, ethical, or political reasons. Members of voluntary organizations would not likely undertake most tasks performed by modern governments.

The Market

By far the most important, and contentious, voluntary instrument is the market. The voluntary interaction between consumers and producers, with the former seeking to buy as much as they can with the limited amount of money at their disposal and the latter searching for highest possible profits, can usually be expected to lead to outcomes that satisfy both. In theory at least, while the primary motive on the part of both sides is self-interest, the society as a whole gains from their interaction because whatever is wanted (backed by the ability to pay) by the society is provided at the lowest possible price. Thus those wanting health care or education simply buy the services from hospitals and schools operating for profit.

The market is a highly recommended instrument in certain circumstances. It is an effective and efficient means of providing most private goods and can ensure that resources are devoted only to those goods and services valued by the society, as reflected in the individuals' willingness to pay. It also ensures that if there is meaningful competition among suppliers valued goods and services are supplied at the lowest possible price. Since most goods and services sought by the population are of a private nature, governments in capitalist societies rely extensively on the market instrument.

In several situations the market may be an inappropriate instrument to use. As we saw in Chapter Two, it cannot adequately provide public goods, precisely the sort of things most public policies are intended to address. Thus it cannot be used for providing defence, policing, street lights, and other similar goods and services valued by the society. Markets also experience difficulties in providing various kinds of toll goods and common pool goods (see Chapter Two for definitions) due to various kinds of market failures. The market is also a highly inequitable instrument, because it meets the needs of only those with the ability to pay. Thus in a purely market-based system of health care delivery, for example, a rich person with money can have a wish for cosmetic surgery fulfilled, while a poor person suffering from kidney failure may not receive essential treatment. It is not surprising that the use of markets in such situations faces tough political opposition.

A 'free market' in the true sense of the term is therefore almost never used as a policy instrument in practice. When the government does choose to resort to this instrument for addressing a public problem, it is usually accompanied by other instruments such as regulation to protect consumers, investors, and workers; it is also accompanied frequently by subsidies for promoting the desired activity. While the market itself is a voluntary organization, it is backed by the coercive powers of the states.

COMPULSORY INSTRUMENTS

Compulsory instruments, also called directive instruments, compel or direct the action of target individuals and firms, who are left with little or no discretion in devising a response. The government, in exercise of its sovereign authority, may instruct a subject citizen to undertake certain activities, may establish government-controlled companies to perform any function it chooses, or directly provide the goods and services in question through the bureaucracy. These are highly coercive instruments because they allow the government to do whatever it chooses within broad constitutional limits and leave little discretion to the target individuals, groups, or organizations.

Regulations

There are numerous definitions of regulation, but most tend to be quite restrictive in focus. A comprehensive definition is offered by Michael Reagan, who defines it as 'a process or activity in which government requires or proscribes certain activities or behaviour on the part of individuals and institutions, mostly private but sometimes public, and does so through a continuing administrative process, generally through specially designated regulatory agencies'.[18] Thus, regulation is a prescription by the government which must be complied with by the intended targets; failure to do so usually involves a penalty.

Some regulations are in fact laws and involve the police and judicial system in their enforcement. Most regulations, however, are administrative edicts created under the terms of enabling legislation and administered on a continuing basis by a government department or specialized government agency (called an Independent Regulatory Commission in the US) which is autonomous of government control in its day-to-day operations. Regulations take various forms and include rules, standards, permits, prohibition, legal orders, and executive orders. Although we may not always be aware of their presence, they govern the price and standards of a wide variety of goods and services we consume, as well as the quality of water we drink and the air we breathe.

The nature of regulations varies somewhat depending on whether they are economic or social. Economic regulations control prices and the volume of production, or return on investment, or the entry into or exit of firms from an industry. Their objective is often to correct perceived imbalances that may emerge as a result of the operation of market forces. Economic regulations have been the traditional form of regulation; their social counterparts are of more recent origin.

Social regulations refer to controls in matters of health, safety, and social practices such as discrimination of various sorts in employment. They have more to do with our physical and moral well-being than with our pocketbooks.[19] Examples of social regulation include rules regarding consumer product safety, occupational hazards, water-related hazards, air pollution, noise pollution, discrimination on the basis of gender or ethnicity, and pornography. Environmental protection is a hybrid between economic and social regulation, because the problems usually have economic origins but their adverse effects are mostly social. Social regulations do not focus on any particular industry (for example, banks or telecommunications), as do economic regulations, but on broader problems or functions such as pollution, safety, or morality. Thus a social regulation might cut across several industries and come under the jurisdiction of several government agencies.

There are several advantages of regulation as a policy instrument.[20] First, the information needed to establish regulation is less because the government need not know in advance the subject's preferences, as is necessary in the case of voluntary and as we shall see, mixed instruments. It can just establish a standard, say the permitted pollution level, and expect compliance, unlike incentives which will not elicit a favourable response unless their intended subjects have a preference for them. Second, where the concerned activity is entirely undesirable, such as films and videos depicting paedophilia, it is easier to establish regulations prohibiting the possession of such products rather than devise ways of discouraging their production and distribution. Third, in administrative terms regulations are more efficient than other instruments if the government has all the relevant information and knows exactly what it wants; it need not deal with the uncertainties involved in the use of less direct instruments. Fourth, regulations allow for better co-ordination of efforts and planning because of the greater predictability they entail. Fifth, and relatedly, their predictability makes them a more suitable instrument in times of crisis when an immediate response is needed. Sixth, regulations may be less costly than other instruments such as subsidies or tax incentives. All that is required is an administrative agency to enforce compliance rather than an agency that not only supervises but offers fiscal incentives as well. Finally, regulations may also be politically appealing if the public or policy subsystem wants to see a quick and definite action on the part of the government.

The disadvantages of regulation are equally telling.[21] First, regulations quite often distort voluntary or private sector activities and can promote economic inefficiencies. Price regulations and direct allocation restrict the operation of the forces of demand and supply and affect the price mechanism, thus causing sometimes unpredictable economic distortions in the market. Restrictions on entry to and exit from industrial sectors, for example, can reduce competition and thus have a negative impact on prices. Second, regulations can, at times, inhibit innovation and technological progress because of the market security they afford existing firms and the limited opportunities for experimentation they permit. Third, regulations are often inflexible and do not permit the consideration of individual circumstances, resulting in decisions and outcomes not intended by the regulation.[22] Social regulations are particularly problematic. It is almost impossible to specify in many instances exactly what is acceptable under regulation. The use of phrases such as 'safe and effective' drugs, for instance, allows for too much uncertainty. If the regulation specifies specific standards, however, then it can become irrelevant in new circumstances.[23] Fourth, in terms of administration, it may simply not be possible to set regulations for every undesired activity. For example, there are millions of pollutants; a special regulation would be required for each if this instrument were chosen for policy purposes. Finally, the cost of enforcement by regulatory commissions may be high because the costs of information, investigation, and prosecution can make policy-making unnecessarily legalistic and adversarial.

Public Enterprise

Public enterprises—also known as state-owned enterprises (SOEs), crown corporations, or parastatal organizations—can be seen as an extreme case of regulation, 'where the rules have been made particular so as to cover all activities, as would be the internal directives of an organizational management'.[24] This makes them more intrusive than regulation because the government can technically do whatever it wishes by virtue of its ownership.

There is no clear-cut way of identifying a public enterprise, which explains why governments quite often do not publish a definitive list of the enterprises they own. The main problem is determining how public an enterprise must be in order to be called a public enterprise. At one extreme it may resemble a private enterprise, and at the other, an ordinary bureaucratic agency.

However, three broad generalizations can be made about the features of public enterprises.[25] First, they involve some degree of public ownership, which may be as high as 100 per cent or less than half. Analysts often use an arbitrary figure of a minimum 51 per cent ownership of a firm by the government to call it a public enterprise. The term 'mixed enterprise' is used to describe firms owned jointly by the government and the private sector. Second, public enterprises entail some degree of control or direct management by the government. Completely passive ownership of a firm which is operated entirely free from government control will not constitute a public enterprise. Third, public enterprises produce goods and services that are sold, unlike public goods such as defence or street lighting for which those receiving the services are not charged directly. As a corollary, their sales revenues must bear some semblance to their costs, though generating profits may or may not be their main objective.

Public enterprises as policy instruments offer a number of advantages to governments.[26] First, they are an efficient economic policy instrument in situations where a socially needed good or service is not produced by the private sector because of high capital outlays or low expected returns. Second, the information required to establish public enterprises is in many instances lower than when using voluntary instruments or regulation. It does not require information on the target activity or the goals and preferences of the subject targeted, because the government as the owner can do whatever it wishes through the enterprise itself. Third, in terms of administration, public enterprises may simplify management if regulation is already extensive. Instead of building layers of regulation, for instance, it might be desirable to establish a company that does the same without the need for the cumbersome processes and legislative oversight provisions attending regulation. Finally, profits from public enterprises may accrue to public funds, which can be used to pay for public expenditures. A significant proportion of the government revenues in Singapore, for example, comes from the profits of its public enterprises.

The disadvantages of public enterprises are no less significant. First, governments often find them difficult to control because managers can adopt various avoidance measures. Moreover the shareholders (the voters) are too diffuse, and their personal interest too distant, to exercise effective control over the company. Second, public enterprise can be inefficient in operation because continued losses do not lead to bankruptcy. Indeed a large number consistently lose money, which is a major reason underlying efforts to privatize them in many countries in recent years. Finally, many public enterprises, such as in the area of electricity and water supply, operate in a monopolistic environment enabling them to pass the costs of their inefficiency to consumers, a strategy no different than that of a private firm enjoying a monopoly position.

Direct Provision

In our effort to understand the more exotic instruments employed by governments, we tend to forget a basic and most widely-used instrument: direct provision. Instead of waiting for the private sector to do something desired by the government, or regulating the private sector's performance of the task, or getting it done through semi-autonomous public enterprise, the government directly performs the task in question, delivering goods and services directly by government employees, funded from the public treasury.[27] Much of what governments do is done through this instrument: national defence, diplomatic relations, policing, firefighting, social security, education, management of public lands, maintenance of parks and roads, and census and geological surveys among others.

Among the advantages of direct provision as an instrument are the following:[28] First, similar to other compulsory instruments, direct provision is easy to establish because of low information requirements. Second, the large size of the agencies required for direct provision enables them to build resources, skills and information necessary for efficient performance of their task. Third, direct provision avoids the problems with indirect provision—discussion, negotiations, and a higher need for information—which may foster more concern with enforcing terms of grants and contracts than with results. Fourth, direct provision permits internalization of transactions, thus minimizing the costs involved in getting something done indirectly.

The disadvantages of direct provision are equally significant: While technically the government can do everything that the private sector can do, in practice this may not be the case. First, delivery of programs by the bureaucracy is often characterized by an inflexibility that is unavoidable in liberal-democratic societies which value the rule of law and must abide by formal operating procedures. Second, political control over the agencies and officials involved in providing good and services may, and often does, promote political meddling to strengthen the government's re-election prospects rather than to serve the public. Political control may also lead to incoherent directives to agencies delivering the goods and services because of the contradictory pressures that beset governments. Third, since bureaucratic agencies are not subject to competition, they are often not sufficiently cost-conscious, for which the tax-payers ultimately pay. Fourth, the delivery of programs may suffer because of inter- and intra-agency conflicts within the government.

Mixed Instruments

Mixed instruments combine the features of both voluntary and compulsory instruments. They permit the government varying levels of involvement in shaping the decisions of non-state actors, while leaving the final decision to private actors. The involvement ranges from a minimum of merely disseminating information to the maximum, punitively taxing an undesired activity. Between the two lie subsidizing a desired activity and establishing a pricing mechanism in areas which would not normally have one. These instruments offer, in some measure, the benefits of both voluntary and compulsory instruments.

Information and Exhortation

Dissemination of information is a passive instrument, providing information to individuals and firms with the expectation of changing their behaviour in a desired manner. The information is often of a general nature, intended to make the population more knowledgeable so that they can make informed choices. For instance, information on tourism, programs, and economic and social statistics is disseminated by the government, leaving it to the population to draw conclusions and respond accordingly. However, the information may also be more precisely targeted to elicit a particular response, as in the case of publicizing information on the ill effects of smoking. In either case, there is no obligation upon the public to respond in a particular manner.

Exhortation, or suasion as it is also called, involves only slightly more government activity than dissemination of information.[29] It entails a concerted effort to change the subjects' preferences and actions, rather than just informing them about a situation with the hope of changing their behaviour in a desired manner. However, it does not include altering the attractiveness of the choice through offer of rewards or imposition of sanctions. Examples of exhortation include advertisements urging people to keep fit and healthy, not to waste water or energy, and to use public transportation. Consultations between government officials and financial, industry, or labour representatives are also a form of exhortation because in these meetings governments often hope to alter the other parties' behaviour. This group of instruments

> assumes one or both of the two things: first, that the realm of private behaviour in question must remain private and government cannot legitimately apply coercive instruments, or second, that motivations are strong enough that they can be themselves relied upon to achieve policy goals once apprised of new information.'[30]

For example, to prevent the spread of AIDS, the government can do little to force behaviour but must instead rely on dissemination of information, hoping that people would make an informed choice to avoid activities that carry risks of infection.

Exhortation offers numerous advantages.[31] It is a good starting point for a government dealing with problems to which definite solutions are unavailable. It is easy to establish and, if the problem is solved through exhortation alone, then nothing more needs to be done. However, if a better instrument is found, then the policy of suasion can be changed or abandoned without much difficulty. It is inexpensive in terms of both financial and personnel costs because it involves little financial commitment or enforcement by the bureaucracy. And finally, exhortation is consistent with the norms of liberal democracy which value arguments, persuasion, individual responsibility, and freedom.

However, exhortation is too weak an instrument when immediate results are required, as in times of crisis. The government may use it to merely portray itself as doing something about a problem, rather than actually doing something meaningful. Thus government exhortation against violence against women, in the absence of other instruments, may be of little use. As Stanbury and Fulton put it, 'In the absence of positive or negative inducements (or more bluntly, leverage), most efforts at suasion probably have either a low probability of success or have a relatively short half life.'[32] At best, it should be used in conjunction with other instruments when they are available.

Subsidy

Subsidy refers to all forms of financial transfers to individuals, firms, and organizations from governments or from other individuals, firms, or organization under government direction. The purpose of the transfer is to financially reward a desired activity, thereby affecting social actors' estimates of costs and benefits of the various alternatives. While the final choice is left to individuals and firms, the likelihood of the desired choice being made is enhanced because of the subsidy it draws.

Subsidy is, however, an extraordinarily heterogeneous instrument. One of the most prominent forms of subsidy is *grants*, 'expenditures made in support of some end worthy in itself, almost as a form of recognition, reward or encouragement, but not closely calibrated to the costs of achieving that end'.[33] Grants are usually offered to producers, with the objective of making them provide more of a desired good or service than they would otherwise provide. The expenditure comes out of the government's general tax revenues, which requires legislative approval. Examples of grants include government funds provided to schools, universities, and public transportation.

Another prominent form of subsidy is the *tax incentive* involving 'remission of taxes in some form, such as deferrals, deductions, credits, exclusions, or preferred rates, contingent on some act (or the omission of some act)'.[34] Tax incentives involve taxes forgone, that is, taxes that would normally have been collected, rather than any direct expenditure by the government. Governments find tax incentives appealing because they are hidden in tax provisions and so escape notice, which makes their establishment and continuation relatively easy.[35] Moreover, in most countries they do not need budgetary approval, for no money is actually spent; rather revenues are forgone, which does not require legislative approval.[36] Nor is their use constrained by availability of funds, because they involve no direct expenditure. They are also easier to administer and enforce because to administer them, no special bureaucracy needs to be created as would be the case with many other instruments. The existing taxation bureaucracy is usually entrusted with the task.

Another much talked-about form of subsidy is *vouchers*. These are papers with a monetary face value offered by the government to consumers of a particular good or service, given by them to their preferred supplier, who in turn presents the voucher to the government for redemption. Vouchers, like grants, are designed to increase the consumption of goods and services which the government deems desirable. But unlike grants, which are provided to producers and restrict consumer choice, the voucher system subsidizes consumers and allows them to exercise relatively free choice in the marketplace. It promotes competition among suppliers, which arguably improves quality and reduces costs to the government.

Loans from the government at an interest rate below the market rate are also a form of subsidy. However, the entire amount of the loan should not be treated as a subsidy, but only the difference between the interest charged and the market rate.

Other policy instruments not technically considered as subsidies may involve some component of subsidy. Thus regulations that restrict the quantity of a particular good or service produced or sold also involve subsidy to the producers because they can often artificially increase prices. Dairy and poultry producers in Canada and the US are subsidized in this manner. Regulations that fix prices to protect competition from driving down prices, and thus hurting other existing producers, also involve subsidy from the consumers. The taxi cab industry in most places receives this kind of subsidy through regulation. Government procurement from local producers at a price higher than the market price is also a subsidy to local producers to the extent of the difference between the purchase price and the market price.

Subsidies offer numerous advantages as policy instruments.[37] First, they are easier to establish if there is a coincidence of preference between what the government wants the people to do and what the latter desire. If the target population believes an action to be desirable but for some reason does not carry it out, then subsidy may make a difference. For instance, firms contemplating plant modernization or labour training may be swayed to act if tax incentives are provided. Second, subsidies are a flexible instrument to administer because the individual participants decide for themselves how to respond to the subsidy in the light of changing circumstances. They similarly permit local and sectoral circumstances to be taken into account, as only those individuals and firms believing a subsidy to be beneficial will take it up. Third, by allowing individuals and firms to devise an appropriate response, subsidies may encourage innovation on their part. In contrast directives, by establishing performance standards, by their very nature would normally discourage innovative responses from the public. (It is, of course, also possible to make a subsidy contingent upon innovation.) Fourth, the costs of administering and enforcing subsidies may be lower because it is up to potential recipients to claim benefits. Finally, subsidies are often politically more acceptable because the benefits are concentrated on a few whereas the costs are spread across the population, with the result that they tend to be supported strongly by the beneficiaries and opposed only weakly by their opponents.

The disadvantages of subsidies are equally telling. Since subsidies (except tax incentives) need financing, which must come from new or existing sources of revenues, their establishment is often difficult. They must compete with other programs needing funds, each backed by its own network of societal groups, politicians, and bureaucrats. Second, the cost of gathering information on how much subsidy would be required to induce a desired behaviour may also be high. Arriving at a correct amount of subsidy by trial and error can be an expensive way of implementing a policy. Third, since subsidies work indirectly, there is also often a time-lag before the desired effects are discernible. This makes them an inappropriate instrument to use in a time of crisis. Fourth, subsidies may be redundant in cases where the activity would have occurred even without the subsidy, thus causing a windfall for the recipients. At the same time, they are hard to eliminate because of the opposition from existing beneficiaries who stand to lose from their removal.

Auction of Property Rights

Auctions of property rights are a particularly interesting mixed instrument. On the basis of the assumption that the market is often the most efficient means of allocating resources, property-rights auctions by the government establish markets in situations where they do not exist. The market is created by setting a fixed quantity of transferable rights to consume a designated resource, which has the effect of creating an artificial scarcity, and enabling the price mechanism to work. The resource can be water or air for the discharge of effluents, fish stocks, or just about anything which would not be scarce unless made so by the government. Those wishing to consume the resource must bid at an auction for the limited amount available. Potential buyers will bid according to the value they attribute to the resource, with those offering the most securing the right.

Many countries have proposed to control the use of dangerous pollutants in this manner. In these schemes, typically, the government fixes the total amount of the pollutant that can enter the market and then through periodic auctions sells the right to discharge the limited amount available. This means that firms intending to use a pollutant in their production process must buy the right to do so at an auction before they can buy the pollutant itself. Those with cheaper alternatives will avoid using the pollutant because of the extra cost of buying the right to it. Manufacturers for whom there is no cheap alternative continue to pay the price for the right to utilize the pollutant. However, even they are under constant pressure to search for alternatives because of the extra costs they must otherwise bear.

The advantage of using an auction of rights is that it restricts the use of an environmentally hazardous material while still making it available to those without alternatives. Of course, the same could be done through regulation, but then the government would have to determine who should be allowed to use the limited amount available, a difficult task because of the high information costs involved. In the case of auctions, the decision is made by the market according to the forces of demand and (artificially limited) supply.

Another example of the use of auctions of property rights is in controlling the number of motor vehicles on city roads. After experimenting with a number of instruments to control the rapidly increasing number of motor vehicles that were causing traffic congestion and posing an environmental hazard in the long run, the government of Singapore decided to resort to the auction of the right to vehicle ownership. The annual supply of new motor vehicles in the country is limited to about 4,000. But before one can buy a car, one must purchase a Certificate of Entitlement at an auction organized by the government. Since the annual demand for new cars is far in excess of 4,000, in recent years the successful bidders have had to pay in excess of Singapore $50,000 just to buy an entitlement (which is over and above the sale price of the car). The instrument has ensured that the government is able to control the number of vehicles on streets without determining which individuals or firms own cars, the latter being determined by the market. Of course the auction is also a highly lucrative source of revenue for the government.

One advantage of auctions of property rights is that they are easy to establish. The government, based on what it considers the maximum amount of a good or service that should be permitted, fixes the ceiling, and then lets the market do the rest. Second, they are a flexible instrument which allows the government to vary the ceiling as and when it wants; the subjects must adjust their behaviour accordingly. Property-rights auctions also allow the subjects to adjust their behaviour according to changing circumstances, such as with respect to development of cost-saving technology, without requiring a corresponding change in the government's policy or instrument. Third, auctions offer the certainty that only a fixed amount of undesired activity occurs, something not possible with other voluntary or mixed instruments.

One of the disadvantages of auctions is that they may encourage speculation, with speculators buying up and hoarding all rights by bidding high, thereby erecting entry barriers to small firms. Second, it is often the case that those who cannot buy the rights, because none may be available for sale, will be forced to cheat, whereas in the case of charges or subsidies they would have an alternative. This can result in very high enforcement costs if grey or black markets are to be avoided. Third, auctions are inequitable to the extent they allocate resources according to ability to pay, rather than need, and can generate fierce opposition from those affected because of the extra costs they must bear in buying the right. Thus in Singapore the rich buy more than one car (because shortage has turned a car into a status symbol) while those who really need one cannot buy any if they do not have the additional money required to buy the certificate of entitlement.

Taxes and User Charges

A tax is a legally prescribed compulsory payment to government by a person or firm.[38] The main purpose of a tax is normally to raise revenues for the government's financing of expenditures. However, it can also be used as a policy instrument to induce a desired behaviour or discourage an undesirable behaviour. Taxes can take a variety of forms and of manners in which they are put into effect.

Payroll taxes of various sorts are used in most countries to fund social security programs. Under such schemes, the employer typically withholds a specified portion of the employee's salary (called the employee contribution), matches the amount by a proportion determined by the government (employer contribution), and then hands the amount thus collected to the government. The purpose of payroll taxes is often to build an insurance pool for designated risks such as sickness, industrial injury, and old age pensions. When the specified contingency occurs, the insured is indemnified from the fund. In a sense this is no different from private insurance one can buy for various risks, except that some risks are regarded as crucial to the society and hence insurance against them is made compulsory by the government. Compulsory membership in an insurance fund expands the number of insured and thus reduces the cost of premiums by spreading the risk.

Taxes can also be used to curb undesirable behaviour. In contrast to a subsidy which is a positive incentive and works by rewarding a desired behaviour, taxes can be applied as a negative incentive (or sanction) which penalizes an undesired behaviour. By taxing a good, service, or activity, the government indirectly discourages its consumption or performance. Many governments' policy objectives of reducing smoking, drinking, and gambling because of their ill effects, for example, can be partially achieved through exceptionally high taxes on cigarettes, alcohol, and gambling revenues. Studies show that the high price of cigarettes caused by high taxes was a key reason for reduction in cigarette consumption in Canada in the early 1990s, although these taxes encouraged smuggling and other forms of tax-avoidance behaviour.

A particularly innovative use of a tax as a policy instrument is a user charge. Instead of inducing a behaviour by rewarding it through subsidy or requiring it through regulations, the government imposes a 'price' on certain behaviours which those undertaking them must pay. The price may be seen as a financial penalty intended to discourage the targeted behaviour. User charges, similar to auctions of property rights, are a combination of regulation and market instruments. The regulatory aspect has to do with the government setting the charge (tax) for an activity without prohibiting or limiting it. How much of the target activity is undertaken is determined by market forces responding to the level of charges. The extra cost involved leads firms to conduct cost-benefit analysis, in order to decide if the activity must be ceased altogether or reduced to a level where benefits exceed costs. Efforts to reduce costs may encourage a search for (cheaper) alternatives that will reduce the chargeable activity. A firm can reap windfalls if it is able to implement technologies which do not involve the target behaviour or the charge associated with it. The success of a user charge is contingent on setting optimal charges so that only an acceptable level of undesired activity occurs.

User charges are most commonly used to control negative externalities. An example from the area of pollution control is that of user charges on pollution, known as effluent charges. Reducing pollution has costs, the marginal rate of which tends to increase with each additional unit of reduction. If a charge is levied on effluent discharge, the polluter will keep reducing its level of pollution to the point at which it becomes more expensive to reduce pollution than to simply pay the effluent charge. The polluter will thus be constantly seeking to devise ways to minimize the charges it has to pay by cutting back on the level of pollution it discharges. The government would ideally set the effluent charge at the point where social benefits equal social costs, assuming that the society knows how much pollution it can live with given the costs of decreasing the level of pollution. Any other price would be inefficient; lower charges would yield excessive pollution and too high a charge would raise costs, and, ultimately, the price which consumers pay. Another innovative example of user charge is provided by Singapore's efforts to control downtown traffic congestion. During peak hours, commuters are required to pay a set fee to enter the downtown area, which forces them to compare the costs of entering the area in their own vehicle with the cost of taking a bus or underground train, which are exempt from the charge. Research shows that the charge has had a marked impact on reducing congestion in the downtown area.

Among the advantages of taxes and user charges as policy instruments are the following. First, they are easy to establish because they enable individuals and firms to gradually find alternatives to paying charges in order to reduce costs. Companies have fewer grounds to oppose the measure; they cannot claim that it is not possible to reduce the activity in question, as they can continue the existing level of activity by paying the charge. Second, taxes and user charges provide a continuing financial incentive to reduce the undesirable activity. Since reducing the charges firms pay would enable them to reduce price or increase profits, it is in their self-interest to minimize the target activity. Regulations, by contrast, provide no incentive to reduce the behaviour below the specified standard. Third, user charges promote innovation by making it in the firms' interest to search for cheaper alternatives. Fourth, they are a flexible instrument, as the government continues to adjust rates until a point is reached where the desirable amount of the target activity occurs. Moreover, unlike regulation, where the discovery of new technology would require a change in the regulation, subjects respond to user charges on their own. Finally, they are desirable on administrative grounds because the responsibility for reducing the target activity is left to individuals and firms, which reduces the need for a bureaucratic machinery to enforce them.

There are some disadvantages of taxes and user charges as well. First, they require a vast amount of information to set the correct level of taxes or charges to elicit desired behaviour. Second, during the process of experimentation to arrive at optimum charges resources may be misallocated. The existing charges might encourage, for example, the installation of machinery which would be unviable when rates are reduced. Third, they are not effective in times of crises when an immediate response is required, nor do they permit planning to occur because of their reliance on private decisions. Finally, they involve cumbersome and possibly damaging administration costs.

CONCLUSION

This chapter has established a simple taxonomy of policy instruments based on the distinction between public or state and private or voluntary provision of goods and services. It has also set out the principal advantages and disadvantages of a range of instruments which offset the technical notion of the 'substitutability' of all policy tools.

While this discussion helps to outline the types of decisions policy-makers must make, it tells us little about why those choices are made. Like the preceding chapter establishing the key actors and institutions affecting public policy-making, this chapter has merely inventoried an important element of the public policy process. How the process actually works and how and why policy actors choose certain instruments is discussed in Part 3.

NOTES

1   For a summary of various classification schemes, see Lester M. Salamon and Michael S. Lund, 'The Tools Approach: Basic Analytics' in Lester S. Salamon (ed.), *Beyond Privatization: The Tools of Government Action* (Washington, DC: Urban Institute, 1989): pp. 32-3.

2   E.S. Kirschen et al., *Economic Policy in Our Time* (Chicago: Rand McNally, 1964).

3   See Robert E. Cushman, *The Independent Regulatory Commissions* (London: Oxford University Press, 1941); Robert A. Dahl and Charles E. Lindblom, *Politics, Economics and Welfare: Planning and Politico-economic Systems Resolved into Basic Social Processes* (New York: Harper and Row, 1953); Theodore J. Lowi, 'Four Systems of Policy, Politics and Choice', *Public Administration* Review 32, 4 (1972): 298-310.

4   Lester M. Salamon, 'Rethinking Public Management: Third-Party Government and the Changing Forms of Government Action', *Public Policy* 29 (1981): 255-75.

5   Christopher C. Hood, *The Tools of Government* (Chatham: Chatham House, 1986).

6   Lorraine M. McDonnell and Richard F. Elmore, *Alternative Policy Instruments* (Santa Monica: Center for Policy Research in Education, 1987).

7   Anne L. Schneider and Helen Ingram, 'Behavioral Assumptions of Policy Tools', *Journal of Politics* 52, 2 (1990): 510-29.

8   G. Bruce Doern and Richard W. Phidd, *Canadian Public Policy: Ideas, Structure, Process*, 2nd ed. (Toronto: Nelson Canada, 1992): 96-8.

9   Nicolas Baxter-Moore, 'Policy Implementation and the Role of the State: A Revised Approach to the Study of Policy Instruments' in Robert J. Jackson, Doreen Jackson, and Nicolas Baxter-Moore (eds), *Contemporary Canadian Politics: Readings and Notes* (Scarborough: Prentice-Hall, 1987): 336-55.

10 See Salamon and Lund, 'The Tools Approach: Basic Analytics' in Salamon (ed.), *Beyond Privatization*: 41.

11 Evert Lindquist, 'Tax Expenditures, Competitiveness and Accountability', in Bryne Purchase (ed.), *Policy Making and Competitiveness* (Kingston: Queen's University School of Policy Studies, 1994).

12 Neil Gilbert and Barbara Gilbert, *The Enabling State: Modern Welfare Capitalism in America* (New York: Oxford University Press, 1989): 281.

13 Robert Lampman, quoted in Gilbert and Gilbert, *The Enabling State*: 19.

14 Robert Wuthnow, 'The Voluntary Sector: Legacy of the Past, Hope for the Future' in Robert Wuthnow (ed.), *Between States and Markets: The Voluntary Sector in Comparative Perspective* (Princeton: Princeton University Press, 1991): 7.

15 Salamon, Lester M., 'Of Market Failure, Voluntary Failure, and Third-Party Government: Toward a Theory of Government-Nonprofit Relations in the Modern Welfare State' in Susan A. Ostrander and Stuart Langton (eds), *Shifting the Debate: Public/Private Sector Relations in the Modern Welfare State* (New Brunswick: Transaction Books, 1987): 31.

16 Norman Johnson, *The Welfare State in Transition: The Theory and Practice of Welfare Pluralism* (Brighton: Wheatsheaf, 1987): 114.

17 Salamon, Lester M., 'Of Market Failure, Voluntary Failure, and Third-Party Government': 31.

18 Michael D. Reagan, *Regulation: The Politics of Policy* (Boston: Little Brown, 1987): 17.

19 Reagan, *Regulation: The Politics of Policy*.

20   B.M. Mitnick, *The Political Economy of Regulation: Creating, Designing, and Removing Regulatory Forms* (New York: Columbia University Press, 1980): 401-04.

21   See James Anderson (ed.), *Economic Regulatory Policies* (Lexington: Lexington Books, 1976).

22   Romano Dyerson and Frank Mueller, 'Intervention by Outsiders: A Strategic Perspective on Government Industrial Policy', *Journal of Public Policy* 13, 1 (1993): 69-88.

23   Eugene Bardach, 'Social Regulation as a Generic Policy Instrument' in Lester M. Salamon (ed.), *Beyond Privatization*: 203-4.

24   B.M. Mitnick, *The Political Economy of Regulation: Creating, Designing, and Removing Regulatory Forms* (New York: Columbia University Press, 1980): 399-400.

25   Yair Ahroni, *Evolution and Management of State Owned Enterprises* (Cambridge, MA.: Ballinger, 1986): 6.

26   B.M. Mitnick, *The Political Economy of Regulation*: 407.

27   Christopher K. Leman, 'The Forgotten Fundamental: Successes and Excesses of Direct Government' in Salamon (ed.), *Beyond Privatization*: 54.

28   Based on Christopher K. Leman, 'The Forgotten Fundamental' in Salamon (ed.), *Beyond Privatization*: 60.

29   W.T. Stanbury and Jane Fulton, 'Suasion as a Governing Instrument' in Allan Maslove (ed.), *How Ottawa Spends 1984: The New Agenda* (Toronto: Lorimer, 1984): 282-324.

30   Leslie A. Pal, *Public Policy Analysis: An Introduction* (Toronto: Methuen, 1987): 148.

31   See Stanbury and Fulton, 'Suasion as a Governing Instrument': 297-301.

32   Stanbury and Fulton, 'Suasion as a Governing Instrument': 300.

33   Pal, *Public Policy Analysis*: 152.

34   B.M. Mitnick, *The Political Economy of Regulation: Creating, Designing, and Removing Regulatory Forms* (New York: Columbia University Press, 1980): 365.

35   Paul R. McDaniel, 'Tax Expenditures as Tools of Government Action' in Salamon (ed.), *Beyond Privatization*: 170-3.

36   Allan Maslove (ed.), *Taxing and Spending: Issues of Process* (Toronto: University of Toronto Press, 1994).

37   See Mitnick, *The Political Economy of Regulation*: 350-3.

38   M.J. Trebilcock et al., *The Choice of Governing Instrument* (Ottawa: Canadian Government Publication Centre, 1982): 53.

FURTHER READING

Atkinson, Michael M. and Robert A. Nigol, 'Selecting Policy Instruments: Neo-Institutional and Rational Choice Interpretations of Automobile Insurance in Ontario', *Canadian Journal of Political Science* 22, 1 (1989): 107-35.

Hood, Christopher, *The Tools of Government*, Chatham: Chatham House Publishers, 1986.

Howlett, Michael, 'Policy Instruments, Policy Styles, and Policy Implementation: National Approaches to Theories of Instrument Choice', *Policy Studies Journal* 19 (1991): 1-21.

Linder, S.H. and B.G. Peters, 'Instruments of Government: Perception and Contexts', *Journal of Public Policy* 9 (1989): 35-58.

Mitnick, B.M., *The Political Economy of Regulation*, New York: Columbia University Press, 1980.

Salamon, Lester M. (ed.), *Beyond Privatization: The Tools of Government Action*, Washington, DC: Urban Institute, 1989: 23-50.

Schneider, Anne and Helen Ingram, 'Behavioral Assumptions of Policy Tools', *Journal of Politics* 52, 2 (1990): 510-29.

Wolf, Charles Jr, *Market or Governments: Choosing Between Imperfect Alternatives*, Cambridge: MIT Press, 1988.

Woodside, K., 'Policy Instruments and the Study of Public Policy', *Canadian Journal of Political Science* 19 (1986): 775-94.

Part 3

THE PUBLIC POLICY PROCESS

Chapter 5

Agenda Setting—
Policy Determinants
and Policy Windows

CONCEPTUAL ISSUES

The first, and perhaps the most critical, stage of the policy cycle is agenda setting. How do issues appear on the governmental agenda for action? Although often taken for granted, the means and mechanisms by which issues and concerns are recognized as candidates for government action are by no means simple. They originate in a variety of factors and must undergo complex processes before they are considered seriously for resolution. What happens at this stage has a decisive impact on the entire policy process and its outcomes. As Cobb and Elder put it:

> pre-political, or at least pre-decisional processes often play the most critical role in determining what issues and alternatives are to be considered by the polity and the probable choices that will be made. What happens in the decision-making councils of the formal institutions of government may do little more than recognize, document and legalize, if not legitimize, the momentary results of a continuing struggle of forces in the larger social matrix. . . . From this perspective, the critical question becomes, how does an issue or a demand become or fail to become the focus of concern and interest within a polity?[1]

The manner and form in which problems are recognized, if they are recognized at all, are important determinants of how they will ultimately be addressed by policy-makers. The demands for government resolution of some public problems come from the society, whereas others are initiated by the government itself. Moreover, the public support for policy initiatives varies across policies which makes generalization difficult.

At its most basic, agenda-setting is about the recognition of a problem on the part of the government. Many of the early works on the subject are American and are deeply imbued with the pluralist sentiments prevalent in mainstream American political science of earlier eras. Thus, for example, Cobb,

Ross, and Ross defined agenda-setting as 'the process by which demands of various groups in the population are translated into items vying for the serious attention of public officials'.[2] This definition is closely linked with the idea that public policy-making is driven by the actions of social groups—a hallmark of Pluralism. Empirical evidence, however, reveals that in many instances the policy process is initiated by members of governments rather than social groups.

A more descriptive and less theoretically biased definition is provided by John Kingdon:

> The *agenda*, as I conceive of it, is the list of subjects or problems to which governmental officials, and people outside of government closely associated with those officials, are paying some serious attention at any given time. . . . Out of the set of all conceivable subjects or problems to which officials could be paying attention, they do in fact seriously attend to some rather than others. So the agenda-setting process narrows this set of conceivable subjects to the set that actually becomes the focus of attention.[3]

This is a clear summary of what is meant by the terms agenda and agenda-setting and forms the basis for our discussion in this chapter.

POLICY DETERMINANTS—CONCEPTIONS OF THE SOURCE OF POLICY PROBLEMS

How a problem comes to be interpreted as a public problem requiring government action raises deeper questions about the nature of human knowledge and the social construction of that knowledge. The policy sciences took many years to evolve a position or theory on the nature of social problems.[4] Most early works on the subject began with the assumption that socio-economic conditions led to the emergence of particular sets of problems to which governments eventually responded. It is now generally agreed, however, that a variety of political, social, and ideological factors determine which problems gain access to the policy agenda for resolution by the government. In the following discussion we will review the various perspectives on how a problem comes to be seen as a public concern requiring policy response.

Economic and Technological Determinism

The idea that public policies originate in the level of 'development' of a society, and that particular sets of problems are common to states at similar levels of development, was first broached by early observers of comparative public policy-making. By the mid 1960s Thomas Dye and others in the United States had concluded that cultural, political, and other factors were less significant for explaining the mix of public policies found in different jurisdictions than were the factors related to the level of economic development of the society in question. In his study of policy development in the US states, for example, Ira Sharkansky concluded that 'high levels of economic development—measured by such variables as per cent urban per capita income; median educational level and industrial employment—are generally associated with high levels of expenditure and service outputs in the fields of education, welfare and health.'[5] The conclusion led him to argue that 'political characteristics long thought to affect policy—voter participation, the strength of each major party, the degree of interparty competition, and the equity of legislative apportionment—have little influence which is independent of economic development.'[6]

This observation about the nature of public policy formation in the American states was soon expanded to the field of comparative public policy dealing with the different mixes of public policies found across nations. Authors such as Harold Wilensky, Philip Cutright, Henry Aaron, and Frederick Pryor all developed the idea that the structure of a nation's economy determined the types of public policies its government would adopt.[7] In its extreme form, this line of analysis led to the emergence of the *convergence thesis*.

The convergence thesis suggests that as countries industrialize, they tend to converge towards the same policy mix.[8] The emergence of similar welfare states in the industrialized countries, its proponents argue, is a direct result of their similar levels of economic wealth and technological development. Although early scholars indicated only a positive correlation between welfare policies and economic development, this relationship assumed causal status in the works of some later scholars. In this 'strong' view, high levels of economic development and wealth created similar problems and opportunities which were dealt with in broadly the same manner in different countries, regardless of the differences in their social or political structures.

Harold Wilensky, for example, noted that 'social security effort', defined as the percentage of a nation's GNP (Gross National Product) devoted to social security expenditures, varied positively with high levels of five key socio-economic and political variables. In a comparative study of sixty countries, he found that 83 per cent of the variance in levels of social security effort could be explained by examining differences in the age of the social security systems, the age of the population, the level of economic development defined in terms of GDP per capita, and whether the state was 'totalitarian' or liberal democratic.[9] He found that the strongest correlation was between social security effort and the level of GDP per capita, a correlation leading him to argue that economic criteria were more significant than political ones in understanding public policies. As he explained it, 'economic growth makes countries with contrasting cultural and political traditions more alike in their strategy for constructing the floor below which no one sinks.'[10]

In Wilensky's view, agenda-setting was thus virtually an automatic process occurring simply as a result of the stresses and strains placed on governments by industrialization and economic modernization. It mattered little whether issues were actually generated by social actors and placed on government agendas, or whether states and state officials took the lead in policy development. What was instead significant was the fact that similar policies emerged in different countries irrespective of the differences in their social and political structures.

The convergence thesis was quickly disputed by critics who argued that it vastly oversimplified the process of policy development and inaccurately portrayed the actual welfare policies found in different jurisdictions, policies characterized by significant divergence as well as convergence.[11] It was noted, for example, that in comparative studies of policy development in the American states, economic measures explained over one half of the inter-state variations in policies in only four per cent of the policy sectors examined. Secondly, the definition of 'political factors' used by investigators was restricted to such things as voter turnout, party strength, and equity of legislative apportionment and did not include such obvious factors affecting program development as tax effort or the nature of intergovernmental grants, both significant factors in the US federal system. Thirdly, it was intimated that the desire to make a strong economic argument had led investigators to overlook the manner in which economic factors varied in significance over time, and by issue.[12]

Similar criticisms were made against the more broadly cross-national comparisons that suggested convergence was occurring. The measures used by Wilensky and others were criticized for failing to capture the various dimensions of social welfare.[13] Instead of focusing on welfare efforts, which is a measure of expenditure on social security as a percentage of GDP, it was argued that analysts need to consider all the ways in which the state affects income distribution in society.[14] The broader approach was said to reveal a great deal of divergence in the social policies of similarly industrialized countries. It was suggested that subtle but significant differences in social welfare policies—such as whether benefits were geared to wage levels or guaranteed basic incomes—were glossed over in the analyses arguing for convergence.[15] Others argued that the issue was not simply social security effort, but the overall level of public expenditures in different countries, a phenomenon felt to be inextricably linked to partisan political factors and the ideological complexion of the government in power.[16]

Interplay of Politics and Economics

One way in which scholars sought to overcome the problems associated with theories of economic and technological policy determinism was by re-integrating political and economic variables in a new 'political economy of public policy'. Here it was argued that both political and economic factors are important determinants of public policy and should therefore be studied together. There are, however, different versions of this argument.

One of the most important versions of this line of argument posits the idea of a *political-business cycle*.[17] Here it was suggested that the economy has its own internal dynamics which are on occasion altered by political 'interference' in the form of public policies. The notion of political-business cycles grew out of the literature on business cycles, which found that the economy grew in fits and starts according to periodic flurries of investment and consumption behaviour. When applied to public policy-making, it was argued that in the modern era governments often intervened in markets in order to smooth out fluctuations in the business cycle. In democratic states, it followed that the nature of these interventions could be predicted on the basis of the political ideology of the governing party—either pro-state or pro-market—while the actual timing of interventions depended on the proximity to elections. Policies which caused difficulties for the voting public were, according to observers, more likely to be implemented when an election did not loom on the immediate horizon. As Edward Tufte put it:

> Although the synchronization of economic fluctuations with the electoral cycle often preoccupies political leaders, the real force of political influence on macroeconomic performance comes in the determination of economic priorities. Here the ideology and platform of the political party in power dominate. Just as the electoral calendar helps set the timing of policy, so the ideology of political leaders shapes the substance of economic policy.[18]

While few disagreed that partisan ideology could have an impact on the economy, this approach was criticized for its limited application to countries in which electoral cycles were fixed, such as the United States. In many other countries, elections are indeterminate and dependent on events in Parliaments or other branches of government, and detailed calculations of policy timing are difficult if not impossible for governments to make.[19] It was also argued that the concept of the business cycle itself was fundamentally flawed and that the model simply pointed out the interdependence of politics and economics already acknowledged by most analysts.[20]

In the mid-1980s, another political-economic explanation of agenda-setting emerged which treated political and economic factors as an integral whole.[21] It argued that industrialization creates a need for social security (because of ageing of the population and urbanization) as well as the economic resources (because of increases in productivity) to address the need. It also creates a working class with a need for social security as well as the political resources (because of the number of voters who belong to this class) to exert pressure on the state to meet the need. The ideology of the government in power and the political threats it faces are also important considerations in determining the extent to which the state meets the demand for social welfare. While some issues, such as the role of international economic forces in domestic policy-formation, are still debated,[22] this view offers a reasonable synthesis of the political-economic explanations of public policy, but remains a high-level theory difficult to apply to specific instances of agenda-setting.

Ideas and Ideology

Problems with 'materialist' explanations of why governments deal with certain social problems led in the 1980s to another set of studies that focused on the effects of social and political ideas on defining the sorts of problems with which governments must deal.

It has long been noted that the ideas individuals hold on an enduring basis have a significant effect on the decisions they make. Although efforts have been made by economists, psychologists, and others to reduce these sets of ideas to a rational calculation of self-interest, it is apparent that traditions, beliefs, and attitudes about the world and society also affect how individuals interpret their interests.[23] These sets of ideas or ideologies, therefore, can be construed to have a significant impact on public policies, for through these ideational prisms individuals conceive of social or other problems that inspire their demands for government action.

In this view, the 'problems' which governments resolve are not considered to have an 'objective' base in the economy or material structure of society, so much as they are constructed in the realm of public and private discourse.[24] As Murray Edelman has argued:

> Problems come into discourse and therefore into existence as reinforcements of ideologies, not simply because they are there or because they are important for well-being. They signify who are virtuous and useful and who are dangerous and inadequate, which actions will be rewarded and which penalized. They constitute people as subjects with particular kinds of aspirations, self-concepts, and fears, and they create beliefs about the relative importance of events and objects. They are critical in determining who exercise authority and who accept it. They construct areas of immunity from concern because those areas are not seen as problems. Like leaders and enemies, they define the contours of the social world, not in the same way for everyone, but in the light of the diverse situations from which people respond to the political spectacle.[25]

Thus, from this perspective, the idea that policy-makers react to objective conditions in a rational manner is deceptive, if not completely misleading. Rather, policy-makers are involved in the same discourse as the public and in the manipulation of the signs, sets, and scenes of a political play or theatre. According to the script of the ideological discourse, different groups of actors are involved and different outcomes prescribed. Michael Shapiro writes,

> Human conduct is controlled and understood within the discourses that give it meaning. Insofar as we do not invent language or meanings in our typical speech, we end up buying into a model of political relations in almost everything we say without making a prior, deliberative evaluation of the purchasing decision.[26]

In this view, the language of politics 'constructs' public policy, since the language of politics is inscribed with interpretations of what a policy 'problem' is. The agenda of politics or policy-making, then, is an agenda which is established out of the history, traditions, attitudes, and beliefs of a people encapsulated and codified in the terms of its political discourse.[27]

In its original formulation, the notion of a political discourse was set out as a tool for understanding the historical evolution of society.[28] The task of historical analysis, and social theory in general, was to understand the nature of the origin and evolution of discursive formations over time, and to situate current discourses into this overall conception of history. This effort was supposed by its proponents to be able to overcome what they saw as the unavoidable limits of other more materialist approaches, which relegated ideological and cultural variables to secondary status. As Anthony Woodiwiss has suggested:

> Using the concept of discourse to specify the structure of the ideological realm enables one to understand its reality and its autonomous determinative capacity. This is something which is, quite simply, impossible otherwise, thanks to the prevalence of such anachronistic dichotomies as 'base/superstructure' and 'thought/behavior', which tend to diminish the significance of the ideological realm.[29]

In the policy realm, this notion of ideas creating claims or demands on governments has recently been taken up by Frank Fischer and John Forester,[30] and applied to agenda-setting by Deborah Stone. In Stone's view, agenda-setting usually involves constructing a 'story' of what caused the policy problem in question.[31] Symbols and statistics, both real and fabricated, are used to back up one's preferred understanding of the causes of the problem. The problems faced by the native Indian population in urban areas, for instance, depending on one's preferences can be attributed to historical, sociological, or political factors. Ancient and contemporary symbols are discovered to make one's case. Convenient statistics are put together to bolster the case. In these statistics, as policy-makers know all too well, one finds what one looks for. As Stone has argued:

> Causal theories, if they are successful, do more than convincingly demonstrate the possibility of human control over bad conditions. First, they can either challenge or protect an existing social order. Second, by identifying causal agents, they can assign responsibility to particular political actors so that someone will have to stop an activity, do it differently, compensate its victims, or possibly face punishment. Third, they can legitimate and empower particular actors as 'fixers' of the problem. And fourth, they can create new political alliances among people who are shown to stand in the same victim relationship to the causal agent.[32]

This conception of the role of ideas in the process of social problem definition has led policy scholars away from the analysis of empirical conditions towards ('post-positivist') concerns with the creation and diffusion of social knowledge. For most analysts, however, the purely 'subjective' (or solipsistic) elements of discourse analyses have been tempered by the need to incorporate institutional elements into the analysis. That is, most policy scholars are unwilling to dispense completely with the results of earlier studies focusing on political and economic conditions, but feel that policy theory must take into account the complex interplay of both ideas and material conditions in the policy-making process.[33]

RE-CONCEPTUALIZING THE AGENDA-SETTING PROCESS

To understand agenda setting we must comprehend how demands for a policy are made by individuals and/or groups and responded to by the government, or vice versa, and the conditions under which these demands emerge and are articulated in prevailing policy discourses.[34] Towards this end, we need to understand the material interests of social and state actors as well as the institutional and ideological contexts in which they operate.[35]

In the late 1970s Anthony King in Great Britain, Richard Hofferbert in the United States, and Richard Simeon in Canada developed models that attempted to capture the general relationships existing among interests, institutions, and ideas in agenda-setting. These models are based on the notion that these variables exist within a *funnel of causality*, in which each variable is 'nested' within another.

The funnel-of-causality approach reviewed and synthesized much of the existing literature on policy formation. Rather than view material and ideational variables as dichotomous or zero-sum, it argued that all these factors are involved in the creation of social or policy problems. More specifically, it identified a series of causal variables, including those related to the socio-economic and physical environment, the distribution of power in society, the prevailing ideas and ideologies, the institutional frameworks of government, and the process of decision-making within governments.[36] Hofferbert and Simeon suggested that these variables are intertwined in a 'nested' pattern of mutual interaction in which decision-making occurs within institutions, institutions exist within prevailing sets of ideas and ideologies, ideologies within relations of power in society, and relations of power within a larger social and material environment.[37]

This synthetic model helped delineate the relations between the multiple material and ideational variables identified in previous studies without bogging down in attempts to specify their exact relationship or causal significance. This is the model's greatest strength as well as its greatest weakness. It is a strength because it allows some discussion between alternate viewpoints to take place, while leaving it to empirical study to determine the exact relationship and mediate between theoretical disputes. It is also a weakness, because it does little to explain the differences which would emerge in specific case studies according to the actual causative agent at work. Why one issue might be influenced by ideas and another by, for example, environmental factors, is not broached, let alone resolved.

Similarly, the funnel-of-causality model says very little about how general forces such as the environmental context, ideas, or economic interests are actually manifested by policy actors in the agenda-setting process. However, several recent efforts have attempted to identify the relevant actors in this process.

Beginning from the observation that the process of agenda-setting involves discussion, debate, and persuasion among those interested in the policy, each presenting a variety of evidence and argument in support of their position,[38] Baumgartner and Jones have developed a model which helps to identify the actors involved in agenda setting.[39] For Baumgartner and Jones, the 'image' of a policy problem is significant because it influences the membership and activities of relevant policy subsystems:

> When [problems] are portrayed as technical problems rather than as social questions, experts can dominate the decision-making process. When the ethical, social or political implications of such policies assume center stage, a much broader range of participants can suddenly become involved.[40]

The key element in the process of agenda-setting, Baumgartner and Jones argue, revolves around the creation of 'policy monopolies' in which specific subsystems gain the ability to control the interpretation of a problem and thus the manner in which it is conceived and discussed. This is an important insight, bringing to the fore the question of the principal actor involved in agenda-setting. However, as currently set out, this model does not allow distinctions to be drawn between typical types or patterns of agenda-setting, and a more specific set of variables and hypotheses about their interrelationships is therefore required.

TYPICAL AGENDA-SETTING PROCESSES

A distinction is often made, following Cobb and Elder, between *systemic* or public agenda and *institutional* or formal agenda. The systemic agenda 'consists of all issues that are commonly perceived by members of the political community as meriting public attention and as involving matters within the legitimate jurisdiction of existing governmental authority'.[41] This is essentially a society's agenda for discussion of *public* problems, such as crime or health care. Each society has literally hundreds of issues that some citizens find to be matters of concern and would have the government do something about. However, only a small proportion of the problems on the systemic agenda are taken up by the government for serious consideration. Once the government has accepted that something needs to be done about a problem, it can be said to have entered the institutional agenda. These are issues that the government has agreed to give serious attention. In other words, the public agenda is an agenda for discussion while the institutional agenda is an agenda for action, indicating that the policy process dealing with the problem in question has begun.

According to Cobb, Ross, and Ross, there are four major phases of agenda-setting as issues move between systemic and institutional agendas. Issues are first *initiated*, their solutions *specified*, support for the issue *expanded*, and if successful, the issue *enters the* institutional agenda.[42] In earlier studies, which were influenced strongly by Pluralism, public problems were viewed as always moving from the systemic to the institutional agenda. However, investigation into actual cases of agenda-building quickly revealed difficulties with such a conception and several different models of agenda-setting were then developed to describe how issues moved from society to state or from state to the society, as they proceeded into the official agenda.

Cobb, Ross, and Ross first developed these different models after having undertaken studies of the agenda-setting process in different countries. According to them, there were three basic patterns or models of agenda-setting: the outside initiation model, the mobilization model, and the inside initiation model, each associated with a particular type of political regime.

They identified the *outside initiation* model with liberal pluralist societies. In this model, 'issues arise in nongovernmental groups and are then expanded sufficiently to reach, first, the public [systemic] agenda and, finally, the formal [institutional] agenda.'[43] In this model the key role is played by social groups. Issues are first initiated when a group articulates a grievance and demands its resolution by the government. Those same groups attempt to expand support for their demand, a process which may involve submerging the specific complaint within a more general one and the formation of alliances across groups. Finally, these groups lobby, contest, and join with others in attempting to get the expanded issue onto the formal agenda. If they have the requisite political resources and skills and can outmanoeuvre their opponents or advocates of other issues and actions, they will succeed in having their issue enter the formal agenda. Thus, as Cobb, Ross, and Ross summarize:

> The outside initiative model applies to the situation in which a group outside the government structure 1) articulates a grievance, 2) tries to expand interest in the issue to enough other groups in the population to gain a place on the public agenda, in order to 3) create sufficient pressure on decision makers to force the issue onto the formal agenda for their serious consideration.[44]

Successful entrance onto the formal agenda does not necessarily mean a favourable government decision will ultimately result. It simply means that the item has been singled out from among a mass of others for more detailed consideration.

The *mobilization* model is quite different and was attributed by Cobb, Ross, and Ross to 'totalitarian' regimes. This model describes 'decision-makers trying to expand an issue from a formal [institutional] to a public [systemic] agenda'.[45]

In the mobilization model, issues are simply placed on the formal agenda by the government with no necessary preliminary expansion from a publicly recognized grievance. There may be considerable debate within government over the issue, but the public may well be kept in the dark about the policy and its development until its formal announcement. The policy may be specified in some detail or it may only establish general principles whose specification will be worked out later. Expansion of support for the new policy is important, however, as successful implementation depends on a favourable public reaction to the policy. Towards this end, government leaders hold meetings and engage in public relations campaigns aimed at mobilizing public support for their decisions. As the authors put it, 'The mobilization model describes the process of agenda building in situations where political leaders initiate a policy but require the support of the mass public for its implementation . . . the crucial problem is to move the issue from the formal agenda to the public agenda.'[46]

In the *inside initiation* model, influential groups with special access to decision-makers initiate a policy and do not necessarily want it to be expanded and contested in public. This can be due to technical as well as political reasons and is a pattern of agenda-setting which one would expect to find in corporatist regimes. In this model, initiation and specification occur simultaneously as a group or government agency enunciates a grievance and specifies some potential solution to the problem. Expansion is restricted to specialized groups or agencies with some knowledge or interest in the subject. Entrance on the agenda is virtually automatic due to the privileged place of those desiring a decision. According to Cobb, Ross, and Ross:

> Proposals arise within governmental units or in groups close to the government. The issue is then expanded to identification and attention groups in order to create sufficient pressure on decision makers to place the item on the formal agenda. At no point is the public greatly involved, and the initiators make no effort to get the issue on the public agenda. On the contrary, they try to keep it off.[47]

This line of analysis identifies several typical patterns or styles of agenda-setting. While it does so on the basis of an (unstated) notion of a relatively crude policy subsystem—one in which state and societal actors are clearly separated—the most important variable in this analysis is regime type. That is, in this model the type of agenda-setting process likely to be found in any sector is ultimately determined by the general nature of the political system; outside initiation is argued to be typical of liberal democracies, mobilization typical of socialist one-party states, and inside initiation typical of authoritarian bureaucratic regimes.

This particular aspect of Cobb, Ross, and Ross's analysis is misleading, and indeed unnecessary. Every kind of political regime is characterized by a variety of agenda-setting styles and no firm generalization of agenda-setting by regime type is possible. Rather than varying by regime type, it is much more likely, as John Kingdon and others have argued, that the key variable is the nature of the problem itself.

In Kingdon's study of agenda-setting in the United States, three sets of variables—'streams' of problems, policies, and politics—are said to interact. The *problem stream* refers to the perceptions of problems as public problems requiring government action and past government efforts to resolve them. In Kingdon's view problems typically come to the attention of policy-makers either because of sudden events like crises or through feedback from the operation of existing programs.[48] People come to see a condition as a 'problem' with reference to their conception of some desired state of affairs. The *policy stream* consists of experts and analysts examining problems and proposing solutions to them. In this stream, the various possibilities are explored and narrowed down. Finally, the *political stream* 'is composed of such factors as swings of national mood, administrative or legislative turnover, and interest group pressure campaign'.[49]

In Kingdon's view, these three streams operate on different paths and pursue courses more or less independent of one another until at specific points in time, or *policy windows*, their paths intersect. As Kingdon argues: 'The separate streams of problems, policies, and politics come together at certain critical times. Solutions become joined to problems, and both of them are joined to favourable political forces.'[50] It is at that point that an item enters the official (or institutional) agenda and the public policy process begins.

Kingdon suggests that agenda-setting is ultimately governed by certain fortuitous happenings, including seemingly unrelated external events and accidents or the presence or absence of 'policy entrepreneurs' both within and outside of governments, and by institutionalized events such as periodic elections or budgetary cycles. As he argues:

> windows are opened either by the appearance of compelling problems or by happenings in the political stream. . . . Policy entrepreneurs, people who are willing to invest their resources in pushing their pet proposals or problems, are responsible not only for prompting important people to pay attention, but also for coupling solutions to problems and for coupling both problems and solutions to politics.[51]

Kingdon's theory of agenda-setting can be seen to add an additional level of insight to the model of agenda-setting developed by Cobb and his colleagues. Unlike Cobb's work, however, Kingdon's theory is extremely contingent. That is, it suggests that the timing at which items emerge on the agenda is set by a host of unpredictable elements such as the behaviour of 'policy entrepreneurs' and various sorts of exogenous and endogenous crises or shocks. While this may be true of specific issues, it ignores the observation of Cobb and others that certain issues tend to emerge on the institutional agenda in only a relatively limited number of ways. Cobb, Ross, and Ross's presentation of the three models of agenda-setting has made a useful contribution to our understanding of the various forms the process can take and should not be abandoned in the effort to arrive at a more precise model of the agenda-setting process.

Nevertheless, Cobb's model requires some improvement. Instead of emphasizing the nature of the regime, a more fruitful avenue is to conceptualize the agenda-setting process in terms of the interaction of the nature of the policy subsystem involved in the issue area and the nature of the problem itself. In this latter dimension, the level of public support for the resolution of a problem is critical. Some problems have a wide-ranging impact on society and therefore the demands for their resolution are likely to be initiated by the public. Others are of significance only to particular groups, which, depending on the closeness of their relations with the government of the day, may be able to undertake inside initiation. Government officials may engage in either mobilization or inside initiation depending on the level of public support for solving the problem in question: if support is forthcoming, then we are likely to see its consolidation, otherwise the government will have to resort to mobilization.

Thus the central question in agenda-setting is not the type of regime involved, but rather the nature of the policy subsystem dealing with the problem, that determines whether the state or societal actors initiate the process, and the level of public support for its resolution.[52] Figure 6 demonstrates the significant aspects of this relationship.

■ Figure 6.
| Models of Agenda-Setting by Policy Type

	Nature of Public Support	
	High	Low
Initiator of Debate		
Societal Actors	*Outside Initiation*	*Inside Initiation*
State	*Consolidation*	*Mobilization*

SOURCE: Adapted from Peter J. May, 'Reconsidering Policy Design: Policies and Publics', *Journal of Public Policy* 11, 2 (1991): 187-206.

In this model, the mode of agenda-setting is determined by the nature of public support for the issue and by the nature of the initiating actor(s). Three of the four possible types of agenda-setting correspond to those put forward by Cobb, Ross, and Ross, although they differ not according to the type of political regime but according to who initiates the process and the level of public support for the issue. The fourth type of agenda-setting, *consolidation*, occurs when the government initiates the process of solving a public problem for which there is already extensive popular support. In such instances the issue does not have to be 'initiated', nor does public support have to be 'mobilized'. It is enough for the state to 'consolidate' the existing support and go ahead with making policy.

CONCLUSION

Little empirical work has been done on agenda-setting in recent years. Although some recent efforts are promising, they are restricted to specific case studies.[53] Nevertheless, the elements necessary for an empirically-driven and theoretically rich analysis of agenda-setting are present within the existing public policy literature.

As our discussion has established, it is possible to construct a model of agenda-setting styles based on the interrelatedness of public and governmental support for a specific claim or demand for government action. Such a model highlights the need to investigate problem definition within the context of both the extent to which material interests affect the interpretation of the society's problems and the manner in which ideas and ideologies condition their realization.[54] Variables relating to the nature of the political regime, dominant ideologies and sets of cultural norms and ideals, and the existence of somewhat fortuitous events which can draw state and social attention to a particular issue are all important in the agenda-setting process. But more significant are variables related to the characteristics of the policy problem, especially in terms of the impact this has on the nature of the policy subsystem involved and the extent of public support (or lack of it) for the resolution of the problem.

NOTES

1   Roger W. Cobb and Charles D. Elder, *Participation in American Politics: The Dynamics of Agenda-Building* (Boston: Allyn and Bacon, 1972): 12.

2   R. Cobb, J.K. Ross, and M.H. Ross, 'Agenda Building as a Comparative Political Process', *American Political Science Review* 70, 1 (1976): 126.

3   John W. Kingdon, *Agendas, Alternatives and Public Policies* (Boston: Little, Brown and Company, 1984): 3-4.

4   Peter L. Berger and Thomas Luckmann, *The Social Construction of Reality: A Treatise in the Sociology of Knowledge* (New York: Doubleday, 1966).

5   Ira Sharkansky, 'Constraints on Innovation in Policy Making: Economic Development and Political Routines' in Frank Marini (ed.), *Toward a New Public Administration: The Minnowbrook Perspective* (Scranton: Chandler, 1971): 263.

6   Sharkansky, 'Constraints on Innovation in Policy Making': 264.

7   H.J. Aaron, 'Social Security: International Comparison' in O. Eckstein (ed.), *Studies in the Economics of Income Maintenance* (Washington, DC: Brookings Institution, 1967): 13-49; P. Cutright, 'Political Structure, Economic Development, and National Security Programs', *American Journal of Sociology* 70, 5 (1965): 537-50; F.L. Pryor, *Public Expenditures in Communist and Capitalist Nations* (Homewood, IL: R.D. Irwin, 1968); H.L. Wilensky, *The Welfare State and Equality: Structural and Ideological Roots of Public Expenditures* (Berkeley: University of California Press, 1975).

8   Colin J. Bennett, 'What is Policy Convergence and What Causes It?', *British Journal of Political Science* 21, 2 (1991): 215-33; Clark Kerr, *The Future of Industrial Societies: Convergence or Continuing Diversity?* (Cambridge: Harvard University Press, 1983).

9   H.L. Wilensky, *The Welfare State and Equality: Structural and Ideological Roots of Public Expenditures* (Berkeley: University of California Press, 1975): 658-9.

10   Wilensky, *The Welfare State and Equality*: 27.

11   Arnold J. Heidenheimer, Hugh Heclo, and Carolyn Teich Adams, *Comparative Public Policy: The Politics of Social Choice in Europe and America* (New York: St Martin's Press, 1975): 257-84.

12   Sharkansky, 'Constraints on Innovation in Policy Making': 261-79.

13   Christopher Hewitt, 'The Effect of Political Democracy and Social Democracy on Equality in Industrial Societies: A Cross-National Comparison', *American Sociological Review*, 42, 3 (1977): 450-64; Leonard S. Miller, 'The Structural Determinants of the Welfare Effort: A Critique and a Contribution', *Social Service Review* 50, 1 (1976): 57-79.

14   Walter Korpi, *The Democratic Class Struggle* (London: Routledge and Kegan Paul, 1983).

15   Gosta Esping-Andersen, *The Three Worlds of Welfare Capitalism* (Cambridge: Polity Press, 1990).

16   Frank Castles and Robert D. McKinlay, 'Does Politics Matter: An Analysis of the Public Welfare Commitment in Advanced Democratic States', *European Journal of Political Research* 7, 2 (1979): 169-86; Francis G. Castles, 'The Impact of Parties on Public Expenditure', in Francis G. Castles (ed.), *The Impact of Parties: Politics and Policies in Democratic Capitalist States* (London: Sage Publications, 1982): 21-96; Douglas A. Hibbs Jr, 'Political Parties and Macroeconomic Policy', *American Political Science Review* 71, (1977): 1467-87; Anthony King, 'What Do Elections Decide?' in David Butler, Howard R. Penniman, and Austin Ranney (eds), *Democracy at the Polls: A Comparative Study of Competitive National Elections* (Washington, DC: American Enterprise Institute for Public Policy Research, 1981); Klaus von Beyme, 'Do Parties Matter? The Impact of Parties on the Key Decisions in the Political System', *Government and Opposition* 19, 1 (1984): 5-29.

17   Bruno S. Frey, 'Politico-Economic Models and Cycles', *Journal of Public Economics* 9, 2 (1978): 203-20; Gareth Locksley, 'The Political Business Cycle: Alternative Interpretations' in Paul Whitely (ed.), *Models of Political Economy* (London: Sage Publications, 1980).

18   Edward R. Tufte, *Political Control of the Economy* (Princeton, NJ: Princeton University Press, 1978): 71.

19   David K. Foot, 'Political Cycles, Economic Cycles and the Trend in Public Employment in Canada' in Meyer W. Bucovetsky (ed.), *Studies in Public Employment and Compensation in Canada* (Toronto: Butterworths for Institute for Research on Public Policy, 1979): 65-80.

20   Raford Boddy and James Crotty, 'Class Conflict and Macro-Policy: The Political Business Cycle', *Review of Radical Political Economics* 7, 1 (1975): 1-19.

21   For a summary of the arguments in this vein, see Hannu Uusitalo, 'Comparative Research on the Determinants of the Welfare State: The State of the Art', *European Journal of Political Research* 12, 4 (1984): 403-22.

22   David R. Cameron, 'Social Democracy, Corporatism, Labour Quiescence and the Representation of Economic Interest in Advanced Capitalist Society' in John H. Goldthorpe (ed.), *Order and Conflict in Contemporary Capitalism* (Oxford: Clarendon Press, 1984): 143-78; Peter J. Katzenstein, *Small States in World Markets: Industrial Policy in Europe* (Ithaca: Cornell University Press, 1985).

23   Richard E. Flathman, *The Public Interest: An Essay Concerning the Normative Discourse of Politics* (New York: Wiley, 1966).

24   Peter L. Berger and Thomas Luckmann, *The Social Construction of Reality: A Treatise in the Sociology of Knowledge*, 1st ed. (New York: Doubleday, 1966); Stephen Hilgartner and Charles L. Bosk, 'The Rise and Fall of Social Problems: A Public Arenas Model', *American Journal of Sociology* 94, 1 (1981): 53-78; Burkhart Holzner and John H. Marx, *Knowledge Application: The Knowledge System in Society* (Boston: Allyn and Bacon, 1979); David A. Rochefort and Roger W. Cobb, 'Problem Definition, Agenda Access, and Policy Change', *Policy Studies Journal* 21, 1 (1993): 56-71; Malcolm Spector and John I. Kitsuse, *Constructing Social Problems* (New York: Aldine de Gruyter, 1987).

25   Murray J. Edelman, *Constructing the Political Spectacle* (Chicago: University of Chicago Press, 1988): 12-13.

26   Michael J. Shapiro, *Language and Political Understanding: The Politics of Discursive Practices* (New Haven: Yale University Press, 1981): 231.

27   Jane Jenson, 'All the World's a Stage: Ideas About Political Space and Time,' *Studies in Political Economy* 36 (1991): 43-72; Andrew Stark, ' "Political-Discourse" Analysis and the Debate Over Canada's Lobbying Legislation,' *Canadian Journal of Political Science* 25, 3 (1992): 513-34.

28   See Michel Foucault, 'The Discourse on Language' in Michel Foucault (ed.), *The Archaeology of Knowledge* (New York: Pantheon, 1972).

29   Anthony Woodiwiss, *Social Theory After Postmodernism: Rethinking Production, Law and Class* (London: Pluto Press, 1990): 29.

30   Fischer, Frank and John Forester (eds), *The Argumentative Turn in Policy Analysis and Planning* (Durham: Duke University Press, 1993).

31   Deborah A. Stone, *Policy Paradox and Political Reason* (Glenview: Scott, Foresman, 1988); Deborah A. Stone, 'Causal Stories and the Formation of Policy Agendas', *Political Science Quarterly* 104, 2 (1989): 281-300.

32   Stone, 'Causal Stories and the Formation of Policy Agendas': 295.

33   Rochefort, David A. and Roger W. Cobb, 'Problem Definition: An Emerging Perspective' in D.A. Rochefort and R.W. Cobb (eds), *The Politics of Problem Definition: Shaping the Policy Agenda* (Lawrence: University of Kansas Press, 1994).

34   Spector and Kitsuse, *Constructing Social Problems*: 75-6

35   John B. Thompson, *Ideology and Modern Culture: Critical Social Theory in the Era of Mass Communication* (Cambridge: Polity Press, 1990).

36   Anthony King, 'Ideas, Institutions and the Policies of Governments: A Comparative Analysis: Part III', *British Journal of Political Science* 3, 4 (1973): 409-23.

37   Richard I. Hofferbert, *The Study of Public Policy* (Indianapolis: Bobbs-Merrill, 1974); Richard Simeon, 'Studying Public Policy', *Canadian Journal of Political Science* 9, 4 (1976): 548-80.

38   Giandomenico Majone, *Evidence, Argument, and Persuasion in the Policy Process* (New Haven: Yale University Press, 1989).

39   Frank R. Baumgartner and Bryan D. Jones, 'Agenda Dynamics and Policy Subsystems', *Journal of Politics* 53, 4 (1991): 1044-74; Frank R. Baumgartner and Bryan D. Jones, *Agendas and Instability in American Politics* (Chicago: University of Chicago Press, 1993); Frank R. Baumgartner and Bryan D. Jones, 'Attention, Boundary Effects, and Large-Scale Policy Change in Air Transportation Policy' in D.A. Rochefort and R.W. Cobb (eds), *The Politics of Problem Definition: Shaping the Policy Agenda* (Lawrence: University of Kansas Press, 1994).

40   Frank R. Baumgartner and Bryan D. Jones, 'Agenda Dynamics and Policy Sub-systems', *Journal of Politics* 53, 4 (1991): 1047

41   Roger W. Cobb and Charles D. Elder, *Participation in American Politics: The Dynamics of Agenda-Building* (Boston: Allyn and Bacon, 1972): 85.

42   R. Cobb, J.K. Ross, and M.H. Ross, 'Agenda Building as a Comparative Political Process', *American Political Science Review* 70, 1 (1976): 127. Kingdon further differentiates within the institutional agenda, locating the specialized agendas of government agencies; the legislative agenda of government; and the decision agenda of the executive: John W. Kingdon, *Agendas, Alternatives and Public Policies* (Boston: Little, Brown and Company, 1984): 4.

43   Cobb, Ross, and Ross, 'Agenda Building as a Comparative Political Process': 127.

44   Cobb, Ross, and Ross: 132.

45   Cobb, Ross, and Ross: 132.

46   Cobb, Ross, and Ross: 135.

47   Cobb, Ross, and Ross: 136.

48   John W. Kingdon, *Agendas, Alternatives and Public Policies* 20.

49   Kingdon: 21.

50   Kingdon: 21.

51   Kingdon: 21.

52   Peter J. May, 'Reconsidering Policy Design: Policies and Publics', *Journal of Public Policy* 11, 2 (1991): 187-206.

53   The best recent study is that of Baumgartner and Jones. Harrison and Hoberg probably represent the state of the art in Canadian studies. See Frank R. Baumgartner and Bryan D. Jones, *Agendas and Instability in American Politics* (Chicago: University of Chicago Press, 1993) and Kathryn Harrison and George Hoberg, 'Setting the Environmental Agenda in Canada and the United States: The Cases of Dioxin and Radon', *Canadian Journal of Political Science* 24, 1 (1991): 3-27.

54   Nelson W. Polsby, *Political Innovation in America: The Politics of Policy Initiation* (New Haven: Yale University Press, 1984); Robert B. Reich (ed.), *The Power of Public Ideas* (Cambridge: Ballinger, 1987).

FURTHER READING

Baumgartner, Frank R. and Bryan D. Jones, *Agendas and Instability in American Politics*, Chicago: University of Chicago Press, 1993.

Bennett, Colin J., 'What is Policy Convergence and What Causes It?', *British Journal of Political Science* 21 (1991): 215-34.

Cobb, Roger W. and Charles D. Elder, *Participation in American Politics: The Dynamics of Agenda-Building*, Boston: Allyn and Bacon, 1972.

Dye, Thomas R., 'Politics Versus Economics: The Development of the Literature on Policy Determination', *Policy Studies Journal* 7 (1978): 652-62.

Edelman, Murray, *Constructing the Political Spectacle*, Chicago: University of Chicago Press, 1988.

King, Anthony, 'Ideas, Institutions and the Policies of Governments: A Comparative Analysis: II', *British Journal of Political Science* 3 (1973): 409-23.

Kingdon, John W., *Agendas, Alternatives and Public Policies*, Boston: Little, Brown and Company, 1984.

Manning, Nick, 'What is a Social Problem?,' pp. 8-23 in Martin Loney et al. (eds), *The State or the Market: Politics and Welfare in Contemporary Britain*, London: Sage, 1987.

May, Peter J., 'Reconsidering Policy Design: Policies and Publics', *Journal of Public Policy* 11 (1991): 187-206.

Rochefort, David A. and Roger W. Cobb, 'Problem Definition, Agenda Access, and Policy Change', *Policy Studies Journal* 21, 1 (1993): 56-71.

Simeon, Richard, 'Studying Public Policy', *Canadian Journal of Political Science* 9 (1976): 548-80.

Stone, Deborah A., *Policy Paradox and Political Reason*, Glenview: Scott, Foresman, 1988.

Wilensky, H.L., *The Welfare State and Equality: Structural and Ideological Roots of Public Expenditures*, Berkeley: University of California Press, 1975.

Chapter 6

Policy Formulation—
Policy Communities and
Policy Networks

CONCEPTUAL ISSUES

When a government has acknowledged the existence of a public problem and the need to do something about it, the policy-makers need to decide on some course of action. In so doing they must explore the various options available for addressing the problem, thus launching into the policy formulation process. According to Charles Jones, the distinguishing characteristic of policy formulation is simply that means are proposed to resolve somebody's perception of the needs that exist in society.[1] The proposals may originate in the agenda-setting process itself, as a problem and its solution are placed simultaneously on the government agenda, or they may be developed after the government has agreed to address a problem. In all cases, the range of available options needs to be considered and narrowed down to those that policy-makers can accept. This process of defining, considering, and accepting or rejecting options is the substance of the second stage of the policy cycle.

Lest it be misunderstood, it needs to be emphasized that choosing a solution to a public problem or fulfilling a societal need does not even remotely resemble the orderly process conceived by the rational theories. We saw in the preceding chapter on agenda-setting that defining and interpreting a problem is a highly nebulous process which does not always lead to clear outcomes. Even if the policy-makers agree on the existence of a problem, they may not share the same understanding of its causes or ramifications. It is therefore to be expected that the search for a solution to a problem will be contentious and subject to a wide variety of pressures, defeating efforts to consider policy options in a rational manner.

The essence of the search for solutions to a problem entails discovering which actions are considered to be possible and which are not.[2] At this stage, options that it is believed will not work or will for some reason be unacceptable to the powerful actors in the policy process are eliminated. Thus those involved in devising health policy to contain health care costs in the industrialized countries do not usually consider the British style of nationalized health service, which is rated highly for its cost-efficiency, because of the opposition it would provoke from the medical profession fearing reduced income. Nor do they consider denying health services to the aged, who account for a disproportionately large proportion of total health care costs, because of the moral and political outrage this will cause. How options are excluded from consideration by policy-makers at this stage of policy formulation tells us a lot about the policy options that are chosen at the decision-making stage of the policy process.

Jones highlights other broad characteristics of policy formulation:

1. Formulation need not be limited to one set of actors. Thus there may well be two or more formulation groups producing competing (or complementary) proposals.
2. Formulation may proceed without clear definition of the problem, or without formulators ever having much contact with the affected groups. . . .
3. There is no necessary coincidence between formulation and particular institutions, though it is a frequent activity of bureaucratic agencies.
4. Formulation and reformulation may occur over a long period of time without ever building sufficient support for any one proposal.
5. There are often several appeal points for those who lose in the formulation process at any one level.
6. The process itself never has neutral effects. Somebody wins and somebody loses even in the workings of science.[3]

The picture of policy formulation this characterization presents is that it is a highly diffuse, and complex, process which varies by case. The nuances of policy formulation in particular instances can be grasped only through empirical case studies.

Policy formulation involves elimination of policy options, until one or only a few are left from amongst which the policy-makers make their final selection. It involves recognizing limitations, which reveals what is not feasible and, by implication, what is feasible. This may seem obvious, but it is yet to be reflected in the voluminous writings proposing what policy-makers ought to be doing without reference to the limitations that constrain the choice of the proposed action. The Public Choice theorists' key assumption that politicians choose policies that best promote their electoral appeal, or the Welfare Economists' prescription that governments must do what is optimal, presumes more room for manoeuvre than is actually the case.[4] Politicians simply cannot do everything they consider appealing to voters or that economists consider optimal.

Before mentioning the limitations that policy-makers typically encounter that lead them to reject certain options, it is worth mentioning that the constraints need not be based on facts. That the significant actors in the policy subsystem believe that something is unworkable or unacceptable is sufficient for its exclusion from further consideration in the policy process. Perception is just as real as reality itself in the policy process.

The constraints the members of policy subsystems encounter may be substantive or procedural. Substantive constraints are innate to the nature of the problem itself. Policy-makers wishing to eliminate poverty thus do not have the option of printing money and distributing it to the poor because inflation will offset the gains, and so they must necessarily address the problem in more indirect ways. Similarly, the goal of promoting excellence in arts or sports cannot be accomplished by ordering people to be the best artist or sportswoman in the world; the pursuit of these goals requires far more delicate measures. The problem of global warming cannot be entirely eliminated because there is no known effective solution that can be employed without causing tremendous economic and social dislocations, which leaves policy-makers to tinker with options that barely scratch the surface of the problem. Substantive problems are thus 'objective' in the sense there is not much anyone can do about them.

Procedural constraints have to do with procedures involved in adopting an option or carrying them out. These constraints may be either institutional or tactical. The institutional constraints, discussed in Chapter Three, include constitutional provisions, the organization of the state and society, and established patterns of ideas and beliefs. They inhibit the choice of some policy options and promote others. Efforts to control hand-guns in the United States thus run up against constraints imposed by the constitutional right to bear arms. Federalism imposes similar constraints on American, Australian, and Canadian policy-makers in many areas of public policy where the two levels of government must agree before anything can be done. How the main social groups are organized internally and are linked with the state also affects what can or cannot be done. In a similar vein, the predominance of liberal ideas in English-speaking societies is said to make difficult a choice of policies that will be considered routine in corporatist societies such as Sweden, Austria, and Japan.

POLICY SUBSYSTEMS

The preceding discussion raises several important questions about the process of policy formulation. Among the most important is, who is actually involved in this process? Is policy formulation a public or private activity? If private, then why are some allowed access to this important part of the policy process and not others? If public, then what are the qualifications for participation? While we will need separate empirical analysis for each case to answer these questions, we can nevertheless set out broad parameters to assist analysis.

As we have seen in our discussion of agenda-setting, the notion of a *policy subsystem* is a powerful concept in policy analysis. Recent studies of policy formulation also emphasize the importance of policy subsystems at this stage of the policy cycle.[5] But unlike agenda-setting, where members of the public are more readily involved, in policy formulation the members of policy subsystems are restricted to those who have some minimal level of knowledge in the subject area, allowing them to comment, at least hypothetically, on the feasibility of options put forward to resolve policy problems.

Not surprisingly, identifying the key actors in policy subsystems, what brings them together, how they interact, and what effect their interaction has on the policy has attracted the attention of many students of public policy-making. Over the years scholars have developed a variety of models, many of which are mutually contradictory and unnecessarily elaborate, to address these questions.[6] In the following pages, we will examine the various models, highlight the points of agreement, and offer a model which is useful for conceptualizing the nature of policy subsystems and the role they play in the process of policy formulation.

Sub-Governments, Iron Triangles, and Issue Networks

The oldest conception of a policy subsystem was developed in the United States by early critics of Pluralism. They developed the notion of the 'sub-government', understood as groupings of societal and state actors into routinized patterns of interaction.[7] This concept was based on the observation that interest groups, congressional committees, and government agencies in the United States had developed a system of mutual support in the course of constant mutual interaction over legislative and regulatory matters. These three-sided relationships in areas such as agriculture, transportation, and education were often dubbed *iron triangles* to capture the essence of their iron-clad control over many aspects of the policy process.[8] Such groupings were condemned for having 'captured' the policy process, which subverted the principles of popular democracy by ensuring that their own self-interests prevailed over those of the general public.[9]

In the 1960s and 1970s, further research into the American case revealed that many of these sub-governments were not all-powerful, and that in fact their influence on policy-making varied across issues and over time.[10] Soon a more flexible and less rigid notion of a policy subsystem evolved, called by Hugh Heclo the *issue network*.[11]

Building on his earlier work on social policies in Britain and Sweden,[12] Heclo argued that while some areas of American political life were organized in an institutionalized system of interest representation, others were not. As he put it: 'Preoccupied with trying to find the few truly powerful actors, observers tend to overlook the power and influence that arise out of the configurations through which leading policy makers move and do business with each other. Looking for the closed triangles of control, we tend to miss the fairly open networks of people that increasingly impinge upon government.'[13] He was not denying the existence of 'iron triangles', but merely pointing out that their membership and functioning were often not as closed or rigid as was suggested by some commentators.

Heclo conceived policy subsystems as a spectrum, with iron triangles at one end and issue networks at the other. He explained the differences between iron triangles and issue networks in the following ways:

> The notion of iron triangles and subgovernments presumes small circles of participants who have succeeded in becoming largely autonomous. Issue networks, on the other hand, comprise a large number of participants with quite variable degrees of mutual commitment or dependence on others in their environment; in fact it is almost impossible to say where a network leaves off and its environment begins. Iron triangles and subgovernments suggest a stable set of participants coalesced to control fairly narrow public programs which are in the direct economic interest of each party to the alliance. Issue networks are almost the reverse image in each respect. Participants move in and out of the networks constantly. Rather than groups united in dominance over a program, no one, as far as one can tell, is in control of the policies and issues. Any direct material interest is often secondary to intellectual or emotional commitment.[14]

Issue networks were thus much less stable, had a constant turnover of participants, and were much less institutionalized than iron triangles.

Heclo's alternative interpretation of the nature of the policy subsystems involved in policy formulation fostered several studies in Europe and North America intended to refine the concept. These studies have indeed done so, but the variety of types of subsystems they have uncovered has necessitated the creation of alternate taxonomies to Heclo's simple spectrum of issue networks and iron triangles.

Advocacy Coalitions

In the US, Paul Sabatier and his colleagues have developed a complex scheme for studying the activities of policy actors in policy subsystems. In their work, an *advocacy coalition* refers to a subset of actors in the policy subsystem.[15] According to Jenkins-Smith and Sabatier, 'An advocacy coalition consists of actors from a variety of public and private institutions at all levels of government who share a set of basic beliefs (policy goals plus causal and other perceptions) and who seek to manipulate the rules, budgets and personnel of governmental institutions in order to achieve these goals over time.'[16]

Jenkins-Smith and Sabatier argue that an advocacy coalition includes both state and societal actors at the national, sub-national, and local levels of government. It also cleverly combines the role of knowledge and interest in the policy process. The actors come together for reasons of common beliefs, often based on their knowledge of the public problem they share and their common interests. The core of their belief system, consisting of views on the nature of human-kind and some desired state of affairs, is quite stable and holds the coalition together. All those in an advocacy coalition participate in the policy process in order to use the government machinery to pursue their (self-serving) goals.

While belief systems and interests determine the policies an advocacy coalition will seek to have adopted, its ability to succeed in this endeavour is affected by a host of factors. These include the coalition's resources such as 'money, expertise, number of supporters, and legal authority'.[17] External factors also affect what it can achieve by making some objectives easier to accomplish than others.[18] Some of these external factors—such as the nature of the problem, natural resource endowments, cultural values, and constitutional provisions—are relatively stable over long periods of time, and are therefore more predictable. Others are subject to a greater degree of change: these include factors such as public opinion, technology, levels of inflation or unemployment, change of the political party in government, and so on. In most cases there will be at least two advocacy coalitions in a subsystem, but there may be more, depending on how many ideational structures are in the policy area concerned.

Policy Networks

In his comparative study of foreign economic policy, Peter Katzenstein referred to policy networks as those links joining the state and societal actors together in the policy process.[19] Although he no more than mentioned the term, other writers combined earlier discussions of policy subsystems with elements of organizational and anthropological analyses to flesh out the concept,[20] which was later applied to the analysis of public policy.[21]

One such application was made in Britain by R.A.W. Rhodes who argued throughout the early 1980s that interactions among various departments and branches of the government and between the government and other organizations in society constituted policy networks which were instrumental in formulating and developing policy.[22] Rhodes argued that networks varied according to their level of 'integration', which was a function of their stability of membership, restrictiveness of membership, degree of insulation from other networks and the public, and the nature of the resources they controlled.[23] In the United States similar attributes were specified by Hamm, who argued that subgovernments could be differentiated according to their 'internal complexity, functional autonomy, and (levels of internal and external) cooperation or conflict'.[24]

In a major study of European industrial policy-making Wilks and Wright endorsed Rhodes' typology, arguing that networks varied along five key dimensions: '[T]he interests of the members of the network, the membership, the extent of members' interdependence, the extent to which the network is isolated from other networks, and the variations in the distribution of resources between the members.'[25] Refining the iron triangle-issue network spectrum developed by Heclo, they argued that this conception allowed a 'high-low' scale to be developed in which highly integrated networks would be characterized by stability of memberships and inter-membership relations, interdependence within the network, and network insulation from other networks. At the other extreme, weakly integrated networks would be large, loosely structured, with multiple and often inchoate links with other groups and actors.[26]

In the United States efforts to clarify and reformulate the concept of policy networks continued. Salisbury, Heinz, Laumann, and Nelson, for example, argued that networks tended to have 'hollow cores' in that even the most institutionalized networks appeared to have no clear leadership.[27] Others argued that networks could be classified according to whether or not state and societal members shared the same goals and agreed on the same means to achieve those goals. Still others argued that the number of discernible interests participating in the network was the crucial variable defining different types of networks.[28]

It is important to note that all of these different conceptions construed policy networks as being essentially interest-based. That is, participants were assumed to participate in these networks in order to further their own ends, which were seen as essentially material and 'objectively recognizable' from outside the network. It is this emphasis on common material interests that sets studies of policy networks apart from those of policy communities.

Policy Communities

The distinction between policy communities and policy networks in studies of policy subsystems was first drawn in the early 1980s, although the two terms continued to be used interchangeably for several more years.[29] Although they endorsed most aspects of Rhodes' scheme, Wilks and Wright reversed earlier conceptualizations of the relationship between policy networks and policy communities within a policy subsystem and, in so doing, captured an important element of the nature of public policy formation. As the two authors argued, 'Community is not the same as network, although they are frequently used synonymously in the literature. . . . The use of community in this very broad sense is of very little help in the analysis of the policy process.'[30] Instead, they sought to make 'community' refer to a more inclusive category of all those involved in policy formulation, and to restrict 'network' to a subset of community members who interacted with each other on a regular basis. In their view, 'Policy community identifies those actors and potential actors drawn from the policy universe who share a common policy focus. Network is the linking process within a policy community or between two or more communities.'[31] They acknowledged their departure from past usage but argued that their own conception passed the test of empirical utility.

This conceptual distinction was to prove useful in subsequent studies. Its main advantage lay in the manner in which it integrated two different sets of motivations guiding the actions of those involved in policy formulation:

knowledge or expertise, and material interest. By associating a policy community with a specific knowledge base and a policy network with the pursuit of some material interest, two different aspects of the process of policy formulation came into sharper focus.[32]

TAXONOMY OF POLICY SUBSYSTEMS

By the end of the 1980s, efforts turned to developing a more consistent method of classifying and analysing policy subsystems.[33] Atkinson and Coleman developed a scheme based on the organization of state and society, and the links between the two. In their view, the two critical questions are whether societal interests are centrally organized and whether the state has the capacity to develop policies independent of them—in other words, the level of state autonomy from societal actors. Although initially clear, this taxonomy was muddied by the addition of a concern for the level of concentration of property owners in affected sectors, generating an eight-fold system of policy subsystems. These ranged from a type of pluralism said to describe situations when all three variables were low, to the 'concertation' network which was said to exist when the interests were centrally organized, capital was concentrated, and the state enjoyed high capacity and autonomy.[34]

Other efforts resulted in even more complex, and confusing, taxonomies. Thus, for example, Frans van Waarden attempted to combine Rhodes' analysis with that of Atkinson and Coleman, arguing that networks varied according to seven criteria: number and type of actors; function of networks; structure; institutionalization; rules of conduct; power relations; and actor strategies.[35] Ultimately, the typology he developed included twelve types of subsystems depending on the number and type of actors and the nature of the functions they performed. Like Atkinson and Coleman's initial effort, it proved difficult to apply in practice.

Utilizing the analytical separation of community and network helps clarify the conceptualization of policy subsystems and the various factors behind their development.[36] It establishes that policy community members are linked together by epistemic concerns—a shared knowledge base—while network members share not only this base, but also some type of material interest allowing or encouraging regularized contact. Although the policy subsystem itself contains elements of both knowledge and interest, these can be distinguished from each other and their impacts on subsystem development analysed separately.[37]

Policy communities can be expected to vary according to whether or not there is a dominant *episteme* or world view in the subsystem and whether these ideas are shared by most of its state and societal members. The types of policy communities which can be identified on the basis of these relationships are set out in Figure 7.

■ Figure 7.
A Taxonomy of Policy Communities

		Dominant Episteme	
		Yes	No
State-Society Consensus	Yes	*Hegemonic Community*	*Leaderless Community*
	No	*Imposed Community*	*Anarchic Community*

SOURCE: Adapted from Karen M. Hult and Charles Walcott, *Governing Public Organizations: Politics, Structures and Institutional Design*, Pacific Grove: Brooks/Cole, 1990.

As Sabatier and others have suggested, in this model a *hegemonic community* or policy monopoly would exist when state and societal actors are in general agreement about the parameters of a problem or issue and there is a clearly identifiable dominant epistemic community. Where there is a dominant episteme but the state and societal members are divided over the appropriateness of an idea, one would expect to find an *imposed community*. When there is a consensus but no dominant episteme, a *leaderless community* of equals will exist. When the state and societal actors are divided and no dominant episteme exists, an *anarchic community* can be expected to develop.

Within each of these different types of communities, however, one would expect some form of regularized interaction among a subset of community members to develop. As van Waarden and others have suggested, these policy networks will vary according to the number and type of participants and their relations with each other, as set out in Figure 8.

■ Figure 8.
A Taxonomy of Policy Networks

		Number/Type of Network Participants			
		State Agencies	One Major Societal Group	Two Major Societal Groups	Three or More Groups
State/Societal Relations With in Network	State Directed	*Bureaucratic Network*	*Clientelistic Network*	*Triadic Network*	*Pluralistic Network*
	Society Dominated	*Participatory Statist Network*	*Captured Network*	*Corporatist Network*	*Issue Network*

SOURCE: Modelled after Frans van Waarden, 'Dimensions and Types of Policy Networks', *European Journal of Political Research* 21, 1/2 (1992): 29-52.

On the basis of the dual criteria of the number and location of policy-relevant interests and knowledge, we find eight basic types of policy networks. A *bureaucratic network* represents the case where the principal interactions among subsystem members takes place exclusively within the state. At the other extreme, an *issue network* is one in which, as Heclo suggested, the principal interactions take place among a large number of societal actors. Between the two extremes there are six other possibilities. *Participatory statist networks* represent those in which state actors play a major role but are dominated by unorganized societal members. *Pluralist networks* are those where a large number of actors are involved in the subsystem but state actors are dominant. When there is only one major societal actor facing the state, two common types of networks exist. In *clientelistic networks* the state dominates the societal actor, while in *captured networks* the reverse is true. When two societal actors face the state, if the state dominates the subsystem it can be termed a *triadic network*. When the societal actors dominate the state, the subsystem is more akin to a traditional *corporatist network*.

What type of subsystem exists in a given sector or issue area is of major significance in understanding the dynamics of policy formulation within that area. Which policy options on the institutional agenda will be considered seriously for adoption is largely a function of the nature and motivation of key actors arrayed in policy subsystems.

CONCLUSION

The concepts of a knowledge-based policy community and an interest-based policy network have had a significant impact on recent studies in public policy. They have, to a certain extent, unified the different approaches to policy determinants—material interests and ideology—as well as many otherwise seemingly disparate writings in public policy, comparative politics, and international relations.[38]

Although the development of these concepts is relatively recent, they have been put to good use in dealing with a number of policy sectors.[39] Studies based on the notion of policy communities and policy networks have revealed a great deal about policy formulation in such areas as fisheries policy,[40] women's issues,[41] environmental policy,[42] pharmaceuticals,[43] information policy,[44] and others.[45]

These studies have also pointed to the need to understand the process of changes in subsystems if the general process of policy change and development is to be understood.[46] Many of the studies cited above, for example, have illustrated how in many economic policy sectors, tight control by governments and industry has given way to a new triadic system in which government sits at the apex of two competing groups, be they labour and capital in the area of industrial relations, or business and environmental groups in the area of environmental policy.[47] The impact of change in policy subsystem on the process of policy change will be addressed in Chapter Ten; in Chapter Seven we will examine the role of subsystems on public policy decision-making.

NOTES

1   Charles O. Jones, *An Introduction to the Study of Public Policy* (Monterey, CA: Brooks/Cole, 1984): 77.

2   Giandomenico Majone, *Evidence, Argument, and Persuasion in the Policy Process* (New Haven: Yale University Press, 1989).

3   Jones, *An Introduction to the Study of Public Policy*: 78.

4   Majone, *Evidence, Argument, and Persuasion in the Policy Process*: 76.

5   Although most use of the concept of a policy subsystem is of quite recent origin, the term itself dates to the mid-1950s. See for example J. Leiper Freeman, *The Political Process: Executive Bureau-Legislative Committee Relations* (New York: Random House, 1955).

6   Grant Jordan has spent much effort cataloguing and categorizing the images and metaphors used to describe policy subsystems involved in policy formulation. See Grant Jordan, 'Iron Triangles, Woolly Corporatism and Elastic Nets: Images of the Policy Process', *Journal of Public Policy* 1, 1 (1981): 95-123; Grant Jordan, 'Policy Community Realism versus "New" Institutionalist Ambiguity', *Political Studies* 38, 3 (1990): 470-84; Grant Jordan, 'Sub-governments, Policy Communities and Networks: Refilling the Old Bottles?', *Journal of Theoretical Politics* 2, 4 (1990): 319-38; Grant Jordan and Klaus Schubert, 'A Preliminary Ordering of Policy Network Labels', *European Journal of Political Research* 21, 1/2 (1992): 7-27.

7   Lance deHaven-Smith and Carl E. Van Horn, 'Subgovernment Conflict in Public Policy', *Policy Studies Journal* 12, 4 (1984): 627-42.

8   Douglas Cater, *Power in Washington: A Critical Look at Today's Struggle in the Nation's Capital* (New York: Random House, 1964).

9   Marver H. Bernstein, *Regulating Business by Independent Commission* (Princeton: Princeton University Press, 1955); Samuel P. Huntington, 'The Marasmus of the ICC: The Commissions, the Railroads and the Public Interest', *Yale Law Review* 61, 4 (1952): 467-509; Theodore Lowi, *The End of Liberalism: Ideology, Policy and the Crisis of Public Authority* (New York: Norton, 1969).

10 Michael T. Hayes, 'The Semi-Sovereign Pressure Groups: A Critique of Current Theory and an Alternative Typology', *Journal of Politics* 40, 1 (1978): 134-61; Randall B. Ripley and Grace A. Franklin, *Congress, the Bureaucracy, and Public Policy* (Homewood, IL: Dorsey Press, 1980).

11 Hugh Heclo, 'Issue Networks and the Executive Establishment, in Anthony King (ed.), *The New American Political System* (Washington, DC: American Enterprise Institute for Public Policy Research, 1978): 87-124.

12 Hugh Heclo, *Modern Social Politics in Britain and Sweden: From Relief to Income Maintenance* (New Haven: Yale University Press, 1974): 308-10.

13 Heclo, 'Issue Networks and the Executive Establishment': 88.

14 Heclo, 'Issue Networks and the Executive Establishment': 102.

15 Paul A. Sabatier and Hank C. Jenkins-Smith, 'The Advocacy Coalition Framework: Assessment, Revisions, and Implications for Scholars and Practitioners' in Paul A. Sabatier and Hank C. Jenkins-Smith (eds), *Policy Change and Learning: An Advocacy Coalition Approach* (Boulder: Westview, 1993).

16 Hank C. Jenkins-Smith and Paul A. Sabatier, 'The Study of Public Policy Processes' in Paul A. Sabatier and Hank C. Jenkins-Smith (eds), *Policy Change and Learning: An Advocacy Coalition Approach* (Boulder: Westview, 1993): 5.

17   Paul Sabatier, 'Knowledge, Policy-Oriented Learning, and Policy Change', *Knowledge: Creation, Diffusion, Utilization* 8, 4 (1987): 664.
18   Jenkins-Smith and Sabatier, 'The Study of Public Policy Processes': 5.
19   Peter J. Katzenstein, 'Conclusion: Domestic Structures and Strategies of Foreign Economic Policy', *International Organization* 31, 4 (1977): 879-920.
20   H. Brinton Milward and Gary L. Walmsley, 'Policy Subsystems, Networks and the Tools of Public Management' in Robert Eyestone (ed.), *Public Policy Formation* (Greenwich: JAI Press, 1984): 3-25. Aldrich and Whetton, for example, talked about 'action sets' and 'networks', the former referring to a group of organizations formed for a specific purpose and the latter to the more general forms of inter-organizational co-ordination in which organizations were bound together by common relationship. Howard E. Aldrich and David A. Whetten, 'Organization-sets, Action-sets, and Networks: Making the Most of Simplicity' in Paul Nystrom and William H. Starbuck (eds), *Handbook of Organizational Design* (Oxford: Oxford University Press, 1980): 385-408.
21   J. Kenneth Benson, 'A Framework for Policy Analysis' in David L. Rogers and David A. Whetton (eds), *Interorganizational Co-ordination: Theory, Research and Implementation* (Ames: Iowa State University Press, 1982): 137-76.
22   R.A.W. Rhodes, 'Power-Dependence, Policy Communities and Intergovernmental Networks', *Public Administration Bulletin* 49 (1984): 4-31.
23   Rhodes, 'Power-Dependence, Policy Communities and Intergovernmental Networks': 14-15
24   Keith E. Hamm, 'Patterns of Influence Among Committees, Agencies, and Interest Groups,' *Legislative Studies Quarterly* 8, 3 (1983): 415.
25   Stephen Wilks and Maurice Wright, 'Conclusion: Comparing Government-Industry Relations: States, Sectors, and Networks' in Stephen Wilks and Maurice Wright (eds), *Comparative Government-Industry Relations: Western Europe, the United States, and Japan* (Oxford: Clarendon Press, 1987): 301.
26   Wilks and Wright, 'Conclusion: Comparing Government-Industry Relations: States, Sectors, and Networks': 301-2.
27   John P. Heinz, Edward O. Laumann, Robert H. Salisbury, and Robert L. Nelson, 'Inner Circles or Hollow Cores', *Journal of Politics* 52 (1990): 356-90; Robert H. Salisbury, John P. Heinz, Edward O. Laumann, and Robert L. Nelson, 'Who Works with Whom? Interest Group Alliances and Opposition', *American Political Science Review* 81, 4 (1987): 1217-34.
28   Andrew S. McFarland, 'Interest Groups and Theories of Power in America', *British Journal of Political Science* 17, 2 (1987): 129-47.
29   See, for example, Jeremy J. Richardson and A.G. Jordan, *Governing Under Pressure: The Policy Process in a Post-Parliamentary Democracy* (Oxford: Martin Robertson, 1979); R.A.W. Rhodes, 'Power-Dependence, Policy Communities and Intergovernmental Networks', *Public Administration Bulletin* 49 (1984): 4-31; H. Brinton Milward and Ronald A. Francisco, 'Subsystem Politics and Corporatism in the United States', *Policy and Politics* 11, 3 (1983); L.J. Sharpe, 'Central Coordination and the Policy Network', *Political Studies* 33, 3 (1985): 361-81.
30   Wilks and Wright, 'Conclusion: Comparing Government-Industry Relations: States, Sectors, and Networks': 296.
31   Wilks and Wright, 'Conclusion: Comparing Government-Industry Relations: States, Sectors, and Networks': 298.

32   At this point, it is worth noting that a similar conception of a policy community has emerged in the International Relations literature in which loose groupings of knowledge actors are said to underlie international institutions and regimes. But instead of calling it a policy community, the term that is used in this literature is *epistemic community*, which is defined as, in the words of Peter Haas, 'a network of professionals with recognized expertise and competence in a particular domain and an authoritative claims to policy-relevant knowledge within that domain or issue-area'. He elaborates: 'Although an epistemic community may consist of professionals from a variety of disciplines and backgrounds, they have (1) a shared set of normative and principled beliefs, which provide a value-based rationale for the social action of community members; (2) shared causal beliefs, which are derived from their analysis of practices leading or contributing to a central set of problems in their domain and which then serve as the basis for elucidating the multiple linkages between possible policy actions and desired outcomes; (3) shared notions of validity—that is, intersubjective, internally defined criteria for weighing and validating knowledge in the domain of their expertise; and (4) a common policy enterprise—that is, a set of common practices associated with a set of problems to which their professional competence is directed, presumably out of the conviction that human welfare will be enhanced as a consequence.' This is a clear elucidation of the knowledge base that binds communities of actors together and how it affects their behaviour. To avoid confusion, however, we will use the term policy community in this book. Peter M. Haas, 'Introduction: Epistemic Communities and International Policy Coordination', *International Organization* 46, 1 (1992): 3. See also Ernst B. Haas, 'Is there a Hole in the Whole? Knowledge, Technology, Interdependence, and the Construction of International Regimes', *International Organization* 29, 3 (1975): 827-76; Robert O. Keohane, 'Multilateralism: An Agenda for Research', *International Journal* 45, 4 (1990): 731-64.

33   Daniel McCool, 'Subgovernments and the Impact of Policy Fragmentation and Accommodation', *Policy Studies Review* 8, 2 (1989): 264-87.

34   Michael Atkinson and William Coleman, 'Strong States and Weak States: Sectoral Policy Networks in Advanced Capitalist Economies', *British Journal of Political Science* 19, 1 (1989): 54.

35   Frans van Waarden, 'Dimensions and Types of Policy Networks', *European Journal of Political Research* 21, 1/2 (1992): 29-52.

36   On policy development and change see Michael M. Atkinson and William D. Coleman, 'Policy Networks, Policy Communities and the Problems of Governance', *Governance* 5, 2 (1992): 154-80.

37   Failing to distinguish between the two leads to many difficulties. See, for example, the difficulties encountered by Sabatier and others operationalizing the notion of an 'advocacy coalition' which combines power and knowledge related actors in one unit. Paul A. Sabatier and Hank C. Jenkins-Smith (eds), *Policy Change and Learning: An Advocacy Coalition Approach* (Boulder: Westview, 1993).

38   Michael M. Atkinson and William D. Coleman, 'Policy Networks, Policy Communities and the Problems of Governance', *Governance* 5 (1992): 154-80; Colin J. Bennett, 'The International Regulation of Personal Data: From Epistemic Community to Policy Sector', Paper presented at Annual Meeting of the Canadian Political Science Association, Charlottetown, Prince Edward Island, 1992.

39   Michael Atkinson and William Coleman, 'Strong States and Weak States: Sectoral

Policy Networks in Advanced Capitalist Economies', *British Journal of Political Science* 19 (1989): 47-67; A. Paul Pross, *Group Politics and Public Policy* (Toronto: Oxford University Press, 1992).

40   A.P. Pross and Susan McCorquodale, 'The State, Interests, and Policy-Making in the East Coast Fishery' in W. Coleman and G. Skogstad (eds), *Policy Communities and Public Policy in Canada: A Structural Approach* (Mississauga, ON: Copp Clark Pitman, 1990).

41   Susan Phillips, 'Meaning and Structure in Social Movements: Mapping the Network of National Canadian Women's Organizations', *Canadian Journal of Political Science* 24, 4 (1991): 755-82.

42   Jim Bruton and Michael Howlett, 'Differences of Opinion: Round Tables, Policy Networks and the Failure of Canadian Environmental Strategy', *Alternatives* 19, 1 (1992): 25.

43   Michael Atkinson and William Coleman, *The State, Business, and Industrial Change in Canada* (Toronto: University of Toronto Press, 1989).

44   Colin J. Bennett, *Regulating Privacy: Data Protection and Public Policy in Europe and the United States* (Ithaca: Cornell University Press, 1992).

45   William D. Coleman and Grace Skogstad (eds), *Policy Communities and Public Policy in Canada: A Structural Approach* (Mississauga, ON: Copp Clark Pitman, 1990).

46   See Hank C. Jenkins-Smith, Gilbert K. St Clair, and Brian Woods, 'Explaining Change in Policy Subsystems: Analysis of Coalition Stability and Defection over Time', *American Journal of Political Science* 35, 4 (1991): 851-80; Frank R. Baumgartner and Bryan D. Jones, 'Agenda Dynamics and Policy Subsystems', *Journal of Politics* 53, 4 (1991): 1044-74.

47   In many cases the interest groups which formed and expanded into the cozy liaison of the state and business were funded by the state itself. See Sandra Burt, 'Canadian Women's Groups in the 1980s: Organizational Development and Policy Influence', *Canadian Public Policy* 16, 1 (1990): 17-28.

FURTHER READING

Atkinson, Michael and William Coleman, 'Policy Networks, Policy Communities and the Problems of Governance', *Governance* 5, 2 (1992): 154-80.

Coleman, William D. and Grace Skogstad, 'Policy Communities and Policy Networks: A Structural Approach', pp. 14-33 in William D. Coleman and Grace Skogstad (eds), *Policy Communities and Public Policy in Canada*, Mississauga: Copp Clark Pitman, 1990.

Jones, Charles O., *An Introduction to the Study of Public Policy*, Monterey, CA: Brooks/Cole, 1984.

Jordan, A. Grant, 'Iron Triangles, Woolly Corporatism and Elastic Nets: Images of the Policy Process', *Journal of Public Policy* 1, 1 (1981): 95-123.

Jordan, Grant, 'Sub-governments, Policy Communities and Networks: Refilling the Old Bottles?', *Journal of Theoretical Politics* 2, 3 (1990): 319-38.

Jordan, Grant and Klaus Schubert, 'A Preliminary Ordering of Policy Network Labels', *European Journal of Political Research* 21, 1/2 (1992): 7-27.

Lindquist, Evert A., 'Public Managers and Policy Communities: Learning to Meet New Challenges', *Canadian Public Administration* 35, 2 (1992): 127-59.

Majone, Giandomenico, *Evidence, Argument, and Persuasion in the Policy Process*, New Haven: Yale University Press, 1989, Chapter 4.

Marin, Bernd and Renate Mayntz (eds), *Policy Networks: Empirical Evidence and Theoretical Considerations*. Boulder: Westview Press, 1991.

Milward, H. Brinton and Gary L. Walmsley, 'Policy Subsystems, Networks and the Tools of Public Management', pp. 3-25 in Robert Eyestone (ed.), *Public Policy Formation*, Greenwich: JAI Press, 1984.

Waarden, Frans van, 'Dimensions and Types of Policy Networks', *European Journal of Political Research* 21 (1992): 29-52.

Wright, Maurice. 'Policy Community, Policy Network and Comparative Industrial Policies', *Political Studies* 36, 4 (1988): 593-612.

Chapter 7

Public Policy Decision-Making—Beyond Rationalism, Incrementalism, and Irrationalism

The decision-making stage of the policy cycle received the most attention in the early development of the policy sciences, when analysts borrowed heavily from the models of decision-making in complex organizations developed by students of public administration and business organization.[1] By the mid-1960s, discussions about public policy decision-making had ossified in the debate surrounding the 'incremental' and 'rational' models.[2] The mainstream position was that while the 'rational' model was more preferable as a model of how decisions ought to be taken, the 'incremental' model best described the actual practice of decision-making in governments.[3] This led to efforts in the 1970s to develop alternative models of decision-making in complex organizations. Some attempted to synthesize the rational and incremental models. Others—including the so-called 'garbage can' model of decision-making—focused on the irrational elements of organizational behaviour in order to arrive at a third path beyond rationalism and incrementalism.[4]

Only recently have efforts been made to go beyond the three general models and develop a nuanced understanding of the complex processes associated with public policy decision-making.[5] The objective of this chapter is to discuss the contending models of public policy decision-making and examine recent developments in the field. It concludes by proposing an alternative model of decision-making in governments which takes into account the questions about constraints on power and the significance of policy subsystems raised in our discussions of earlier stages of the policy cycle.

CONCEPTUAL ISSUES

Gary Brewer and Peter DeLeon describe the decision-making stage of the public policy process as:

the choice among policy alternatives that have been generated and their likely effects on the problem estimated. . . . It is the most overtly political stage in so far as the many potential solutions to a given problem must somehow be win- nowed down and but one or a select few picked and readied for use. Obviously most possible choices will not be realized and deciding not to take particular courses of action is as much a part of selection as finally settling on the best course.[6]

This definition makes several key points about the decision-making stage of public policy-making. First, decision-making is not a self-contained stage, nor a synonym for the entire public policy-making process, but a specific stage rooted firmly in the previous stages of the policy cycle. It involves choosing from among a relatively small number of alternative policy options, as identified in the process of policy formulation, to resolve a public problem. Secondly, this definition underlines the point that public policy decision-making is not a tech- nical exercise, but an inherently political process. It recognizes that public policy decisions create 'winners' and 'losers', even if the decision is to do nothing or to retain the *status quo*.

Brewer and DeLeon's definition says nothing about the desirability, likely direction, or scope of public decision-making. To deal with these issues, differ- ent theories have been developed to describe how decisions are made in gov- ernment as well as to prescribe how decisions ought to be made. Although they have significant differences these models also exhibit several similarities. It is to discussion of these that we now turn.

First, each of the models acknowledges that the number of relevant policy actors decreases with the progress of the public policy process. Thus agenda- setting involves a wide variety of state and societal actors. At the stage of pol- icy formulation, the number of actors remains large, but includes only those state and societal actors forming the policy subsystem. The public policy deci- sion-making stage involves even fewer actors, as it normally excludes virtually all non-state actors, including those from other levels of government. Only those politicians, judges, and government officials empowered to make author- itative decisions in the area in question participate in this stage of the policy cycle.[7]

Second, the models also recognize that in modern governments the degree of freedom enjoyed by each decision-maker is circumscribed by a host of rules governing political and administrative offices and constraining the actions of each office-holder. These rules range from the country's constitution to the specific mandate conferred on individual decision-makers by various laws and regulations.[8] The rules usually set out not only which decisions can be made by which government agency or official, but also the procedure that must be followed. As Allison and Halperin have noted, such rules and operating proce- dures provide decision-makers with 'action channels'—a regularized set of pro- cedures for producing certain types of decisions.[9] These rules and standard operating procedures explain why so much of the decision-making in government is of a routine and repetitive nature.[10] While they circumscribe the freedom available to decision-makers, considerable discretion remains with individual decision-makers to arrive at their own judgement of the 'best' course of action to follow in specific circumstances. Exactly what process is followed and which decision is considered 'best' varies among decision-makers and the contexts in which they operate.

At the macro-level, different countries have different constitutional arrangements and different sets of rules governing the structure of governmental agencies and the conduct of officials. Some political systems concentrate decision-making authority in the elected executive and the bureaucracy, while others permit the legislature and judiciary to play a greater role. Parliamentary systems tend to fall in the former category and presidential systems in the latter. Thus in Australia, Britain, and Canada and other parliamentary democracies, the cabinet and bureaucracy are solely responsible for making policy decisions. They may at times have decisions imposed upon them by the legislature in situations when the government does not enjoy a majority in the parliament or by the judiciary, in its role as the interpreter of the constitution, but these are not routine occurrences. In the United States and other Republican systems, although the authority to make decisions rests with the President (and the cabinet and bureaucracy acting on the president's behalf), those requiring legislative approval often involve negotiation with members of the Congress, while some are modified or overturned on a regular basis by the judiciary on constitutional or other grounds. At the micro-level, decision-makers themselves vary greatly in terms of background, knowledge, and predilections that affect how they interpret a problem and the solutions to it.[11] Different decision-makers operating in similar institutional set-ups respond differently when dealing with the same or similar problems.

Beyond these areas of similarity the numerous models developed to describe the decision-making process differ substantially. Three of the most commonly used in this respect are the Rational, Incremental, and Garbage Can models. We will discuss these in turn.

MODELS OF DECISION-MAKING

The two best known models of public policy decision-making are usually referred to as the *rational* model and the *incremental* model. The former is essentially a model of business decision-making applied to the public arena, while the latter is a political model applied to public policy. Other models seek to combine rationality and incrementalism in varying measures. In contrast to all these models admitting varying degrees of rationality, the *garbage can* model portrays decision-making as an essentially non-rational (but not completely irrational) process based on convenience and ritualized decision-making behaviour.

The Rational Model

An idealized model of rational policy-making process consists of a 'rational individual' undertaking the following sequential activities:

1. A goal for solving a problem is established.
2. All alternative strategies of achieving the goal are explored and listed.
3. All significant consequences of each alternative strategy are predicted and the probability of those consequences occurring is estimated.
4. Finally, the strategy that most nearly solves the problem or solves it at least cost is selected.[12]

The rational model is 'rational' in the sense that it prescribes procedures for decision-making that will lead to the choice of the most efficient means of achieving policy goals. Rationalist theories are rooted in enlightenment rationalism and positivism, schools of thought which seek to develop detached, scientific knowledge to improve human conditions.[13] They are based on the belief that society's problems ought to be solved in a 'scientific' or 'rational' manner, by gathering all relevant information on the problems and the alternative solutions to them, and then selecting the best alternative.[14] The task of the policy analyst is viewed as developing the relevant knowledge and then offering it to the government for application.[15] Policy-makers are assumed to operate as technicians or business managers, who identify a problem and then adopt the most effective or efficient way of solving it. It is for its problem-solving orientation that this approach is also known as 'scientific', 'engineering', or 'managerialist'.

In decision-making studies, the rational model is rooted in early attempts to establish a science of organizational behaviour and public administration. Elements of the model can be found in the work of early students of public administration such as Henri Fayol in France and Luther Gulick and Lyndal Urwick in Britain and the United States. Drawing on the insights gleaned by Fayol from his studies of the turn-of-the-century French coal industry,[16] Gulick and Urwick codified a model by which they argued the best decisions could be taken. The PODSCORB model they developed suggests that organizations can maximize their performance by systematically Planning, Organizing, Deciding, Selecting, Co-ordinating, Recruiting, and Budgeting.[17] 'Deciding' on a particular course of action, for Gulick and Urwick, amounted to weighing the benefits of any decision against its expected costs.

Later, many analysts subscribing to this perspective began to argue that this form of decision-making would generate maximal results only if all possible alternatives and the costs of each alternative were assessed before a decision was made—the 'rational-comprehensive' model of decision-making.[18] The new emphasis on comprehensiveness proved problematic, as critics were quick to point out. There are limits to the ability of human decision-makers to be comprehensive in establishing alternatives and calculating benefits and costs. There are also political and institutional constraints that condition the selection of options and decision choices. The rational-comprehensive model was criticized as misguided at best and mischievous at worst.

Perhaps the most noted critic of the rational model is the American behavioural scientist Herbert Simon, the only student of public administration ever to win a Nobel prize. Beginning in the early 1950s, he argued in a series of books and articles that several hurdles prevented decision-makers from attaining 'pure' comprehensive rationality in their decisions.[19] First, there are cognitive limits to the decision-makers' ability to consider all possible options, forcing them to selectively consider alternatives. If this is so, then it is likely they choose from among options selected on ideological or political grounds, if not randomly, without reference to their implications for efficiency. Second, the model assumes that it is possible for decision-makers to know the consequences of each decision in advance, which is rarely the case in reality. Third, each policy option entails a bundle of favourable and adverse consequences which makes comparisons among them difficult indeed. Since the same option can be efficient or inefficient depending on circumstances, it is not possible for decision-makers to arrive at unambiguous conclusions about which alternative is superior.

Simon's assessment of the rational model concluded that public decisions in practice did not maximize benefits over costs, but merely tended to satisfy whatever criteria decision-makers set for themselves in the instance in question. This 'satisfycing' criterion, as he put it, was a realistic one given the bounded rationality with which human beings are endowed.

The Incremental Model

Doubts about the practicality or even usefulness of the rational model led to efforts to develop a theory of decision-making more closely approximating the actual behaviour of decision-makers in practical situations. This fostered the emergence of the *incremental* model which portrayed public policy decision-making as a political process characterized by bargaining and compromise among self-interested decision-makers. The decisions that are eventually made represent what is politically feasible rather than desirable.

The credit for developing the incremental model of public decision-making is attributed to Yale University political scientist Charles Lindblom.[20] He summarized the model as consisting of the following 'mutually supporting set of simplifying and focusing stratagems':

> a. Limitation of analysis to a few somewhat familiar policy alternatives . . . differing only marginally from the status quo;
> b. An intertwining of analysis of policy goals and other values with the empirical aspects of the problem (that is, no requirement that values be specified first with means subsequently found to promote them);
> c. A greater analytical preoccupation with ills to be remedied than positive goals to be sought;

d. A sequence of trials, errors, and revised trials;

e. Analysis that explores only some, not all, of the important possible consequences of a considered alternative;

f. Fragmentation of analytical work to many (partisan) participants in policy making (each attending to their piece of the overall problem domain).[21]

In Lindblom's view, decision-makers develop policies through a process of making 'successive limited comparisons' with earlier decisions, those they are familiar with. As he put it in his oft-cited article on 'The Science of "Muddling Through",' decision-makers work through a process of 'continually building out from the current situation, step-by-step and by small degrees'.[22] Decisions thus arrived at are usually only marginally different from those that exist; in other words, the changes from the *status quo* are incremental.

There are two reasons why decisions do not usually vary substantially from the *status quo*.[23] First, since bargaining requires distribution of limited resources among various participants, it is easier to continue the existing pattern of distribution rather than try to impute values to radically new proposals. The benefits and costs of the present arrangements are known to the policy actors, unlike the uncertainties surrounding new arrangements, which make agreement on changes difficult to reach. The result is either continuation of the *status quo*, or small changes from it. Second, the standard operating procedures that are the hallmark of bureaucracy tend to promote the continuation of existing practices. The methods by which bureaucrats identify options and the methods and criteria for choice are often laid out in advance, inhibiting innovation and perpetuating the existing arrangements.

Lindblom also argued that the rational model's requirement of separation between ends and means was unworkable in practice not only for the time and information constraints identified by Simon, but also because it assumed policy-makers could clearly separate means and ends in assessing policies, and could then agree upon both. Lindblom argued that in most policy areas, ends are inseparable from means, and which goals are pursued often depends on whether or not there are viable means available to accomplish them. Since agreement on a policy choice is difficult to achieve, decision-makers avoid re-opening old issues or considering choices that are so different from existing practices as to make agreement difficult. The result is, again, policy decisions that differ only incrementally from the old policies.

The incremental model views decision-making as a practical exercise concerned with solving problems at hand rather than achieving lofty goals. In this model the means chosen for solving problems are discovered through trial-and-error rather than through the comprehensive evaluation of all possible means. Decision-makers consider only a few familiar alternatives for appropriateness and stop the search when they believe an acceptable alternative has been found.

In earlier writings, Lindblom and his co-authors held out the possibility that incremental decision-making could co-exist with efforts to achieve more 'rational' decisions. Thus Braybrooke and Lindblom, for example, argued that four different types of decision-making could be discerned depending upon the amount of knowledge at the disposal of decision-makers, and the amount of change the decision involved from earlier decisions.[24] This generated the two-by-two matrix shown in Figure 9.

■ Figure 9.
Four Types of Decision-Making

		Level of Available Knowledge	
		High	Low
Amount of Change	High	*Revolutionary*	*Analytic*
Involved	Low	*Rational*	*Disjointed Incremental*

SOURCE: Adapted from David Braybrooke and Charles Lindblom, *A Strategy of Decision: Policy Evaluation as a Social Process*, New York: Free Press of Glencoe, 1963.

In this view, the overwhelming majority of decisions were likely to be taken in an incremental fashion, involving minimal change in situations of low available knowledge. However three other possibilities existed, the rational model emerging as one possibility and two other poorly defined styles—'revolutionary' and 'analytic'—also existing as infrequently utilized alternatives.

Later in his career, however, Lindblom was to argue that a spectrum of decision-making styles existed. These ranged from 'synoptic' or rational-comprehensive decision-making to 'blundering', that is, simply following hunches or guesses without any real effort at systematic analysis of alternative strategies. The spectrum is illustrated in Figure 10.

■ Figure 10.
A Spectrum of Decision-Making Styles

Synoptic —— Strategic —— Disjointed —— Simple —— Blundering
                           Incremental   Incremental

SOURCE: Adapted from Charles E. Lindblom and D.K. Cohen, *Usable Knowledge: Social Science and Social Problem Solving*, New Haven: Yale University Press, 1979.

Although admitting the theoretical possibility of different styles of decision-making, Lindblom in his later works rejected all other alternatives to the incremental on practical grounds. He argued that any kind of synoptic analysis which attempted to arrive at decisions on the basis of maximizing criteria of any kind would end in failure, and that all decision-making was based on what he termed 'grossly incomplete' analysis. The essence of incrementalism, he argued, was to try to systematize decisions reached in this fashion by stressing the need for political agreement and learning by trial-and-error, rather than simply bumbling into random decisions.[25]

While the incremental model may be an accurate description—and that too is debatable—of how public policy decisions are often made, critics have found several faults with the implications of the line of inquiry it suggests.[26] First, it is criticized severely for its lack of any kind of goal orientation. As Forester puts it, incrementalism 'would have us cross and recross intersections without knowing where we are going'.[27] Second, the model is criticized for being inherently conservative, given its suspicion of large-scale change and innovation. Third, it is criticized for being undemocratic, to the extent it confines decision-making to bargaining within a select group of senior policy-makers.[28] Fourth, by discouraging systematic analysis and planning and undermining the need to search for promising new alternatives, it is said to promote short-sighted decisions which can have adverse consequences for society in the long run. In addition to criticisms of the desirability of decisions made incrementally, the model is criticized for its narrow analytic usefulness. Yehezkel Dror, for example, notes that incrementalism can only work when there is a great deal of continuity in the nature of problems policies are intended to address and in the means available to address them, a continuity that does not always exist.[29] Incrementalism is also more characteristic of decision-making in a relatively stable environment, rather than in situations that are unusual, such as a crisis.[30]

The Garbage Can Model

The limitations of rational and incremental models led students of public policy-making to look for alternatives. Amitai Etzioni developed his *mixed scanning* model to bridge the shortcomings of both rational and incremental models by combining elements from both.[31] His model suggests that optimal decision-making would consist of a cursory search ('scanning') for alternatives, followed by a detailed probe of the most promising alternative. This would allow for more innovation than permitted by the incremental model, without imposing the unrealistic demands prescribed by the rational model. Etzioni goes further and suggests that indeed this is how decisions are made in reality. It is not uncommon to find a series of incremental decisions followed by a substantially different decision when faced with a problem significantly different from those dealt with before. Thus, mixed scanning is presented as both a prescriptive and descriptive model of decision-making.

This and other approaches, however, remained largely within the framework established by the rational model and its incremental critics. In the 1970s, a very different model asserted the inherent lack of rationality in the decision-making process. March and Olsen proposed a so-called *garbage can model* of decision-making which denied even the limited rationality permitted by incrementalism.[32] They began with the assumption that the other models presumed a level of intentionality, comprehension of problems, and predictability of relations among actors that simply does not obtain in reality. In their view, decision-making was a highly ambiguous and unpredictable process only distantly related to searching for means to achieving goals. Rejecting the instrumentalism that characterized most other models, March and Olsen argued that decision opportunities were:

> a garbage can into which various problems and solutions are dumped by participants. The mix of garbage in a single can depends partly on the labels attached to the alternative cans; but it also depends on what garbage is being produced at the moment, on the mix of cans available, and on the speed with which garbage is collected and removed from the scene.[33]

March and Olsen deliberately used the garbage-can metaphor to strip away the aura of science and rationality attributed to decision-making by earlier theorists. They sought to drive home the point that goals are often unknown to policymakers, as are causal relationships. In their view, actors simply define goals and choose means as they go along in a process which is necessarily contingent and unpredictable.

Several case studies[34] have substantiated the proposition that public decisions are often made in too *ad-hoc* and haphazard a fashion to be called incremental, much less rational. Anderson, for example, has argued that even decisions with respect to the Cuban Missile Crisis, admittedly one of the most critical issues of the post-World War Two period, were made in terms of simplistic yes/no binary choices on proposals that would emerge in the course of discussion.[35]

Be that as it may, the garbage can model is perhaps an exaggeration of what actually occurs. While its key tenets may well be a fairly accurate description of how at times organizations make decisions, in other instances it would be reasonable to expect more order. Its main strength was in breaking the logjam which surrounded the rather sterile rational-incremental debate, allowing for more nuanced studies of decision-making within institutional contexts to be undertaken.

A SUBSYSTEM MODEL OF PUBLIC DECISION-MAKING

By the early 1980s, it had become apparent to many observers that the continuing debate between the advocates of rationalism and those of incrementalism was interfering with empirical work and the theoretical development of the subject. As Smith and May argued, 'A debate about the relative merits of rationalistic as opposed to incrementalist models of decision-making has featured for some years now and although the terms of this debate are relatively well known it has had comparatively little impact upon empirical research in the areas of either policy or administrative studies.'[36] Rather than continue with this debate, the authors argued that:

we require more than one account to describe the several facets of organizational life. The problem is not to reconcile the differences between contrasting rational and incremental models, nor to construct some third alternative which combines the strongest features of each. The problem is to relate the two in the sense of spelling out the relationship between the social realities with which each is concerned.[37]

At present, some progress has been made in the direction suggested by Smith and May. Although few advocate a return to a comprehensive rational model, or completely reject incrementalism at least as a description of much actual public policy decision-making, most argue that Braybrooke and Lindblom's notion of multiple decision-making styles is correct and that it is important to spell out exactly under which conditions different styles will tend to be adopted.[38]

One of the most interesting developments in this direction can be found in the works of John Forester. He argues that there are at least five distinct decision-making styles associated with six key sets of conditions.[39] According to him, 'what is rational for administrators to do depends on the situations in which they work.'[40] That is, the decision-making style and the type of decision made by decision-makers vary according to issue and institutional contexts. As he put it in his 1984 article:

> Depending upon the conditions at hand, a strategy may be practical or ridiculous. With time, expertise, data, and a well-defined problem, technical calculations may be in order; without time, data, definition, and expertise, attempting those calculations could well be a waste of time. In a complex organizational environment, intelligence networks will be as, or more, important than documents when information is needed. In an environment of inter-organizational conflict, bargaining and compromise may be called for. Administrative strategies are sensible only in a political and organizational context.[41]

Forester suggests that for decision-making along the lines suggested by the rational model to take place, the following conditions must be met.[42] First, the number of *agents* (decision-makers) will need to be limited, possibly to as few as one person. Second, the organizational *setting* for the decision will have to be simple, and will be closed off from the influences of other policy actors. Third, the *problem* must be well defined; in other words, its scope, time horizon, value dimensions, and chains of consequences must be well understood. Fourth, *information* must be as close to perfect as possible; in other words it must be complete, accessible, and comprehensible. Finally, there must be no urgency for the decision; that is, *time* must be infinitely available to the decision-makers to consider all possible contingencies and their present and anticipated consequences. When these conditions are met completely, rational decision-making can be expected to prevail.

To the extent these five conditions are not met, as is almost always the case, Forester argues that we will find other styles of decision-making. Thus the number of agents (decision-makers) can expand and multiply almost to infinity; the setting can include many different organizations and can be more or less open to external influences; the problem can be ambiguous or susceptible to multiple competing interpretations; information can be incomplete, misleading or purposefully withheld or manipulated; and time can be limited or artificially constrained and manipulated. These are set out in Figure 11.

Figure 11.
Parameters of Decision-Making

Variables	Dimensions
1. *Agent*	*Single—Multiple*
2. *Setting*	*Single, Closed—Multiple, Open*
3. *Problem*	*Well-Defined—Multiple, Vague*
4. *Information*	*Perfect—Contested*
5. *Time*	*Infinite—Manipulated*

SOURCE: Adapted from John Forester, 'Bounded Rationality and the Politics of Muddling Through', *Public Administration Review* 44, 1 (1984): 26.

From this perspective, Forester suggests that there are five possible styles of decision-making: Optimization, Satisfycing, Search, Bargain, and Organizational. *Optimization* is the strategy that obtains when the conditions (mentioned above) of the rational-comprehensive model are met. The prevalence of other styles depends on the degree to which the conditions are not met. When the limitations are cognitive, for reasons mentioned earlier, we are likely to find the *Satisfycing* style of decision-making. The other styles mentioned by Forester are overlapping and therefore difficult to distinguish clearly. A *Search* strategy is one which is likely to occur when the problem is vague. A *Bargaining* strategy is one which is likely to be found when multiple actors deal with a problem in the absence of information and time. The *Organizational* strategy involves multiple settings and actors with both time and informational resources but also multiple problems. Suffice it to say that these types involve greater number of actors, more complex settings, more intractable problems, incomplete or distorted information, and limited availability of time for making a decision.

While a major improvement over earlier classifications and taxonomies, and certainly an improvement over the rational and incremental models and their 'garbage can' opponents, Forester's was only a first step in establishing an improved model of decision-making. A major problem with his taxonomy of decision-making is that it does not follow from his arguments. That is, a close examination of his discussion of the factors shaping decision-making[43] reveals that one would expect to find many more possible styles than five flowing from the possible combinations and permutations of the variables he cites. Although many of these categories are indistinguishable in practice and, in any event, seem to serve little analytical purpose, it remains unclear why one should expect only the five styles he cites to emerge.

An improvement on Forester's model can be made by re-casting his variables. Study of 'agent' and 'setting' can be accomplished by focusing on the policy subsystem, while the notions of the 'problem', 'information', and 'time' resources can all be seen as relating to the types of constraints which are placed upon decision-makers. Thus the two significant variables become (1) the complexity of the policy subsystem dealing with the problem and (2) the severity of the constraints it faces. The complexity of the policy subsystem affects the likelihood of attaining a high level of agreement or opposition to an option within the subsystem. Some options accord with the core values of the subsystem members while other do not, thereby structuring decisions into hard and soft choices.[44] Similarly, the making of decisions is constrained to varying degrees by information and time limitation, as well as the intractability of the problem.[45] Figure 12 outlines the four basic decision-making styles that emerge on the basis of the two dimensions emerging from this analysis: the complexity of the policy subsystem and the severity of constraints.

■ Figure 12.
┐ **Basic Decision-Making Styles**

		Complexity of the Policy Subsystem	
		High	Low
Severity of Constraints	High	*Incremental Adjustment*	*Satisfycing Search*
	Low	*Optimizing Adjustment*	*Rational Search*

SOURCE: Modelled after Martin J. Smith, 'Policy Networks and State Autonomy' in *The Political Influence of Ideas: Policy Communities and the Social Sciences*, eds S. Brooks and A.-G. Gagnon. New York: Praeger, 1994.

In this model, complex policy subsystems are more likely to be involved in adjustment strategies than in searches. Situations of high constraint are likely to result in a bargaining approach to decision-making while low constraint situations are more likely to generate rational or optimizing activity.

Taken together, these two variables result in four basic decision-making styles. Lindblom-style *incremental adjustments* are likely to occur where policy subsystems are complex and constraints on decision-makers are high. In such situations one would expect large-scale, high-risk decisions to be rare. In the opposite scenario, where the policy subsystem is simple and constraints are low, more traditional *rational searches* for new and possibly major changes are possible. When a complex subsystem exists and constraints are low, an adjustment strategy is likely, but one which may tend towards *optimization*. Finally, where constraints are high but subsystems simple, then *satisfycing* decisions are quite likely.

CONCLUSION

The essential character of the public decision-making process is very much the same as that of the other stages. Like the earlier stages of the public policy process, the decision-making stage varies according to the nature of the policy subsystem involved and the constraints under which decision-makers operate. As John Forester sums up the argument, what is rational for administrators and politicians to do 'depends on the situations in which they work. Pressed for quick recommendations, they cannot begin long studies. Faced with organizational rivalries, competition and turf struggles, they may justifiably be less than candid about their plans. What is reasonable to do depends on the context one is in, in ordinary life no less than in public administration.'[46]

NOTES

1   Anthony Cahill and E. Sam Overman, 'The Evolution of Rationality in Policy Analysis' in Stuart S. Nagel (ed.), *Policy Theory and Policy Evaluation* (New York: Greenwood, 1990); Herbert A. Simon, 'Proverbs of Administration', *Public Administration Review* 6, 1 (1946): 53-67; Herbert A. Simon, 'A Behavioral Model of Rational Choice', *Quarterly Journal of Economics* 69, 1 (1955): 99-118; Herbert A. Simon, *Administrative Behavior: A Study of Decision-Making Processes in Administrative Organization* (New York: Macmillan, 1957); Herbert A. Simon, *Models of Man, Social and Rational: Mathematical Essays on Rational Human Behavior in a Social Setting* (New York: Wiley, 1957).

2   David Braybrooke and Charles Lindblom, *A Strategy of Decision: Policy Evaluation as a Social Process* (New York: Free Press of Glencoe, 1963); Robert A. Dahl and Charles E. Lindblom, *Politics, Economics and Welfare: Planning and Politico-economic Systems Resolved into Basic Social Processes* (New York: Harper and Row, 1953); Charles E. Lindblom, 'The Science of Muddling Through', *Public Administration Review* 19, 2 (1959): 79-88.

3   Yehezkel Dror, *Public Policymaking Re-examined* (San Francisco: Chandler Publishing Co., 1968); Amitai Etzioni, 'Mixed-Scanning: A "Third" Approach to Decision-Making', *Public Administration Review* 27, 5 (1967): 385-92; S. Kenneth Howard, 'Analysis, Rationality, and Administrative Decision-Making' in Frank Marini (ed.), *Toward a New Public Administration: The Minnowbrook Perspective* (Scranton: Chandler, 1971): 285-301.

4   M. Cohen, J. March, and J. Olsen, 'A Garbage Can Model of Organizational Choice', *Administrative Science Quarterly* 17, 1 (1972): 1-25, and James G. March and Johan P. Olsen, 'Organizational Choice Under Ambiguity' in J.G. March and J.P. Olsen (eds), *Ambiguity and Choice in Organizations* 2nd ed. (Bergen: Universitetsforlaget, 1979).

5   Gilbert Smith and David May, 'The Artificial Debate Between Rationalist and Incrementalist Models of Decision-Making', *Policy and Politics* 8, 2 (1980): 147-61.

6   Garry Brewer and Peter DeLeon, *The Foundations of Policy Analysis* (Homewood: Dorsey, 1983): 179.

7   Joel D. Aberbach, Robert D. Putnam, and Bert A. Rockman, *Bureaucrats and Politicians in Western Democracies* (Cambridge: Harvard University Press, 1981). On legitimacy and authority, see Max Weber, *Economy and Society: An Outline of Interpretive Sociology* (Berkeley: University of California Press, 1978).

8   John Markoff, 'Governmental Bureaucratization: General Processes and an Anomalous Case', *Comparative Studies in Society and History* 17, 4 (1975): 479-503; Edward C. Page, *Political Authority and Bureaucratic Power: A Comparative Analysis* (Brighton, Sussex: Wheatsheaf, 1985).

9   Graham T. Allison and Morton H. Halperin, 'Bureaucratic Politics: A Paradigm and Some Policy Implications', *World Politics* 24 (Supplement, 1972): 40-79.

10   See Richard R. Nelson and Sidney G. Winter, *An Evolutionary Theory of Economic Change* (Cambridge: Harvard University Press, 1982). For an excellent review of the literature, see Evert Lindquist, 'What Do Decision Models Tell Us about Information Use?' *Knowledge in Society* 1, 2 (1988): 86-111.

11   Ralph K. Huitt, 'Political Feasibility' in Austin Rannay (ed.), *Political Science and Public Policy* (Chicago: Markham Publishing Co., 1968).

12   Adapted from Michael Carley, *Rational Techniques in Policy Analysis* (London: Heinemann, 1980): 11.

13   Bruce Jennings, 'Interpretation and the Practice of Policy Analysis' in Frank Fischer and John Forester (eds), *Confronting Values in Policy Analysis: The Politics of Criteria* (Newbury Park: Sage, 1987): 128-52; Douglas Torgerson, 'Between Knowledge and Politics: Three Faces Of Policy Analysis', Policy Sciences 19, 1 (1986): 33-59.

14   Carol H. Weiss, 'Research for Policy's Sake: The Enlightenment Function of Social Science Research', *Policy Analysis* 3, 4 (1977): 531-45.

15   Jon Elster, 'The Possibility of Rational Politics' in David Held (ed.), *Political Theory Today* (Oxford: Polity, 1991): 115.

16   Henri Fayol, *Studies in the Science of Administration*, 1895.

17   Luther Gulick, 'Notes on the Theory of Organizations' in Luther Gulick and Lyndal Urwick (eds), *Papers on the Science of Administration* (New York: Institute of Public Administration, 1937).

18   Ward Edwards, 'The Theory of Decision-Making', *Psychological Bulletin* 51, 4 (1954): 380-417.

19   Herbert A. Simon, 'A Behavioral Model of Rational Choice', *Quarterly Journal of Economics* 69, 1 (1955): 99-118; Herbert A. Simon, *Models of Man, Social and Rational: Mathematical Essays on Rational Human Behavior in a Social Setting* (New York: Wiley, 1957).

20   Robert A. Dahl and Charles E. Lindblom, *Politics, Economics and Welfare: Planning and Politico-economic Systems Resolved into Basic Social Processes* (New York: Harper and Row, 1953); Charles Lindblom, *Bargaining* (Los Angeles: Rand Corporation, 1955); Charles E. Lindblom, 'The Science of Muddling Through', *Public Administration Review* 19, 2 (1959): 79-88; Charles E. Lindblom, 'Policy Analysis', *American Economic Review* 48, 3 (1958): 298-312.

21   Charles E. Lindblom, 'Still Muddling, Not Yet Through', *Public Administration Review* 39, 6 (1979): 517.

22   Lindblom, 'The Science of Muddling Through': 81.

23   Harold Gortner, Julianne Mahler, and Jeanne Bell Nicholson, *Organization Theory: A Public Perspective* (Chicago: Dorsey Press, 1987): 257.

24   David Braybrooke and Charles Lindblom, *A Strategy of Decision: Policy Evaluation as a Social Process* (New York: Free Press of Glencoe, 1963).

25   Charles E. Lindblom and D.K. Cohen, *Usable Knowledge: Social Science and Social Problem Solving* (New Haven: Yale University Press, 1979).

26   For a review of the criticisms of the incrementalist model, see Andrew Weiss and Edward Woodhouse, 'Reframing Incrementalism: A Constructive Response to Critics', *Policy Sciences* 25, 3 (1992): 255-73.

27   John Forester, 'Bounded Rationality and the Politics of Muddling Through', *Public Administration Review* 44, 1 (1984): 23.

28   Louis Gawthrop, *Administrative Politics and Social Change* (New York: St Martin's Press, 1971).

29   Yehezkel Dror, 'Muddling Through—"Science" or Inertia', *Public Administration Review* 24, 3 (1964): 154-7.

30   D.C. Nice, 'Incremental and Nonincremental Policy Responses: The States and the Railroads', *Polity* 20 (1987): 145-56.

31   Amitai Etzioni, 'Mixed-Scanning: A "Third" Approach to Decision-Making', *Public Administration Review* 27, 5 (1967): 385-92.

32   James March and Johan Olsen, 'Organization Choice Under Ambiguity' in James March and Johan Olsen (eds), *Ambiguity and Choice in Organizations*.

33   Michael Cohen, James March, and Johan Olsen, 'People, Problems, Solutions, and the Ambiguity of Relevance' in March and Olsen (eds), *Ambiguity and Choice in Organizations*: 26.

34   See the case studies in March and Olsen (eds), *Ambiguity and Choice in Organizations*.

35   Paul Anderson, 'Decision Making by Objection and the Cuban Missile Crisis', *Administrative Science Quarterly* 28 (1983): 201-22.

36   Gilbert Smith and David May, 'The Artificial Debate Between Rationalist and Incrementalist Models of Decision-Making', *Policy and Politics* 8, 2 (1980): 147

37   Smith and May, 'The Artificial Debate': 156.

38   Ian Lustick, 'Explaining the Variable Utility of Disjointed Incrementalism: Four Propositions', *American Political Science Review* 74, 2 (1980): 342-53.

39   John Forester, 'Bounded Rationality and the Politics of Muddling Through', *Public Administration Review* 44, 1 (1984): 23-31; John Forester, *Planning in the Face of Power* (Berkeley: University of California Press, 1989).

40   Forester, 'Bounded Rationality': 23.

41   Forester, 'Bounded Rationality': 25.

42   Forester, 'Bounded Rationality': 25.

43   See summary table, Forester, 'Bounded Rationality': 26.

44   Philip H. Pollock III, Stuart A. Lilie, and M. Elliot Vittes, 'Hard Issues, Core Values and Vertical Constraint: The Case of Nuclear Power', *British Journal of Political Science* 23, 1 (1993): 29-50.

45   On these constraints see Evert A. Lindquist, 'What do Decision Models Tell Us about Information Use?' *Knowledge in Society* 1, 2 (1988): 86-111; David A. Rochefort and Roger W. Cobb, 'Problem Definition, Agenda Access, and Policy Choice', *Policy Studies Journal* 21, 1 (1993): 56-71; David J. Webber, 'The Distribution and Use of Policy Knowledge in the Policy Process' in W.N. Dunn and

R.M. Kelly (eds), *Advances in Policy Studies Since 1950* (New Brunswick, NJ: Transaction Publishers, 1992).
46   Forester, 'Bounded Rationality': 23.

FURTHER READING

Cahill, Anthony and E. Sam Overman, 'The Evolution of Rationality in Policy Analysis', pp. 11-27 in Stuart S. Nagel (ed.), *Policy Theory and Policy Evaluation*, New York: Greenwood, 1990.

Cohen, M., J. March, and J. Olsen, 'A Garbage Can Model of Organizational Choice', *Administrative Science Quarterly*, 17, 1 (1972): 1-25.

Etzioni, Amitai, 'Mixed-Scanning: A "Third" Approach to Decision-Making', *Public Administration Review* 27 (1967): 385-92.

Forester, John, 'Bounded Rationality and the Politics of Muddling Through', *Public Administration Review* 44 (1984): 23-30.

Lindblom, Charles, 'The Science of Muddling Through', *Public Administration Review* 19 (1959): 79-88.

MacRae, Duncan Jr, and James A. Wilde, *Policy Analysis For Public Decisions*, Lanham, MD: University Press of America, 1985.

Simon, Herbert, 'A Behavioral Model of Rational Choice', *Quarterly Journal of Economics* 69, 1 (1955): 99-118.

Smith, Gilbert and David May, 'The Artificial Debate Between Rationalist and Incrementalist Models of Decision-Making', *Policy and Politics* 8 (1980): 147-61.

Chapter 8

Policy Implementation— Policy Design and the Choice of Policy Instrument

CONCEPTUAL ISSUES

After a public problem has made its way to the policy agenda, various options have been proposed to resolve it, and a government has made some choice among those options, what remains is putting the decision into practice. This is the policy implementation stage of the policy cycle. It is defined as 'the process whereby programs or policies are carried out; it denotes the translation of plans into practice.'[1]

Until the early 1970s, implementation was regarded as unproblematic in a policy sense; it was assumed that once a policy was made, it would simply be carried out. This view began to change with the publication of Pressman and Wildavsky's work on program implementation. Their study of federal programs for unemployed inner-city residents of Oakland, California showed that job creation programs were not being carried out in the manner anticipated by policy-makers.[2] Other studies confirmed that the Great Society programs instituted by the Johnson Administration (1963-1968) in the US were not achieving their intended objectives and that the problem was rooted in the manner in which they were being implemented. Research in other countries arrived at similar conclusions. The upshot of all these studies was a more systematic effort to understand the factors that facilitated or constrained implementation of public policies.

Some of these efforts generated analyses and prescriptions that perceived policy implementation to be a 'top-down' process concerned with how the implementing officials could be made to do their job more effectively. This approach was opposed by those who subscribed to a 'bottom-up' approach, which starts from the perspective of those affected by and involved in the implementation of a policy. Later a third approach emerged which, rather than studying the purely administrative concerns of putting a program into practice, looked at the implementation process as one in which various tools of government were applied to concrete cases in policy design.[3] Since the general contours of the available policy instruments are reasonably well known, studies in this mould tend to concentrate on the reasons or rationales for the choice of particular tools by the government and the potential for their use in future circumstances.

In this chapter we set out the factors that make policy implementation a difficult task and discuss the main perspectives on the subject before examining the factors affecting the choice of instruments for implementing policy.

THE REALITIES OF POLICY IMPLEMENTATION

Translating programs into practice is not as simple as may first appear. For a host of reasons relating to the nature of the problems, the circumstances surrounding them, or the organization of the administrative machinery in charge of the task, programs may not be implemented as intended. These are the realities of implementation, as distinct from the stated objectives and the procedures prescribed for achieving them. It is important to recognize these limitations if we are to understand the public policy process.

The *nature of the problems* themselves affects the implementation of programs designed to address them in several ways. First, policy decisions involve varying degrees of technical difficulties during implementation, some of which are more intractable than others.[4] Implementing some programs can be expected to be unproblematic, as in the case of closing down a casino or opening a new school in a new neighbourhood, because these are single decisions whose translation into practice is usually rather routine. The same is not true for programs designed to eliminate gambling or improve pupils' educational standards. Similarly, programs designed to eliminate pollution or tax and welfare frauds must face the reality that no available technology will allow complete achievement of these objectives. Even if the technology is available, it may be more expensive than the society is willing to pay. Some problems are simply more difficult to tackle because of their complex, novel, or interdependent nature and because they involve not a single decision but a series of decisions on how to carry out the government's policy.

Second, the diversity of problems targeted by a government program may make its implementation difficult. Public problems such as domestic violence or educational under-achievement are rooted in so many causes that programs designed to address single or even multiple causes can normally be expected to fall short of their objectives. The problem of speeding on the city streets has more simple origins and can therefore be solved more easily.

Third, the size of the target group is also a factor, insofar as the larger and more diverse the group, the more difficult it is to affect its behaviour in a desired fashion. Thus, because of the small number of manufacturers involved, a policy designed to improve safety features of automobiles would be easier to implement than a policy design to make thousands of careless drivers observe traffic safety rules.

Finally, the extent of the behavioural change the policy requires of the target group determines the level of difficulty faced in its implementation. A policy of eradicating sexism and racism is more difficult to implement, because of their deep roots in societies' cultural belief systems, than one of increasing the electricity supply, which requires almost no change in behaviour on the part of consumers.

In addition to the nature of the problem being addressed by the policy, implementation is affected by its social, economic, technological, and political contexts.

First, changes in *social conditions* may affect the interpretation of the problem and thus the manner in which the program is implemented. Thus many of the problems being faced by social security programs in the industrialized countries arise from the fact that they were not designed to cope with the ever-increasing proportion of the aged or high rates of unemployment which impose a very heavy burden on public finance.

Second, changes in *economic conditions* have a similar impact on policy implementation. A program targeting the poor and unemployed, for instance, can be expected to undergo changes after an economic upturn or downturn. Economic conditions also vary by region, necessitating greater flexibility and discretion in implementation.[5]

Third, the availability of new *technology* can also be expected to cause changes in policy. Policies towards pollution control, for example, often change in the course of implementation after a more effective or cheaper technology has been discovered.

Fourth, variations in *political circumstances* have an impact on policy implementation. A change of government may lead to changes in the way policies are implemented without change in the policy itself. Many conservative governments, for example, have been known to tighten the availability of social security programs established by labour or socialist governments without necessarily changing the policy itself.

The organization of the *administrative apparatus* in charge of implementing a policy has no less impact than the other factors mentioned so far. Policy implementation is inadvertently subject to the intra- and inter-organizational conflicts endemic to the public policy process. There are often different bureaucratic organizations within the government and at other levels of government (national, state or provincial, and local) involved in implementing policy, each with its own interests, ambitions, and traditions that can hamper the implementation process and shape its outcomes.[6] For many agencies, implementation may simply be another opportunity for continuing the fight they may have lost at the policy formulation stage.

The *political and economic resources* of the target groups also affect implementation of policies. Powerful groups affected by a policy can condition the character of implementation by supporting or opposing it. It is therefore quite common for implementors to strike compromises with groups in order to make the task of implementation easier. *Public support* for a policy can also affect implementation. Many policies witness a decline in support after the policy has been adopted, giving greater opportunity to implementors to vary the original intent. Of course, the implementors themselves may use polling surveys to justify continuing the programs in the face of policy-makers' or groups' demands to change the policy.

Many noble efforts on the part of governments and citizens to create better and safer worlds have foundered on these 'realities' of implementation. This has led not only to a greater appreciation of the difficulties encountered in policy implementation, but also to attempts to design policies in a manner offering a reasonable chance of success in implementation. While many government decisions continue to be taken without adequate attention to the difficulties of implementation, there is a broad recognition now of the need to take these concerns into account at earlier stages of the policy process. It is easier for the policy makers to take the limitation into account, and devise an appropriate response, *ex ante* rather than *ex post*.[7]

Among the measures policy-makers can take to improve policy design to facilitate policy implementation are the following.[8] First, the decision-makers must state the goals of the policy and their relative ranking as clearly as possible. This serves as clear instruction to implementors what exactly they are expected to do and the priority they must attribute to their tasks. Second, the policy must be backed implicitly or explicitly by a viable causal theory as to why the prescribed measure is expected to resolve the problem. A policy designed to encourage people to save sufficiently for their retirement years must outline clearly why people are not now saving enough so that the policy is necessary. Third, the policy must have sufficient funds allocated to it for successful implementation. One of the surest ways of killing a program is to starve it of necessary funds. Fourth, the policy should set out clear procedures that implementing agencies must adhere to when carrying out the policy. Fifth, the task of implementation must be allocated to an agency with relevant experience and commitment.

PERSPECTIVES ON POLICY IMPLEMENTATION

Studies on policy implementation emphasizing policy design are usually referred to as the 'top down' approach to the subject. This approach 'assumes that we can usefully view the policy process as a series of chains of command where political leaders articulate a clear policy preference which is then carried out at increasing levels of specificity as it goes through the administrative machinery that serves the government.'[9] The 'top down' approach starts with the decisions of the government, examines the extent to which administrators carry out or fail to carry out the decisions, and seeks to find the reasons underlying the extent of the implementation.[10]

This approach provides clear directions for implementation research. Its emphasis on the extent of achievement of stated objectives and on the activities of the legally-mandated implementation machinery offers clear indications of what implementors are to understand and what end to have in mind. However, this approach assumes that policies have clear goals when, as we have seen in earlier chapters, in reality they are often unclear or even contradictory. The most serious shortcoming of this approach, however, concerns its focus on senior decision-makers, who often play only a marginal role in implementation compared to lower level officials and members of the public.

Criticism of the 'top-down' approach's neglect of a focus on lower level officials led to the development of a 'bottom-up' approach to the study of public policy implementation.[11] This approach starts with all the public and private actors involved in implementing programs and examines their personal and organizational goals, their strategies, and the network of contacts they have built. It then works its way upward to discover the goals, strategies, and contacts of those involved in designing, financing, and executing of programs. Studies conducted in bottom-up fashion have shown that the success or failure of many programs often depends on the commitment and skills of the actors at the bottom directly involved in implementing programs.[12]

The key advantage of the 'bottom-up' approach is that it directs attention to the formal and informal relationships constituting the policy networks involved in making and implementing policies. As we have seen, policy subsystems consisting of key private and public actors in a policy sector play a crucial role in the policy process. This is just as true of policy implementation as it is of policy formulation. The bottom-up approach orients the study of implementation away from policy decisions and back towards policy problems, thus enabling the study of all private and public actors and institutions involved in the problem.

The distinction between the 'top-down' and 'bottom-up' approaches to policy implementation, while useful, tends to blur the fact that both approaches bring insights to policy implementation and should be combined to reach a comprehensive understanding of the subject.[13] To put these insights together in a fashion which sheds light on their operation in specific circumstances and aids in the overall conceptualization of the policy process, many students of public policy have turned to examining policy implementation as an instance of instrument choice.

RATIONALES FOR INSTRUMENT CHOICE

The instrument-choice approach to policy implementation begins from the observation that, to a great extent, policy implementation involves applying one or more of the basic techniques of government to policy problems. These basic techniques, as discussed at length in Chapter Four, are variously known as *policy tools*, *policy instruments* or *governing instruments*. Regardless of whether we study the implementation process in a top-down 'design' fashion or a more traditional bottom-up administrative one, the process of giving form or substance to a government decision always involves choosing one or several tools from those available in the government toolbox.[14] This perspective addresses why a government chooses particular instruments from among the many available, and whether any distinct patterns or styles of instrument choice can be discerned in the policy implementation process. Answering these questions moves policy analysis away from simply the study of public administration and helps to integrate implementation research with the general inquiries and concerns of the policy sciences. To date two different groups of scholars have been working on the question of instrument choice, and the solutions they have put forward to answer this question vary dramatically. Economists have for the most part tended to interpret the choice of policy instrument as, at least in theory, a technical exercise of matching the attributes of specific tools to the job at hand. Political scientists, on the other hand, have tended to argue that instruments are more or less substitutable on a purely technical basis, and have instead focused on the political forces they feel govern instrument selection.

Economic Models

Studies by economists are shaped by the theoretical debates between neoclassical and welfare economists on the proper role of the state in the economy which were set out in Chapter Two. While both prefer voluntary instruments, welfare economists permit greater scope for the use of compulsory and mixed instruments to correct market failures.[15] In contrast, neoclassical economic theorists approve the use of such instruments only for providing pure public goods; their use for any other reason is viewed as distorting the market process and leading to sub-optimal outcomes.[16] The welfare economists' greater theoretical acceptance of state intervention leads them to more systematic analyses of instrument choice.[17] However, they tend to treat the choice of instrument as a strictly technical exercise that consists of evaluating the features of various instruments, matching them to different types of market failures, estimating their relative costs, and choosing that instrument which most efficiently overcomes the market failure in question.

The neo-classical economists generally rely on Public Choice theory to explain patterns of instrument use. They argue that in a democracy the dynamics of self-serving behaviour by voters, politicians, and bureaucrats promotes an increasing tendency to tax and spend, and to regulate and nationalize private activity. It is argued that democratic politics leads states to choose instruments that provide concentrated benefits to marginal voters while spreading the costs to the entire population.[18] For electoral reasons, governments make efforts to choose instruments that do not reveal their true costs to the voters who ultimately pay for them. While the incorporation of political factors into the analysis is an improvement upon some aspects of the welfare economic approaches, such analyses do little to further the explanation of systematic patterns of instrument choices. It is very difficult, for example, to match types of instruments with patterns of the distribution of costs and benefits[19] since one must first know whether governments want to claim credit or avoid blame for the action to be undertaken.[20] Most instruments can be used for both purposes, and which purpose is chosen depends on highly idiosyncratic and contextual factors.

The economic theories of instrument choice of both welfare and neo-classical economists are overly deductive and lack a solid empirical base in studies of actual decision-making by governments. Their rationales for policy instrument choice are based on their theoretical assumptions concerning what governments do or ought to do, rather than on empirical investigations into what they actually do. Studies by political scientists, as the following discussion will show, tend to display a wider variety and are generally more empirical in nature. They may not appear as elegant as those generated by economists to those looking for theoretical parsimony, but they represent sincere efforts to grapple with the complexity of policy instruments and inductively develop a plausible theory of instrument choice.[21]

Political Models

One oft-cited political science approach to theorizing the question of policy instrument choice has been developed by Bruce Doern and several of his Canadian associates.[22] Assuming that all instruments are technically substitutable, they argue that in a liberal democratic society governments prefer to use the least coercive instruments available and would 'move up the scale' as necessary to overcome societal resistance to effective regulation. That is, any instrument can theoretically accomplish any chosen aim, but governments prefer less coercive instruments unless forced by either recalcitrance on the part of the subject and/or continued social pressure for change to utilize more coercive instruments. Overall, this conception led Doern and his colleagues to suggest that a typical pattern of instrument use would be for governments to begin with minimal activities such as exhortation and move slowly, if at all, toward direct provision.

There are serious problems with this understanding of substitutability among instruments, and the rationales for instrument choice. First, no government has the complete range of instruments available to it: social and political constraints favour the choice of some instruments and inhibit the choice of others.[23] Second, the conception of changes in instrument choice consisting of a slow movement up the coercion scale does not conform to the empirical evidence. Many governments, for example, have begun towards the top of the scale in creating public enterprises to deal with elements of emerging technologies, without ever having experimented with less coercive tools. Third, the idea of social resistance provoking governments to move towards more coercive instruments is also problematic. While in some policy areas—notably the economy—it may be true that there is often societal resistance to further government action, in many other fields this is not the case. In the area of social policy, for example, social pressure often runs the other way, urging greater regulation and expenditures than governments for fiscal or ideological reasons may be willing to provide.

Policy implementation and instrument choice is an complex process which cannot be encapsulated in a simplified assumption of movement from less to most coercive instruments. It is possible that policy-makers will choose the strongest instrument in the first instance if that is what the political circumstances or the nature of the problem being addressed warrants.

A second widely cited political model of instrument choice has been developed by Christopher Hood. He argues that instrument choice is not a technical exercise but 'a matter of faith and politics'.[24] He posits that the choice is shaped by resource constraints, political pressures, legal constraints, and the lessons learnt from past instrument failures.[25] Although he does not spell out the exact nature of these forces, Hood does discuss a number of 'normal' patterns of government 're-tooling' over time. These include: '1. A shift from information-based instruments to those based on other resources. 2. A shift from reliance on coercion alone to the use of financial and organizational resources'.[26] Furthermore, he argues that technological change may erode the usefulness of old instruments and lead to the application of new ones, often on the basis of analogies between historical and present circumstances drawn by policy-makers.

While Hood admits the essentially contingent nature of the process of instrument choice, he argues that the process is driven by identifiable forces based on the governments' experience with various instruments and their effects on social actors. According to him, different instruments vary in effectiveness according to the nature of the social groups they are intended to influence; if large and well-organized social groups exist, governments will utilize persuasion and expenditure instruments. He notes that the size of the target group is significant since the larger the group to be affected, the more likely governments will use passive (voluntary) rather than active (compulsory) instruments. However, he also argues that, regardless of the size of the social group affected, governments will not utilize coercive instruments if they want voluntary compliance from a social group. On the other hand, if a government wants to re-distribute resources among those groups, it will utilize coercive instruments.[27]

Thus, for Hood, instrument choice is a function of the nature of the state's goals and resources and the organization and capacity of targeted societal actors. Overall, he argues, these lead governments to practise the ethos of 'using bureaucracy sparingly': that is, towards a distinct preference for use of information and authority instruments since those instruments are 'non-depletable'.[28]

In fact, the most preferred resource is nodality or information-based influence, since Hood argues that only instruments based on this resource are both non-depletable and place minimum constraints on citizens. When coercion is required, it is primarily due to the desire to more closely target societal groups for action. Even then, authority is preferred to organization because the former is less resource-intensive.

Hood's model improves on some elements of Doern's formulations but also has its own problems. Why should governments inherently desire to use bureaucracy sparingly? Why should resources like treasure and organization be considered less replenishable than resources such as information or organiza-tion, when it is apparent to most observers that the extended use of either pro-paganda or force has diminishing returns? These questions remain unanswered in Hood's analysis.

In one of the most sophisticated works on the subject, Linder and Peters have developed a third model integrating many of the various conceptions of instrument choice put forward in both the economics and political science liter-atures.[29] They list the following factors as playing a critical role in shaping instrument choice.

First, the *features of the policy instruments* are important for selection purposes, because some instruments are more suited for a task at hand than are others. They argue that instruments vary according to four general categories of features, each ranging on a scale from low to high:

1) *Resource intensiveness*, including administrative cost and operational simplicity;
2) *Targeting*, including precision and selectivity;
3) *Political risk*, including nature of support and opposition, public visibility and chances of failure; and
4) *Constraints on state activity*, including difficulties with coerciveness and ideological principles limiting government activity.[30]

Second, they argue that a nation's *policy style and political culture*, and the depth of its social cleavages, have a critical bearing on the choice of an instrument. Each nation has a peculiar national style, culture, and pattern of social conflicts which predispose its decision-makers to choose a particular instrument.

Third, they argue that the choice of an instrument is circumscribed by the *organizational culture* of the concerned agencies and the nature of their links with clients and other agencies.

Fourth, they argue that the *context of the problem situation*, its timing and the scope of actors it includes will also affect the choice of instrument.

Ultimately, however, for Linder and Peters instrument choice is a matter of the decision-makers' subjective preferences, based on their professional back-ground, institutional affiliation, and cognitive make-up. They are the ones who define the situational context constraining choice and, in the process, implant their professional and personal preferences on instrument choice.

The three political models, taken together, suggest that the choice of policy instruments is shaped by the characteristics of the instruments, the nature of the problem at hand, governments' past experiences in dealing with the same or similar problems, the subjective preference of the decision-makers, and the likely reaction to the choice by affected social groups. Taken separately, however, each political model leaves out at least one aspect of the selection process. Thus Doern examines the preferences of decision-makers, the likely response of social actors, and decision-makers' experiences with past instrument uses, while failing to deal with the characteristics of the instruments or the nature of the task at hand. Hood does much the same, and both Hood and Doern make several simplifying assumptions about the preferences of decision-makers and social actors, and the nature of the lessons drawn from past experiences, which limit the ability of their models to explain patterns of instrument choice found in different countries. Linder and Peters, on the other hand, focus intently on the features of policy instruments, the task at hand, and the preferences of state and societal actors. Their main shortcoming lies in inadequate conceptualization of how the actors' preferences are formed and realized or thwarted.

A Synthetic Model of Policy Instrument Choice

It is only a start to say that instrument choices are conditioned by a variety of contextual factors which affect the preferences of implementors. For the instrument choice perspective to say anything meaningful about policy implementation requires a model linking specific choice of instruments to specific rationales. Such a model can be developed combining the insights afforded by economists and political scientists into the rationales of instrument choice. Despite their different approaches and backgrounds, the analysts agree that while there are almost an infinite number of permutations, the actual number of different types of instruments at the disposal of implementors is rather limited. The range of policy tools can be reduced to four categories: 1) market, 2) family or community, 3) regulation, public enterprise, or direct provision, and 4) mixed instruments.

What is needed, then, is a model which links these four general categories of instruments to specific rationales for their choice. In this regard, both sets of theorists discussed above rely either explicitly or implicitly on two interlinked general variables in setting out their frameworks. These are, first, the extent of state planning capacity, or the organizational ability of states to affect societal actors; and second, subsystem complexity and especially the number and type of actors governments must face in implementing their programs and policies. Setting these variables out allows a model of instrument choice to be developed which includes specific instrument orientations. This model is laid out in Figure 13, opposite.

■ Figure 13.
❘ **A Model of Instrument Preferences**

Policy Subsystem Complexity

		High	Low
State Capacity	High	*Market Instruments*	*Regulatory Public Enterprise, or Direct Provision Instruments*
	Low	*Voluntary, Community or Family Based Instruments*	*Mixed Instruments*

SOURCE: Adapted from Stephen H. Linder and B. Guy Peters, 'Instruments of Government: Perceptions and Contexts', *Journal of Public Policy* 9, 1 (1989): 35-58.

This model suggests that a high level of state capacity is required to utilize market-based instruments and regulatory or direct-provision ones. While it may seem odd to associate market, a voluntary instrument, with high state capacity, it must be remembered that market is a highly contentious instrument which is opposed by those who are likely to lose out from its operation. When the state is lacking in policy capacity, it will tend to utilize incentives or propaganda, or to rely on existing voluntary, community, or family-based instruments. The tendency to choose a particular instrument within these categories, however, is ultimately determined not only by state capacity but by the level of subsystem complexity. Thus those policies involving numerous and conflicting groups in implementing a complex subsystem will favour the use of either market or voluntary instruments which are capable of dealing with multiple actors and interests. In situations where the number of actors is smaller and the subsystem less complex, governments can choose to use directive or mixed instruments.

This model sets out only the general expectations which an instrument choice perspective brings to the study of policy implementation. It does not delve into the detail of fine gradients of instruments within each category, or the specific contexts of individual decisions. However, it suggests that although a complex process, general patterns of policy implementation can be discerned within states and policy sectors which can greatly aid the understanding of this stage of the policy cycle.

CONCLUSION

Economists and political scientists differ significantly in their approach to the choice of policy instruments. Unlike economic approaches, which are deductive in nature and assume the superiority of market forces, the approaches espoused by political scientists are much more inductive and derive hypotheses concerning the state and the nature of state activities from empirical investigations into actual instances of instrument choices. Despite somewhat different methodologies and frameworks, the political approaches share the view that instrument choice involves much more than simply executing previously arrived-at decisions, or matching goals with means. They endorse the notion that public policies can be meaningfully understood and evaluated only in terms of the existing range of ideas and institutions within which actors make their decisions.[31]

The central assumption of the political science approaches to instrument choices is that the decision process and its outcomes are shaped by political factors related to state capacity and subsystem complexity.[32] That is, all three approaches note that patterns of choice exist in which governments tend to rely on similar instruments in widely divergent circumstances. Thus what the British policy-makers accomplish through public enterprises are implemented in the US through regulations. This is something economists repeatedly find, to their displeasure, when their proposals for utilizing new types of economic instruments to control pollution are rejected in favour of continuing to use regulation, as has become almost habitual in many countries for dealing with this type of problem. A focus on relatively long-standing political factors related to state capacity and subsystem complexity helps to explain why these national styles of instrument choice exist.

NOTES

1   Milbrey W. McLaughlin, 'Implementation Realities and Evaluation Design' in R. Lance Shotland and Melvin M. Mark (eds), *Social Science and Social Policy* (Beverly Hills: Sage, 1985): 97.

2   Jeffrey L. Pressman and Aaron B. Wildavsky, *Implementation*, 3rd ed. (Berkeley: University of California Press, 1984 [1st ed. 1973]).

3   Lester M. Salamon, 'Rethinking Public Management: Third-Party Government and the Changing Forms of Government Action', *Public Policy* 29, 3 (1981): 255-75.

4   The following discussion draws heavily on Daniel A. Mazmanian and Paul A. Sabatier, *Implementation and Public Policy* (Glenview: Scott, Foresman, 1983): 21-5.

5   Mazmanian and Sabatier, *Implementation and Public Policy*: 31.

6   See Eugene Bardach, *The Implementation Game* (Cambridge: MIT Press, 1977); Richard F. Elmore, 'Organizational Models of Social Program Implementation', *Public Policy* 26, 2 (1978): 185-228.

7   See Stephen H. Linder and B. Guy Peters, 'From Social Theory to Policy Design', *Journal of Public Policy* 4, 3 (1984): 237-59; Stephen H. Linder and B. Guy Peters, 'The Analysis of Design or the Design of Analysis?' *Policy Studies Review* 7, 4 (1988): 738-50; Stephen H. Linder and B. Guy Peters, 'Research Perspectives on the Design of Public Policy: Implementation, Formulation, and Design' in Dennis J. Palumbo and Donald J. Calista (eds), *Implementation and the Policy Process: Opening up the Black Box* (New York: Greenwood Press, 1990).

8   Paul A. Sabatier, 'Top-down and Bottom-up Approaches to Implementation Research' in Michael Hill (ed.), *The Public Policy Process: A Reader* (London: Harvester Wheatsheaf, 1993): 266-93.

9   Michael Clarke, 'Implementation' in Martin Harrap (ed.), *Power and Policy in Liberal Democracies* (Cambridge: Cambridge University Press, 1992): 222.

10   See Sabatier, 'Top-down and Bottom-up Approaches to Implementation Research': 266-93.

11   See Benny Hjern and David O. Porter, 'Implementation Structures: A New Unit of Administrative Studies' in Michael Hill (ed.), *The Public Policy Process: A Reader* (London: Harvester Wheatsheaf, 1993): 248-65; Benny Hjern, 'Implementation Research—The Link Gone Missing', *Journal of Public Policy* 2, 3 (1982): 301-8. Also see S. Barrett and C. Fudge, *Policy and Action* (London: Methuen, 1981).

12   Michael Lipsky, *Street-Level Bureaucracy: Dilemmas of the Individual in Public Services* (Cambridge: MIT Press, 1980).

13   Charles J. Fox, 'Implementation Research: Why and How to Transcend Positivist Methodology' in Dennis J. Palumbo and Donald J. Calista (eds), *Implementation and the Policy Process: Opening up the Black Box* (New York: Greenwood Press, 1990): 199-212.

14   Christopher C. Hood, *The Tools of Government* (Chatham: Chatham House, 1986); Stephen H. Linder and B. Guy Peters, 'The Logic of Public Policy Design: Linking Policy Actors and Plausible Instruments', *Knowledge in Society* 4 (1991): 125-51.

15   Francis M. Bator, 'The Anatomy of Market Failure', *Quarterly Journal of Economics* 72, 3 (1958): 351-79; Economic Council of Canada, *Responsible Regulation: An Interim Report* (Ottawa: Supply and Services Canada, 1979); M.A. Utton, *The Economics of Regulating Industry* (Oxford: Basil Blackwell, 1986).

16   Stephen Breyer, 'Analyzing Regulatory Failure: Mismatches, Less Restrictive Alternatives, and Reform', *Harvard Law Review* 92, 3 (1979): 549-609; Stephen Breyer, *Regulation and Its Reform* (Cambridge: Harvard University Press, 1982); Richard A. Posner, 'Theories of Economic Regulation', *Bell Journal of Economics and Management Science* 5, 2 (1974): 335-58; George J. Stigler, *The Citizen and the State: Essays on Regulation* (Chicago: University of Chicago Press, 1975); Charles Wolf Jr, 'Markets and Non-Market Failures: Comparison and Assessment', *Journal of Public Policy* 7, 1 (1987): 43-70.

17   Barry M. Mitnick, *The Political Economy of Regulation: Creating, Designing, and Removing Regulatory Forms* (New York: Columbia University Press, 1980); Edith Stokey and Richard Zeckhauser, *A Primer for Policy Analysis* (New York: W.W. Norton, 1978); David L. Weimer and Aidan R. Vining, *Policy Analysis: Concepts and Practice* (Englewood Cliffs: Prentice Hall, 1992).

18   James M. Buchanan, 'Rent Seeking and Profit Seeking' in James M. Buchanan, Robert D. Tollison, and Gordon Tullock (eds), *Toward a Theory of the Rent-Seeking Society* (College Station: Texas A&M University Press, 1980).

19   James Q. Wilson, 'The Politics of Regulation' in J.W. McKie (ed.), *Social Responsibility and the Business Predicament* (Washington: Brookings Institution, 1974): 135-68.

20   R. Kent Weaver, 'The Politics of Blame Avoidance', *Journal of Public Policy* 6, 4 (1986): 371-98.

21   See Michael Howlett, 'Policy Instruments, Policy Styles, and Policy Implementation: National Approaches to Theories of Instrument Choice', *Policy Studies Journal* 19, 2 (1991): 1-21.

22   G. Bruce Doern, *The Nature of Scientific and Technological Controversy in Federal Policy Formation* (Ottawa: Science Council of Canada, 1981); Richard Phidd and G. Bruce Doern, *Canadian Public Policy: Ideas, Structures, Process* (Toronto: Methuen, 1983); Allan Tupper and G. Bruce Doern, 'Public Corporations and Public Policy in Canada' in Allan Tupper and G. Bruce Doern (eds), *Public Corporations and Public Policy in Canada* (Montreal: Institute for Research on Public Policy, 1981): 1-50.

23   Kenneth Woodside, 'Policy Instruments and the Study of Public Policy', *Canadian Journal of Political Science* 19, 4 (1986): 775-93.

24   Christopher C. Hood, *The Tools of Government* (Chatham: Chatham House, 1986): 9.

25   Hood, *The Tools of Government*: 118-20, 141-3.

26   Hood, *The Tools of Government*: 126-31.

27   Hood, *The Tools of Government*: 138-9.

28   Christopher Hood, 'Using Bureaucracy Sparingly', *Public Administration* 61, 2 (1983): 197-208.

29   Stephen H. Linder and B. Guy Peters, 'Instruments of Government: Perceptions and Contexts', *Journal of Public Policy* 9, 1 (1989): 35-58.

30   Linder and Peters, 'Instruments of Government': 47.

31   Stephen H. Linder and B. Guy Peters, 'The Logic of Public Policy Design: Linking Policy Actors and Plausible Instruments', *Knowledge in Society* 4 (1991): 131.

32   Michael M. Atkinson, 'Selecting Policy Instruments: Neo-Institutional and Rational Choice Interpretations of Automobile Insurance in Ontario', *Canadian Journal of Political Science* 22, 1 (1989): 114.

FURTHER READING

Baxter-Moore, Nicolas, 'Policy Implementation and the Role of the State: A Revised Approach to the Study of Policy Instruments' in R.J. Jackson, D. Jackson and N. Baxter-Moore (eds), *Contemporary Canadian Politics: Readings and Notes*, Scarborough: Prentice-Hall, 1987.

Doern, G. Bruce and Richard W. Phidd, *Canadian Public Policy: Ideas, Structure, Process*, 2nd ed. Toronto: Nelson, 1992.

Hjern, Benny, 'Implementation Research—The Link Gone Missing', *Journal of Public Policy* 2, 3 (1982): 301-8.

Hood, Christopher C., *The Tools of Government*, Chatham: Chatham House, 1986.

Howlett, Michael and M. Ramesh, 'Patterns of Policy Instrument Choice: Policy Styles, Policy Learning and the Privatization Experience', *Policy Studies Review* 12, 1-2 (1993): 1-22.

Ingram, Helen and Anne Schneider. 'Improving Implementation Through Framing Smarter Statutes'. *Journal of Public Policy* 10, 1 (1990): 67-88.

Linder, Stephen H. and B. Guy Peters. 'Instruments of Government: Perceptions and Contexts', *Journal of Public Policy* 9, 1 (1989): 35-58.

Palumbo, Dennis J. and Donald J. Calista, 'Opening Up the Black Box: Implementation and the Policy Process,' pp. 1-17 in Dennis J. Palumbo and Donald J. Calista (eds), *Implementation and the Policy Process*, New York: Greenwood Press, 1990.

Sabatier, Paul A., 'Top-down and Bottom-up Approaches to Implementation Research', pp. 266-93 in Michael Hill (ed.), *The Public Policy Process: A Reader*, London: Harvester Wheatsheaf, 1993. First published in 1986 in *Journal of Public Policy*.

Winter, Soren, 'Integrating Implementation Research', pp. 19-38 in Dennis J. Palumbo and Donald J. Calista (eds), *Implementation and the Policy Process: Opening up the Black Box*, New York: Greenwood Press, 1990.

Woodside, K., 'Policy Instruments and the Study of Public Policy', *Canadian Journal of Political Science* 19, 4 (1986): 775-93.

Chapter 9

Policy Evaluation— Policy Analysis and Policy Learning

CONCEPTUAL ISSUES

Once the need to address a public problem has been acknowledged, various possible solutions considered, and some among them selected and put into practice, the government often initiates an assessment of how the policy is working. At the same time, various interested members of policy subsystems and of the public are engaged in their own assessment of the workings and effects of the policy in order to express support for or opposition to the policy, or to demand changes to it. The concept of policy evaluation thus refers broadly to the process of finding out about a public policy in action, the means being employed and the objectives being served. How deep or thorough the evaluation is depends on those ordering its initiation and/or those undertaking it.

Policy evaluation almost always involves bureaucrats and politicians within government dealing with the policy in question, and it usually involves non-governmental members of policy subsystems as well. It may also involve members of the public, who will have the ultimate say when they vote at elections.[1] The sites of policy evaluation are broader than often presented in the literature, which tends to concentrate overwhelmingly on evaluation by bureaucrats and private consultants hired by them.

After a policy has been evaluated, the problem and solutions may be rethought completely, in which case the cycle may swing back to agenda-setting or some other stage of the cycle, or the *status quo* may be maintained. Reconceptualization may consist of minor changes or fundamental reformulation of the problem, including terminating the policy altogether.[2] How evaluation is conducted, the problems the exercise entails, and the range of results to which it typically leads are the concerns of this chapter. It then outlines the patterns of policy change to which policy evaluation typically leads.

The study of policy evaluation is dominated by those whom we described as rationalists in Chapter Two. For them, policy evaluation consists of assessing whether a public policy is achieving its stated objective and, if not, what could be done to eliminate the hurdles in the way. David Nachmias, an influential figure in the discipline, defines policy evaluation as 'the objective systematic, empirical examination of the effects ongoing policies and public programs have on their targets in terms of the goals they are meant to achieve'.[3] Discerning readers will have no difficulty detecting the rationalist orientation of this definition. It specifies explicitly that the examination of a policy's effects on the achievement of its goals should be objective, systematic, and empirical. However, as we have mentioned before, goals in public policy are often not stated clearly enough to find out if and to what extent they are achieved. The possibilities for objective analysis are also limited because of insurmountable difficulties in developing objective standards by which to evaluate government success in dealing with subjective claims and socially constructed problems.

Developing adequate and acceptable measures for policy evaluation is a difficult and contentious task, as many authors have noted.[4] Analysts often resort to such fuzzy concepts as success or failure to conclude their evaluation. But, as Ingram and Mann caution,

> the phenomenon of [policy] failure is neither so simple nor certain as many contemporary critics of policy and politics would have us believe. Success and failure are slippery concepts, often highly subjective and reflective of an individual's goals, perception of need, and perhaps even psychological disposition toward life. The old story about asking two individuals how much milk is in the bottle and receiving two replies that appear to reflect their different approaches to life—one says half-full and the other half-empty—seems relevant.[5]

The same condition can be interpreted very differently by different evaluators, and there is no definitive way of determining who is right. Which interpretation prevails is ultimately determined by political conflicts and compromises among the various actors.

Policy evaluation, like other stages of the policy process, is a political activity. It is naïve to believe that policy evaluation is always designed to reveal the effects of a policy. In fact, it is at times employed to disguise or conceal certain facts, facts which it is feared will show the government in poor light. It is also possible for governments to design the terms of evaluation in such a way as to lead to conclusions that would show it in a better light. Or, if it wants to change or scrap a policy, it can adjust the terms of the evaluation accordingly. Similarly, evaluations by those outside the government are not always designed to improve a policy, but often to criticize it to gain partisan political advantage or reinforce ideological postulates.

That is not to suggest that policy evaluation is an irrational or a completely political process, devoid of genuine intentions to find out about the functioning of a policy and its effects. It is rather to caution against undue reliance upon formal evaluation for drawing conclusions about a policy. To get the most out of policy evaluation, the limits of rationality and the political forces that shape it must clearly be recognized.

Perhaps the greatest benefit of policy evaluation is not the direct results it generates but the process of policy learning that accompanies it.[6] Policy actors learn constantly from the formal and informal evaluation of policies they are engaged in, and are led to modify their positions. The lessons they draw from their evaluation, based on both objective facts and subjective interpretations of the facts, lead to conclusions about both the means and the objectives of public policy. An integral part of this process is the discussion, debate, argument, and persuasion that occur constantly among policy actors.[7]

TYPES OF POLICY EVALUATION

At a general level, policy evaluations can be classified in three broad categories—administrative evaluation, judicial evaluation, and political evaluation—which differ in the way they are conducted, the actors they involve, and their effects.

Administrative Evaluation—Managerial Performance and Budgeting Systems

Administrative evaluation is the focus of many published academic studies on policy evaluation. It is undertaken within the government, occasionally by specialist agencies whose only task is evaluation of policies, but more often by financial, legal, and political overseers attached to existing government departments, specialized executive agencies, legislatures, and judiciaries. Private consultants may also be hired by the various branches and agencies of the government to conduct evaluation for a fee.

Administrative evaluation is usually, though not always, restricted to examining the efficient delivery of government services and attempting to determine whether or not 'value for money' is being achieved while still respecting principles of justice and democracy. It is intended to ensure that policies are accomplishing their expected goals at the least possible cost and with the least possible burden on individual citizens. This concern for efficiency lies behind managerial performance and personnel reviews, as well as the conduct of annual audits and the creation of budgeting systems that attempt to match goals and expenditures. Administrative evaluation requires collection of precise information on program delivery and its compilation in a standardized fashion to allow comparisons of costs and outcomes over time and across policy sectors. As such, these efforts are quite technical and increasingly sophisticated, although the increase in complexity is not necessarily matched by a similar increase in usefulness.

Administrative policy evaluations come in a variety of forms and differ widely in levels of sophistication and formality. Those undertaken by government agencies in the effort to minimize costs are generally of five different types: 1) Effort Evaluation; 2) Performance Evaluation; 3) Adequacy of Performance Evaluation; 4) Efficiency Evaluation; and 5) Process Evaluation.[8]

Effort evaluation attempts to measure the quantity of program inputs, that is, the amount of effort which governments put into accomplishing their goals. The input may be personnel, office space, communication, transportation, and so on–all of which are calculated in terms of the monetary costs they involve. The purpose of the evaluation is to establish a baseline for data which can be used for further evaluations of efficiency or quality of service delivery.

Performance evaluation examines program outputs rather than inputs. Examples of the output may be hospital beds or places in schools, number of patients seen or children taught. Performance evaluation's main aim is simply to determine what the policy is producing, regardless of the stated objectives. This type of evaluation produces data which are used as inputs into more comprehensive and intensive evaluations mentioned below.

Adequacy of performance evaluation (also known as *Effectiveness evaluation*) involves more complexity than simply adding up the program inputs or outputs; it is intended to find out if the program is doing what it is supposed to be doing. In this type of evaluation, the performance of a given program is compared to its intended goals in order to determine whether the program is meeting its goals and/or whether the goals need to be adjusted in the light of the program's accomplishments. On the basis of the findings recommendations for altering or changing programs or policies may be made. While this type of evaluation is most useful to policy-makers, it is also the most difficult to undertake. The information needs are immense and the level of sophistication required to carry out the process is higher than is generally available.

Efficiency evaluation attempts to assess the costs of a program and judge if the same amount and quality of outputs could be achieved more efficiently, that is, at a lower cost. Input and output evaluations are the building blocks of this form of evaluation, which is of great significance in the present climate of budgetary restraint. The difficulties involved in the more comprehensive effectiveness evaluation means that policy-makers must often content themselves with efficiency evaluations.

Finally, *process evaluations* examine the organizational methods, including rules and operating procedures, used to deliver programs. The objective is usually to see if the processes can be streamlined and made more efficient.[9] Towards this objective, implementation of a policy is usually broken down into discrete tasks, such as strategic planning, financial management, or clients' claim evaluation, and then one or more of the tasks is evaluated for efficiency, effectiveness, and/or accountability.

These different types of administrative evaluation of public policy have generated a variety of techniques. In the 1970s and 1980s these included such systems as the Program Planning and Budgeting System (PPBS) first developed at the Ford Motor Company and then adopted by the US Department of Defence and ultimately the entire US federal government; Zero-Based Budgeting (ZBB), a variant of PPBS which was implemented in the US and in many other countries; and Management by Objectives (MBO), a PPBS substitute developed at the Xerox Corporation and adopted by the Carter administration in the US.[10] These techniques have been utilized to varying degrees by different governments around the world. In addition, different countries and governments developed their own evaluative systems. Thus in Canada, for example, in the 1980s a new Policy and Expenditure Management System (PEMS) was established at the federal level, along with a new Office of the Controller General (OCG) mandated specifically to carry out evaluation research, while the federal Treasury Board tried to introduce a new government-wide Operational Performance Measurement System (OPMS).[11]

While much effort has been put into developing these techniques of policy evaluation, they have largely failed to overcome the limitations innate to ratio-nalist analysis.[12] The prerequisites for its success are too steep to be met in the rough-and-tumble world of public policy. Any emphasis on examining the extent to which policy objectives are accomplished by a program must contend with the reality that policies usually do not state their objectives precisely enough to permit rigorous analysis of whether they are being achieved. More-over, the same policy may be directed at achieving a variety of objectives, without indicating their relative priority, thus making it difficult to find out if a particular objective is being achieved.[13] Social and economic problems tend to be enormously inter-related, and it is virtually impossible to isolate and evalu-ate the effects of policies directed at them. Relatedly, each policy has effects on problems other than those intended, which a comprehensive evaluation must consider but which may make the task unmanageable. The difficulties involved in gathering reliable and usable information further aggravate the problem.

The limitations faced by administrative evaluation—and we have noted only a few—increase with the level of sophistication and comprehensiveness expected of them. Thus effectiveness evaluations, which would clearly be of most use to policy-makers, are the most difficult to undertake. Considering the difficulties, the enthusiasm for rational administrative evaluation has been on the wane in many industrialized countries since the early 1980s. Frustration with the difficulties involved in administrative evaluation, for example, led the Auditor-General of Canada to conclude in his 1983 Annual Report that 'a significant proportion of evaluation assessments did not form an adequate basis for sound advice.'[14] This is a polite way of saying that the evaluations were next to useless. Ten years later, the Auditor General's review of Program Evaluation in the Canadian federal government found numerous changes in form but little in substance. According to the Report, evaluations are:

less likely to be an important source of information in support of program and policy decisions addressing questions of continued relevance and cost-effectiveness. Evaluations are more likely to provide information for accountability purposes but are often partial. The most complete information available is related to operational effectiveness, the way a program is working.[15]

In order to broaden administrative evaluation, many governments have experimented with promoting public participation in the evaluation process. The intention is to head off challenges to policies on the grounds of a 'lack of consultation' with interested or affected members of the public. But usefulness and/or the legitimacy of public forums has been challenged on the grounds that only those capable of affording the costs of preparing briefs and travelling to the hearings can meaningfully participate, and that the hearings are more concerned with legitimizing conclusions already reached by the government than altering their content on the basis of input from the public.[16] These concerns have led in some consultations to the provision of funding to the participants. As sounding boards for discontent, these consultations can be an effective means of administrative evaluation.

Judicial Evaluation—Judicial Review and Administrative Discretion

A second major type of policy evaluation is not concerned with budgets, priorities, efficiencies, and expenditures, but with the legal issues relating to the manner in which government programs are implemented. Such evaluations are carried out by the judiciary and are concerned with possible conflicts between government actions and constitutional provisions or established standards of administrative conduct and individual rights.

The judiciary is entitled to review government actions either on its own initiative or when asked to do so by an individual or organization filing a case against a government agency in a court of law. The grounds for review differ considerably across countries but usually extend to the examination of the constitutionality of the policy being implemented, or whether its implementation or development violated principles of natural rights and/or justice in democratic societies. That is, the judges assess whether the policy was developed and implemented in a non-capricious and non-arbitrary fashion according to principles of due process and accepted administrative law.[17]

In many countries such as Canada or Britain, judicial courts concentrate on whether or not an inferior court, tribunal, or government agency has acted within its powers or jurisdiction. If it has, and if it has also abided with key principles of natural justice and has not acted in a capricious or arbitrary fashion, then its decision will stand subject to any existing statutory appeal provisions. Stated simply, judicial reviews in these two countries focus on issues or errors in law.[18] Since administrative courts in these countries do not review cases on the facts specific to the case, it means that as long as administrative agencies operate within their jurisdiction and according to principles of fundamental justice and due process, their decisions are unlikely to be overturned. American courts, on the other hand, have a very different constitutional role and are much more active, willing to consider errors of fact as well as errors of law in their evaluations of administrative behaviour.[19]

Political Evaluation—Consultations with Policy Subsystems and the Public

Political evaluation of government policy is undertaken by just about everyone with any interest in politics. Unlike administrative and judicial evaluations, political evaluations are usually neither systematic nor necessarily technically sophisticated. Indeed, many are inherently one-sided and biased. This does not undermine their significance, however, because their objective is rarely to improve the government's policy, but rather to support or challenge it. Political evaluations attempt to label a policy a success or failure, followed by demands for continuation or change. Praise or criticism at this stage can lead to new iterations of the cycle as governments attempt to respond to criticisms, or carry over lessons from past experiences into new or reformed policies.

While political evaluation is on-going it enters the policy process only on specialized occasions. One of the most important occasions in democracies is at election time, when citizens get their opportunity to render judgement on the government's performance. Votes at elections or referendums express the voters' informal evaluations of the efficiency and effectiveness of governments, their programs and policies. However, in most democratic countries, referendums or plebiscites on particular policies are relatively rare. While elections are held regularly, by their very nature they involve a range of issues which makes it inappropriate to draw conclusions about the voters' opinion on individual policies. When citizens express their preferences and sentiments at elections, the evaluation made is usually an aggregate judgement on a government's record rather than about the effectiveness or usefulness of specific policies. Nevertheless, public perceptions of the ineffectiveness or harmful effects of government activities can and do affect voting behaviour, a reality governments ignore at their electoral peril.

A more common type of political policy evaluation involves consultation with other members of the relevant policy subsystem. There are many mechanisms for such consultations, including setting up administrative forums for public hearings or establishing special consultative committees and task forces for consultation purposes. These can range from small meetings of less than a dozen participants and lasting several minutes, to multi-million dollar inquiries which hear thousands of individual briefs and can take years to complete.[20]

These political mechanisms for policy evaluation are usually capable of ascertaining the views of the members of the policy subsystem and affected public on specific policy issues. However, it is not certain that simply because these views have been made known, they will be reflected in the revision of government policy. Effectiveness often depends on whether the views heard are congruent with those of the government,[21] which in turn depends on the criteria utilized to assess success or failure of a particular policy or program.

POLICY EVALUATION—POLICY LEARNING

Fundamental to policy evaluation is its impact on effecting changes to the policy in question. After all, the implicit purpose of policy evaluation is to change the policy if it is deemed necessary as a result of undertaking the exercise. To understand the nexus between policy evaluation and policy change, we need to comprehend the larger process of learning.[22] From a learning perspective, public policy evaluation is conceived as an iterative process of active learning on the part of policy actors about the nature of policy problems and the solutions to them.[23]

Like other concepts in the policy science, there are different interpretations of what is meant by the term 'policy learning'.[24] Peter Hall adopts an instrumental definition of learning and argues that in the realm of public policy, learning serves the purpose of better goal attainment by governments. As he puts it, learning is a 'deliberate attempt to adjust the goals or techniques of policy in the light of the consequences of past policy and new information so as to better attain the ultimate objects of governance.'[25] Hugh Heclo, on the other hand, suggests that learning is a less conscious activity, often occurring as a government's response to some kind of societal or environmental stimulus. According to him, 'learning can be taken to mean a relatively enduring alteration in behaviour that results from experience; usually this alteration is conceptualized as a change in response made in reaction to some perceived stimulus.'[26] Learning, in Heclo's view, is what governments do in response to a new situation on the basis of their past experience.

The two definitions describe the nature of the relationship between policy learning and policy change, but differ substantially in their approach to the issue. For Hall, learning is a part of the normal public policy process in which decision-makers attempt to understand why certain initiatives may have succeeded while others failed. If policies change as a result of learning, the impetus for change originates within the formal policy process of the government. For Heclo, on the other hand, policy learning is seen as an activity undertaken by policy-makers largely in reaction to changes in external policy 'environments'. As the environment changes, policy-makers must adapt if their policies are to succeed. These two contrasting conceptions raise the critical theoretical question, whether policy learning occurs endogenously or exogenously. That is, whether learning is a process imposed upon policy-makers from outside the policy process, or whether it originates within the process as policy-makers attempt to refine and adapt their policies in the light of their past actions.

It is our contention that the use of similar terminology has somewhat disguised the fact that at least two separate aspects of policy learning should be clearly distinguished. The characteristics of these two different types of learning are set out in Figure 14.

■ Figure 14.
**Exogenous and Endogenous Concepts
of Policy Learning**

	Endogenous Learning	Exogenous Learning
Subject of Learning	*Small, Technically Specialized Policy Networks*	*Large, Publicly Participative Policy Communities*
Object of Learning	*Policy Settings, or Policy Instruments*	*Perception of Problem, or Policy Goals*

SOURCE: Adapted from Colin J. Bennett and Michael Howlett, 'The Lessons of Learning: Reconciling Theories of Policy Learning and Policy Change', *Policy Sciences* 25, 3 (1992): 275-94.

Endogenous learning takes place among small, focused policy networks; its objective is to learn about policy settings or policy instruments. In contrast, exogenous learning occurs in broad policy communities and may involve questioning the interpretation of the problem or the goal of the policy designed to address it.

The first type of endogenous learning, following Richard Rose, can be referred to as *lesson-drawing*.[27] This type of learning originates within the formal policy process and affects the choice of means or technique employed by policy-makers in their efforts to achieve their goals.[28] These lessons are likely to concern practical suggestions about different aspects of the policy cycle as it has operated in the past—for example, which policy instruments have 'succeeded' in which circumstances and which have 'failed', or which issues have enjoyed public support in the agenda-setting process and which have not.

Following Hall, the second refers to a more general type of learning, known as *social learning*. It originates outside the policy process and affects the constraints or capacities of policy-makers to alter or change society. The second form of learning is about the goals themselves. This is the most fundamental type of learning, which is accompanied by change in the thinking underlying the policy. The move in many countries in the 1980s towards privatization, and consideration of inflation as a more serious problem than unemployment, are instances of this second type of learning.[29]

Policy evaluations can involve either type of learning. Administrative evaluations virtually by definition occur within the established administrative institutions of government and tend to take the form of lesson-drawing—in both the negative and positive senses of the term. Both judicial and political evaluations are much more susceptible to changes in social values and mores and thus are means by which the lessons of social learning can be brought into the administrative process.

In the cases of both exogenous and endogenous learning, however, whether or not any lessons will be learned by policy-makers depends on their capacity to absorb new information. As Cohen and Levinthal have argued in the case of the private firm:

> the ability to evaluate and utilize outside knowledge is largely a function of the level of prior related knowledge. At the most elemental level, this prior knowledge includes basic skills or even a shared language but may also include knowledge of the most recent scientific or technological developments in a given field. Thus, prior related knowledge confers an ability to recognize the value of new information, assimilate it, and apply it to commercial ends. These abilities collectively constitute what we call a firm's 'absorptive capacity'.[30]

In a complex organization such as a firm or government, this implies that learning is a cumulative process and that the existing store of knowledge largely determines what will be done with any new information that flows into the organization. Critical in this regard are 'boundary-spanning' links between the organization and its environment, links receptive to new information and capable of disseminating it within the organization.

In the case of policy-making, this implies that the two relevant variables affecting the potential for evaluations to lead to learning and hence to some form of policy change are (1) the organizational capacity of the state, including especially its expertise in the subject area, and (2) the nature of the policy subsystem, especially whether and to what extent links exist between its state and societal members. Taken together, the two variables sets up further relationships between policy evaluation and policy learning (see Figure 15).

■ Figure 15.
**A Model of Policy Evaluation and
Learning Propensity**

		Links Between State and Societal Actors in Policy Subsystem	
		High	Low
State Administrative Capacity	High	*Social Learning*	*Lesson-Drawing*
	Low	*Formal Evaluations*	*Informal Evaluations*

SOURCE: Adapted from Wesley M. Cohen and Daniel A. Levinthal, 'Absorptive Capacity: A New Perspective on Learning and Innovation', *Administrative Science Quarterly* 35 (1990): 128-52.

In this model, a state must have a high administrative capacity for any true 'learning' activity to take place. If the state is the dominant actor, then a form of endogenous lesson-drawing can be expected to occur. If societal actors dominate the policy subsystem, then the conditions for social learning may be present. If, on the other hand, state administrative capacity is low, then one would expect simpler forms of formal and informal evaluations to occur without the necessity for any learning to actually occur within the state itself.

CONCLUSION

This chapter has set out the different forms of evaluation—administrative, judicial, and political—that take place in the public policy process. The literature on the subject, however, concentrates overwhelmingly on developing, criticizing, and refining the techniques of administrative evaluation. In the process, the limits of rational methods are often forgotten. Policy evaluation, like other stages of the policy cycle, is an inherently political exercise and must be recognized explicitly as such.

Analysts who do take the politics underlying policy evaluation into account see policy evaluation both as a continuation of the struggle over scarce resources or ideologies occurring in the political arena and as part of a process of learning in which policies develop and change largely on the basis of conscious recognition of past successes and failures and conscious efforts to emulate successes and avoid failures. This conception not only helps make sense of policy evaluation and removes it from the narrow technocratic concerns characteristic of administrative evaluation, but also helps to highlight the significant role played by all forms of evaluation in the ongoing policy process. Somewhat less obviously, this reconceptualization of policy evaluation as part of a process of policy learning also helps to clarify how and why policies change. This question of policy change is addressed more fully in Chapter Ten.

NOTES

1   Garry Brewer and Peter DeLeon, *The Foundations of Policy Analysis* (Homewood: Dorsey, 1983): 319-26.

2   Peter DeLeon, 'Policy Evaluation and Program Termination', *Policy Studies Review* 2, 4 (1983): 631-47.

3   David Nachmias, *Public Policy Evaluation* (New York: St Martin's Press, 1979): 4.

4   Charles W. Anderson, 'The Place of Principles in Policy Analysis', *American Political Science Review* 73, 3 (1979): 711-23; Donna H. Kerr, 'The Logic of "Policy" and Successful Policies', *Policy Sciences* 7, 3 (1976): 351-63; Ronald Manzer, 'Policy Rationality and Policy Analysis: The Problem of the Choice of Criteria for Decision-making' in O.P. Dwivedi (ed.), *Public Policy and Administrative Studies* (Guelph: University of Guelph, 1984): 27-40.

5   Helen M. Ingram and Dean E. Mann, 'Policy Failure: An Issue Deserving Analysis' in Helen M. Ingram and Dean E. Mann (eds), *Why Policies Succeed or Fail* (Beverly Hills: Sage, 1980): 852.

6   Jeffrey L. Pressman and Aaron Wildavsky, *Implementation* (Berkeley: University of California Press, 1984).

7   For a brilliant exposition of this point, see Giandomenico Majone, *Evidence, Argument, and Persuasion In The Policy Process* (New Haven: Yale University Press, 1989).

8   Edward A. Suchman, *Evaluative Research* (New York: Sage, 1967).

9   David Nachmias, *Public Policy Evaluation* (New York: St Martin's Press, 1979); Edward A. Suchman, *Evaluative Research* (New York: Sage, 1967); E.A. Suchman, *Social Sciences in Policy-Making* (Paris: Organization of Economic Co-operation and Development, 1979).

10   T.E. Reid, 'The Failure of PPBS: Real Incentives for the 1980s', *Optimum* 10, 4 (1979): 23-37; Harry Rogers, 'Management Control in the Public Service', *Optimum* 9, 3 (1978): 14-28; Aaron Wildavsky, 'Rescuing Policy Analysis From PPBS', *Public Administration Review* March-April (1969): 189-202.

11   Treasury Board Canada, *A Manager's Guide to Performance Measurement* (Ottawa: Treasury Board of Canada, 1976); Treasury Board Canada, *The Policy and Expenditure Management System* (Ottawa: Treasury Board of Canada, 1981); H.G. Rogers, M.A. Ulrick, and K.L. Traversy, 'Evaluation in Practice: The State of the Art in Canadian Governments', *Canadian Public Administration* 24, 3 (1981): 371-86.

12   R. Dobell and D. Zussman, 'An Evaluation System for Government: If Politics is Theatre then Evaluation is (mostly) Art', *Canadian Public Administration* 24, 3 (1981): 404-27; J.M. Jordan and S.L. Sutherland, 'Assessing the Results of Public Expenditure: Program Evaluation in the Federal Government', *Canadian Public Administration* 22, 6 (1979): 581-609.

13   Anthony Cahill and E. Sam Overman, 'The Evolution of Rationality in Policy Analysis' in Stuart S. Nagel (ed.), *Policy Theory and Policy Evaluation* (New York: Greenwood, 1990): 11-27; Robert Formaini, *The Myth of Scientific Public Policy* (Bowling Green, OH: Social Philosophy & Policy Center; New Brunswick, NJ: Transaction Publishers, 1990); Milbrey W. McLaughlin, 'Implementation Realities and Evaluation Design' in R. Lance Shotland and Melvin M. Mark (eds), *Social Science and Social Policy* (Beverly Hills: Sage, 1985): 96-120; Dennis J. Palumbo, *The Politics of Program Evaluation* (Beverly Hills: Sage, 1987); Carol H. Weiss, *Using Social Research in Public Policy Making* (Lexington: Lexington Books, 1977).

14   Canada, Auditor General of, *Annual Report of the Auditor General* (Ottawa: Parliament of Canada, 1983): 95.

15   Canada, Auditor General of, *Report of the Auditor General of Canada to the House of Commons* (Ottawa: Supply and Services Canada, 1993).

16   Jack De Sario and Stuart Langton, *Citizen Participation in Public Decision-Making* (Westport: Greenwood, 1987); Kenneth G. Englehart and Michael J. Trebilcock, *Public Participation in the Regulatory Process: The Issue of Funding* (Ottawa: Economic Council of Canada, 1981); Carole Pateman, *Participation and Democratic Theory* (Cambridge: Cambridge University Press, 1970); N. Wengert, 'Citizen Participation: Practice in Search of a Theory' in A.E. Utton (ed.), *Natural Resources for a Democratic Society: Public Participation in Decision-Making* (Boulder: Westview, 1976).

17   R. Dussault and L. Borgeat, *Administrative Law: A Treatise* (Toronto: Carswell, 1990); N. Finkelstein and B.M. Rogers (eds), *Recent Developments in Administrative Law* (Agin-

court, ON: Carswell, 1987); Gerald L. Gall, *The Canadian Legal System* (Toronto: Carswell, 1983); H.W.R. Wade, 'Anglo-American Administrative Law: Some Reflections', *Law Quarterly Review* 81 (1965): 357-79; H.W.R. Wade, 'Anglo-American Administrative Law: More Reflections', *Law Quarterly Review* 82 (1966): 226-52.

18 Louis L. Jaffe, *English and American Judges as Lawmakers* (Oxford: Clarendon, 1969).

19 Louis L. Jaffe, *Judicial Control of Administrative Action* (Boston: Little Brown, 1965).

20 G. Bruce Doern, 'The Role of Royal Commissions in the General Policy Process and in Federal-Provincial Relations', *Canadian Public Administration* 10, 4 (1967): 417-33; Liora Salter, *Public Inquiries in Canada* (Ottawa: Science Council of Canada, 1981); V. Seymour Wilson, 'The Role of Royal Commissions and Task Forces' in G. Bruce Doern and Peter Aucoin (eds), *The Structures of Policy-Making in Canada* (Toronto: Macmillan, 1971).

21 Thomas Dye, *Understanding Public Policy* (Englewood Cliffs: Prentice Hall, 1992) 353-75.

22 Jurgen Feick, 'Comparing Comparative Policy Studies—A Path Towards Integration?' *Journal of Public Policy* 12, 3 (1992): 257-86.

23 Ray C. Rist, 'The Preconditions for Learning: Lessons from the Public Sector' in F.L. Leeuw, R.C. Rist, and R.C. Sonnischen (eds), *Can Governments Learn: Comparative Perspectives on Evaluation and Organizational Learning* (New Brunswick, NJ: Transaction Publishers, 1994).

24 A variety of terms are utilized to describe this phenomena including 'policy learning', 'social learning', and 'government learning'. A fourth use, 'organizational learning', exists in the somewhat tangential field of organizational behaviour. See Paul A. Sabatier, 'An Advocacy Coalition Framework of Policy Change and the Role of Policy-Oriented Learning Therein', *Policy Sciences* 21, 2/3 (1988): 129-68; Peter A. Hall, 'Policy Paradigms, Social Learning and the State: The Case of Economic Policy Making in Britain', *Comparative Politics* 25, 3 (1993): 275-96; Lloyd S. Etheredge, 'Government Learning: An Overview' in S.L. Long (ed.), *The Handbook of Political Behavior* (New York: Plenum, 1981); George P. Huber, 'Organization Learning: The Contributing Processes and the Literatures', *Organization Science* 2, 1 (1991): 88-115.

25 Peter A. Hall, 'Policy Paradigms, Social Learning and the State: The Case of Economic Policy-making in Britain', *Comparative Politics* 25, 3 (1993): 278.

26 Hugh Heclo, *Modern Social Politics in Britain and Sweden: From Relief to Income Maintenance* (New Haven: Yale University Press, 1974): 306.

27 Richard Rose, 'Comparative Policy Analysis: The Program Approach' in M. Dogan (ed.), *Comparing Pluralist Democracies: Strains on Legitimacy* (Boulder: Westview Press, 1988): 219-41; Richard Rose, 'What is Lesson-Drawing?' *Journal of Public Policy* 11, 1 (1991): 3-30.

28 We tend to think of learning chiefly across time, within the confines of domestic historical actions; thus 'learning from experience' implies 'learning from one's own experience'. This is the dominant, possibly exclusive, meaning in oft-cited studies by Heclo and Hall. A recognition that has taken somewhat longer to affect the research of policy analysts is that states may not only learn from their own experiences, but also from the actions of other states. Various concepts have been employed to depict how policy makers from one country 'emulate', 'imitate', or 'draw lessons from' their counterparts abroad. As Rose points out, in any effort to reduce dissatisfaction, 'policymakers have three alternatives: to turn to their national past; to speculate about the future; or to seek lessons from current experience in

other places.' Richard Rose, 'What is Lesson-Drawing?' *Journal of Public Policy* 11, 1 (1991): 21. Learning in this sense can be both positive and negative. That is, learning is both about what to do, and about what not to do, so the same program can act as a model or exemplar for one country, and exactly the reverse for another. Colin Bennett and Michael Howlett, 'The Lessons of Learning: Reconciling Theories of Policy Learning and Policy Change', *Policy Sciences* 25, 3 (1992): 275-94. Yet, obviously, drawing negative lessons is very different from 'nonlearning'; the former denotes that policy-makers in one country examined the policy lessons of another, and decided to avoid that program of action; the latter suggests that they never knew about it. Hugh Heclo, *Modern Social Politics in Britain and Sweden: From Relief to Income Maintenance* (New Haven: Yale University Press, 1974).

29   Peter A. Hall, 'Policy Paradigms, Social Learning and the State: The Case of Economic Policy Making in Britain', *Comparative Politics* 25, 3 (1993): 275-96; M. Howlett and M. Ramesh, 'Patterns of Policy Instrument Choice: Policy Styles, Policy Learning and the Privatization Experience', *Policy Studies Review* 12, 1 (1993): 1-21.

30   Wesley M. Cohen, and Daniel A. Levinthal, 'Absorptive Capacity: A New Perspective on Learning and Innovation', *Administrative Science Quarterly* 35 (1990): 128-52.

FURTHER READING

Bennett, Colin and Michael Howlett, 'The Lessons of Learning: Reconciling Theories of Policy Learning and Policy Change', *Policy Sciences* 25, 3 (1992): 275-94.

Cohen, Wesley M. and Daniel A. Levinthal, 'Absorptive Capacity: A New Perspective on Learning and Innovation', *Administrative Science Quarterly* 35 (1990): 128-52.

DeLeon, Peter, 'Policy Evaluation and Program Termination', *Policy Studies Review* 2, 4 (1983): 631-47.

Hall, Peter A., 'Policy Paradigms, Social Learning and the State: The Case of Economic Policy-making in Britain', *Comparative Politics* 25, 3 (1993): 275-96.

Huber, George P., 'Organization Learning: The Contributing Processes and the Literatures', *Organization Science* 2, 1 (1991): 88-115.

May, Peter J., 'Policy Learning And Failure', *Journal Of Public Policy* 12, 4 (1992).

Mayne, John and Joe Hudson, 'Program Evaluation: An Overview' in Joe Hudson, John Mayne, and Ray Thomlinson (eds), *Action-Orientated Evaluation in Organizations*, Toronto: Wall and Emerson, 1992.

McLaughlin, Milbrey W., 'Implementation Realities And Evaluation Design' in R. Lance Shotland and Melvin M. Mark (eds), *Social Sciences And Social Policy*, Beverly Hills: Sage, 1985.

Palumbo, Dennis J., *The Politics of Policy Evaluation*, Beverly Hills: Sage, 1987

Rose, Richard, *Lesson-Drawing in Public Policy: A Guide to Learning Across Time and Space*, Chatham: Chatham House, 1993.

Sabatier, Paul, 'Knowledge, Policy-Oriented Learning, and Policy Change', *Knowledge: Creation, Diffusion, Utilization* 8 (1987): 649-92.

Part 4

CONCLUSION

Chapter 10

Policy Styles, Policy Paradigms, and the Policy Cycle

Studying a disaggregated and sequential model of the public policy process—the policy cycle—helps to underline the dynamic nature of public policy-making and to organize the otherwise difficult-to-grasp relations binding actors, institutions, and policy instruments together in the process. However, while disaggregation permits the detailed examination of the policy process, it begs the question of what that process looks like when all its constitutive pieces are reassembled. Is there a pattern or patterns of policy development and change which are in any sense typical of policy-making in liberal democratic states?[1] Or does each issue, sector, and country develop and change policies in a different and idiosyncratic fashion?[2] These are the issues we will examine in this concluding chapter.

NORMAL AND PARADIGMATIC PATTERNS OF POLICY CHANGE

It is our contention that two common types or patterns of change are typical of public policy-making. In Chapter Nine it was argued that there are two distinctive types of policy learning—'lesson-drawing' and 'social learning'—that affect the manner in which governments, members of policy subsystems, and the public evaluate and alter public policies. These two types of learning imply that at least two distinct patterns of policy change can be expected. One, the more 'normal' pattern, involves relatively minor tinkering with policies and programs on the basis of lesson-drawing. The second, a more substantial pattern, fundamentally transforms policies on the basis of social learning, and can be referred to as 'paradigmatic policy change'.

Normal Policy Change—Policy Style

There is a surprising degree of continuity in public policy, as evident in literally thousands of case studies of disparate policy sectors in a multitude of countries showing that most policies made by governments are in some way a continuation of past policies and practices. Thus the policy to expand access to education or health services usually consists of opening new schools, universities, or hospitals based on existing practices. Similarly, what are often portrayed as 'new' industrial and environment policies initiatives are often comprised of offering extra subsidies to existing industries or tightening the regulation of polluting activities.[3] We call this pattern of policy change 'normal' policy-making.

This pattern of policy change can be explained in several ways, but most analyses attribute continuity in policy-making to the fact that the same set of actors is typically involved in the policy process over a long period of time. In his analysis of 'incremental' decision-making, Lindblom attributed a propensity for policy change to analysis of the marginal differences between existing and proposed policy options; policy-makers must bargain among themselves to arrive at a decision, and therefore are unlikely to overturn agreements based on past negotiations and compromises.[4] Baumgartner and Jones argued that subsystems tend to construct policy monopolies in which the interpretation and general approach to a subject are more or less fixed. Only when a monopoly is broken by the emergence of new members or subsystems would one expect a policy to change in any significant sense of the term.[5] Both of these interpretations suggest that in normal circumstances policy problems are dealt with within the context of the existing approach to the subject in question, or what some studies describe as a *policy style.*

The first users of the term argued that each country or jurisdiction had a peculiar pattern of policy-making. It was soon found that the concept was more appropriately focused at the sectoral level since distinctive patterns of policy-making were found to exist at that level rather than at the national one.[6] Some deal with long-term patterns in details of policies, such as the rigid and legalistic nature of American environmental regulations, compared to the flexibility and self-regulation that characterize their counterparts in Britain.[7] Others have found patterns at a broader level, such as the American preference for regulation in instances when other countries employ public enterprises, as in the area of public utilities.[8]

The most prominent studies of policy styles to date have classified styles in terms of the twin dimensions of a government's typical problem-solving methodology and the pattern of its relationship with societal groups. Richardson, Gustafsson, and Jordan—who together have done the most to develop the concept—define a policy style as 'the interaction between (a) the government's approach to problem solving and (b) the relationship between government and other actors in the policy process'.[9] They mention 'anticipatory/active' and 'reactive' as the two general approaches to problem-solving. Relationships are similarly divided into two categories: 'consensus' and 'imposition' relationships (see Figure 16). According to them, German policy style is anticipatory and based on consensus, whereas British style is characterized by reactiveness, though also based on consensus. French policy style is anticipatory, but effected

■ Figure 16.
⌐ **An Early Model of National Policy Styles**

	Dominant Approach to Problem-Solving	
	Anticipatory	Reactive
Relationship Between Government and Society		
Consensus	German 'Rationalist Consensus' Style	British 'Negotiation' Style
Imposition	French 'Concertation' Style	Dutch 'Negotiation and Conflict' Style

SOURCE: Adapted from Jeremy Richardson, Gunnel Gustafsson, and Grant Jordan, 'The Concept of Policy Style' in *Policy Styles in Western Europe*, ed. J.J. Richardson. London: George Allen and Unwin, 1982.

through imposition rather than consensus. In contrast, Dutch policy style is both reactive and impositional.

These simple classifications do not, however, do justice to the complexity of the subject matter they are intended to describe.[10] No government is entirely active or reactive, nor does any government always work through either consensus or imposition. The model's parsimony is clearly at the expense of analytical usefulness. A better way to conceptualize a government's approach to problem-solving would be to conceive it in terms of all the variables affecting public policy at each stage of the policy cycle, without presuming the style in advance. The components of a policy style thus conceived are set out in Figure 17.

At all stages of the policy cycle, the nature of the policy subsystem is a crucial variable. In agenda setting, the extent of public support for the definition of a policy problem is a significant variable in identifying typical patterns of agenda-setting, along with the question of whether the state or societal members of a subsystem dominated or initiated debate on the subject. In policy formulation the role of policy subsystems is crucial in defining the options placed before decision-makers. The factors affecting their role include whether or not there is a dominant or hegemonic set of ideas circulating within the subsystem, whether state and societal actors are equally united around a certain idea or set of ideas, and how many network participants there are and whether they are led by their state or societal components. At the decision-making stage, the complexity of the subsystem, that is, whether or not it is characterized by multiple membership, and what sorts of constraints decision-makers operate under, are important variables in explaining the typical pattern of government decision-

Figure 17.
Components of a Policy Style

Elements Which Together Form a Policy Style

Policy Cycle Stage				
Agenda-Setting				
(Model Followed)	*Outside Initiation*	*Inside Initiation*	*Consolidation*	*Mobilization*
Policy Formulation				
(Type of Policy Community)	*Hegemonic*	*Imposed*	*Leaderless*	*Anarchic*
(Type of Policy Network)	*Bureaucratic/ Participatory Statist*	*Clientelistic/ Captured*	*Triadic/ Corporatist*	*Pluralist/ Issue*
Decision-Making				
(Decision-Making Style)	*Incremental*	*Satisfycing*	*Optimizing*	*Rational*
Policy Implementation				
(Instrument Preferences)	*Market-Based*	*Regulatory/ Direct*	*Exhortory/ Subsidy*	*Voluntary/ Community/ Family*
Policy Evaluation				
(Propensity for Learning)	*Lesson- Drawing*	*Formal Evaluations*	*Social Learning*	*Informal Evaluations*

making. At the stage of implementation, significant variables are policy sub-system complexity and the administrative capacity of the state. Both these variables also figure prominently in the discussion of policy evaluation, as the two types of learning identified involve different types of subsystems. Whether or not learning from evaluations occurs at all is tied to state administrative capacity.

Hence, it should be apparent that the two most significant variables affecting a policy style are (1) the structure of the relevant policy subsystem, including the range of ideas and actors found within it, their relations to each other, and the extent to which they enjoy public support, and (2) state autonomy, including its administrative capacity and the nature of the resource constraints under which it operates. However, since these variables manifest themselves sectorally and through each of the five stages of the policy cycle, the range of possible variations in policy styles they permit is too large to catalogue in a simple matrix. Rather, the exact combination of elements forming a country's or sector's policy style must be arrived at empirically and described in detail.

The resulting characterization will not be elegant or parsimonious, but it will accurately depict the policy style in the country or sector in question.

A Punctuated Equilibrium Model of Paradigmatic Policy Change

The second type of typical policy change is less frequent and involves a dramatic change in policy style. As the discussion in Chapter Nine suggested, this form of change is likely to result from some process of social learning altering relatively long-lasting policy subsystems. Some authors have likened this second process of change in policy communities to the general process of change in scientific communities, a phenomenon associated with shifts in the major elements of scientific thought, or 'paradigms'.[11]

In this sense, a *paradigm* is a common epistemological vision shared by members of some knowledge-based community—such as physicists or economists, and even policy-makers—to the extent that knowledge is a significant factor binding them together and shaping their behaviour.[12] According to the American philosopher of science, Thomas Kuhn, not only do the ideas on which scientific and other knowledge-based communities change, but they change in a particular fashion. In his view, scientific progress is revolutionary and not, as many philosophers and historians of science argued in the past, evolutionary in nature. As he put it in his book *The Structure of Scientific Revolutions*, 'Led by a new paradigm, scientists adopt new instruments and look in new places. Even more important, during revolutions scientists see new and different things when looking with familiar instruments in places they have looked before . . . we may want to say that after a revolution scientists are responding to a different world.'[13] Paradigm shifts represent such a fundamental break from the past that they cannot possibly be considered evolutionary. As Derek Phillips has noted:

> Since Kuhn defines paradigms as closed logical systems, change can only be revolutionary—all at once. The entire paradigm must be totally accepted or totally rejected, there is no middle way. . . . [By] formulating paradigms as coherent wholes, all of whose parts 'hold together' Kuhn has forced upon us a distinction between normal and revolutionary phases in sciences.[14]

Paradigms in Kuhn's work are thus linked to a particular pattern of change. This is a specific process of change which has elsewhere been termed a *punctuated equilibrium* model. In this model, change is envisioned as involving alternations between long periods of stability involving incremental adaptations and brief periods of revolutionary upheaval.[15] Scientific revolutions punctuate long-standing periods of equilibrium, so to speak, and lead to substantial changes in the way a phenomenon is perceived.

Exactly why this pattern of change occurs is controversial. Some explanations are essentially metaphysical, but one of the more convincing explanations is that individuals in any epistemic community hold some sort of a 'deep structure' of basic values and beliefs which inhibits anything but marginal changes from occurring. This deep structure shapes our understanding of a phenomenon by directing our attention to a particular set of relations, while ignoring others. As Gersick has argued, the deep structure 'generates a strong inertia, first to prevent the system from generating alternatives outside its own boundaries, then to pull any deviations that do occur back into line. According to this logic, the deep structure must first be dismantled, leaving the system temporarily disorganized, in order for any fundamental change to be accomplished.'[16]

But what causes, however infrequently, changes in deep structures to occur? Kuhn's work highlights endogenous sources of change. He suggests that accumulation of anomalies, or observations of occurrences which cannot be explained adequately by the existing paradigm, leads to efforts to understand the phenomenon in an entirely new fashion, resulting eventually in the emergence of a new paradigm.[17] This account begs several questions, including: why do some members of scientific communities attempt to reconcile anomalies while others formulate new paradigms? And why do some resist a new paradigm while others readily adopt it?

Although this is an under-theorized aspect of Kuhn's work, Jack Walker has suggested—drawing on work in the sociology of science undertaken by Robert K. Merton—that the individual community members' personal motivations, unrelated to the pursuit of 'objective' knowledge, may account for the variations. He argues that the members' desire for prestige and recognition within the scientific community play a large part in this process. 'Scientists are said to be involved in an elaborate system of social exchange in which they provide information and new ideas and are repaid with professional notoriety and recognition.'[18] As inquiry within the existing paradigm matures, creative individuals are led to look for new challenges, weakening the prevailing framework and thus rendering the ground hospitable for the emergence of a new framework. The entry of new scholars into the discipline leads to similar pressures for challenging existing ideas and replacing them with new, as each scholar looks for fresh opportunities for career advancement.

Thus politics is very much present in this process. As Hernes has argued, 'acceptance is to a large extent a question of power and a conversion process which shifts professional allegiances over time.'[19] The process of paradigmatic change is complete when the new paradigm is perceived as normal, or hegemonic, by the members of the community in question.[20]

Although the term paradigm was developed originally to describe developments in the 'hard' sciences, it was later applied to social sciences as well. In the social sciences the concept bears a close relationship to traditional philosophical notions of 'ideologies' or to more recent sociological notions of 'discourses' or 'discursive regimes'. Both are relevant to the discussion of the applicability of the notion of paradigms to public policy-making.[21]

According to Jane Jenson a *societal paradigm* is

> a shared set of interconnected premises which make sense of many social relations. Every paradigm contains a view of human nature, a definition of basic and proper forms of social relations among equals and among those in relationships of hierarchy, and specification of relations among institutions as well as a stipulation of the role of such institutions.[22]

It is thus both a descriptive and prescriptive account of the relationships among actors and institutions. What makes the concept of a paradigm useful to social scientists is not just its description of underlying ideas and beliefs, but the way it is used to visualize changes in them.

The notion of a paradigm shift as a metaphor for describing significant policy change is a recent development in the discipline, capturing fundamental long-term change in the underlying beliefs, values, and attitudes towards the nature of public problems and the solutions to them on the part of policy-makers.[23] A strong trend in this literature is to discuss the process of change in terms similar to changes in scientific paradigm.[24]

Peter Hall, who has perhaps done the most to develop the concept in recent times, defines a *policy paradigm* as establishing

> the broad goals behind policy, the related problems or puzzles that policy-makers have to solve to get there, and, in large measure, the kind of instruments that can be used to attain these goals. Like a gestalt, this framework is all the more powerful because it is largely taken for granted and rarely subject to scrutiny as a whole. It seems likely that policy-makers in all fields are guided by some such paradigm, even though the complexity and coherence of the paradigm may vary considerably across fields.[25]

A policy paradigm is thus an intellectual construct intimately linked to policy subsystems. It is essentially a set of ideas held by relevant policy subsystem members—a doctrine or school of thought such as Keynesianism or Monetarism in the case of economic policy subsystems—which shapes the broad goals policy-makers pursue, the way they perceive public problems, and the kinds of solutions they consider for adoption. Its effects are pervasive because policy-makers take it so for granted that they are often not even aware of its influences. While a considerable amount of thinking usually goes into the formation of a paradigm, it is not always coherent, reflecting the limitations innate to the study of public problems and the complex compromises public policy-makers must contend with.

Hall accepts the general notion that policy change proceeds in a 'punctuated equilibrium' fashion and accepts the Kuhnian argument that the discovery of 'anomalies' eventually undermines existing paradigms and leads to their replacement. Initially, policy-makers stretch the paradigm to the limit to cover the discrepancies between paradigmatic expectations and empirical reality, but eventually this becomes impossible, precipitating a search for a new paradigm.[26]

Unlike Kuhn, however, and of some significance for the application of the term to the policy sciences, Hall argues that the transition between paradigms results from a sociological rather than a purely intellectual process. Like Walker, Hall suggests that the length of a transitionary period will depend on how deeply held is the existing order, as well as upon the level of opposition apologists for the old order can mount. Hall's model of this process of change in a policy paradigm is set out in Figure 18.

■ Figure 18.
The Process of Policy Paradigm Change

Stage	Characteristics
1. Paradigm Stability	*in which the reigning orthodoxy is institutionalized and policy adjustments are made, largely by a closed group of experts and officials.*
2. Accumulation of Anomalies	*in which 'real-world' developments occur which are neither anticipated nor fully explicable in terms of the reigning orthodoxy.*
3. Experimentation	*in which efforts are made to stretch the existing paradigm to account for the anomalies.*
4. Fragmentation of Authority	*in which experts and officials are discredited and new participants challenge the existing paradigm.*
5. Contestation	*in which debate spills into the public arena and involves the larger political process, including electoral and partisan considerations.*
6. Institutionalization of a New Paradigm	*in which, after a shorter or longer period of time, the advocates of a new paradigm secure positions of authority and alter existing organizational and decision-making arrangements in order to institutionalize the new paradigm.*

SOURCE: Adapted from Peter A. Hall, 'Policy Paradigms, Social Learning and the State: The Case of Economic Policy Making in Britain', *Comparative Politics* 25, 3 (1993): 275-96.

The figure shows that the period of an entrenched paradigm has two stages: one in which the paradigm is largely unchallenged, and one in which challenges begin to build up. The period of transition also involves two stages, one in which the challenges lead to some tentative or experimental changes, and a second in which experts disagree openly with each other. The period in which a new paradigm exists also has two stages: one in which the disagreement between experts goes public and the relevant policy community is dramatically enlarged, and a second in which the new paradigm is institutionalized.

In Hall's view, competition between paradigms is likely to be resolved not simply by the endogenous effects of scientific inquiry and intellectual debate, but in terms of 'exogenous shifts in the power of key actors and a broader strug-gle among competing interests in the community'.[27] Jane Jenson and Paul Sabatier take positions similar to that of Hall. While Jenson, like Hall, does not specify the exogenous variables responsible for the changes, she suggests that external 'crises'—economic, social, political—are responsible for paradigm changes.[28] Sabatier is more precise in his efforts to define these exogenous vari-ables. He suggests that significant changes in policy subsystems occur ulti-mately due to shifts in advocacy coalitions: individuals within subsystems holding similar core beliefs. While this can occur through endogenous learning or the development and perception of anomalies, changes in core beliefs must await favourable external events.[29] These events include: (1) change in socio-economic conditions and technology; (2) changes in systemic governing coali-tions; and (3) policy decisions and impacts from other subsystems.[30]

However, Sabatier and his colleagues also recognize that internal subsystem behaviour must be such that the opportunities presented by external shocks lead to internal change.[31] These changes affect the resources—'money, expertise, number of supporters, and legal authority'[32]—available to the subsystem mem-bership and are reflected in alterations in their behaviour.[33] Baumgartner and Jones also argue that the behaviour of non-subsystem members is the crucial variable, as those who fail to benefit or who disagree with the direction policy has taken will attempt to link their interests and ideas to other institutions and settings. This activity, they argue, can sometimes allow an issue to be expanded along with subsystem membership and thereby result in a significant change in how a problem is dealt with.[34]

Thus a paradigm shift ultimately occurs because anomalies build up between the paradigm and the reality it claims to describe. The change is pre-cipitated by innovative individuals—described as 'policy entrepreneurs'—within the subsystem responding to the changed circumstances and to their own career ambitions. The process of paradigmatic change is initially quite unstable as con-flicting ideas emerge and compete for dominance. The process is complete, at least until the next upheaval, when a new set of ideas wins out over the others and is accepted by most, or at least the most powerful, members of the policy subsystem. The hegemony of the new paradigm is eventually established and its legitimacy is recognized to the point that it appears normal and alternatives that do not fit appear unusual.

A much-cited example of change in policy paradigm pertains to economic policy in the years following World War Two, when Keynesianism emerged as the dominant paradigm. Unlike the previous era in which the state was seen as having little direct role in determining the level of economic activity, Keyne-sianism (the term refers to Keynes' ideas in practice, rather than what he actu-ally said and wrote) promoted an active government role in the management of the economy.[35] The challenge for the policy-makers was to devise ways of manipulating market processes in order to create jobs and raise the population's standard of living. A range of compulsory and mixed policy instruments—such as public enterprises, regulations, and subsidies—was used to put economic policies into effect; voluntary instruments were relatively less prominent. While there were some staunch critics of the overall direction of government policies, the main thrust of the policies was broadly accepted by the policy-makers as well as the politically-involved segments of the population.

It has been argued that the 1980s was a period of similar paradigmatic change, when Monetarism replaced Keynesianism as the dominant paradigm. It emerged in the context of high unemployment and inflation throughout much of the 1970s and the Keynesian policies' perceived inability to adequately address these concerns. Unlike Keynesianism, which favours an expanded role for the state in economic affairs, Monetarism sought to 'roll back the state'. It regarded the primary policy goal as maintaining low inflation rather than full employment, leaving the latter largely to market forces. It sought to conceptualize public problems in terms of their economic costs and benefits. Voluntary instruments involving market, community, and family are preferred to compulsory instruments in implementing policy, reflecting Monetarism's scepticism toward state intervention.[36]

CONCLUSION—POLICY SUBSYSTEMS, POLICY LEARNING, AND POLICY CHANGE

The two types of policy change—Normal and Paradigmatic—discussed here differ in many respects. Both, however, are improvements upon the notion of the staged-sequential model of policy development and change associated with conventional models of the policy cycle.

The key actors in both forms of change are policy subsystems. In the case of normal policy development, the critical activity undertaken by a subsystem is a form of policy learning—'lesson-drawing'—which allows for changes to occur within an established policy style without altering the fundamental elements of that policy. Change, in this sense, is evolutionary and 'path-dependent'.

Paradigmatic policy changes represent a significant, though not necessarily total, break from the past in terms of the overall policy goals, the understanding of public problems, the solutions to them, and the policy instruments used to put decisions into effect. Such deep changes occur in circumstances when normal changes to the policy come to be regarded as insufficient for the task at hand. By their very nature, their occurrence is infrequent, but when they do take place, their effects are felt far beyond the confines of the policy in question.

In the case of these more dramatic, revolutionary paradigm changes, the main agents are still members of policy subsystems, which are to public policy what scientific communities are to the natural sciences. In the course of interaction among themselves and in their day-to-day dealings with a public problem, members of policy subsystems develop a common episteme, world view, or paradigm.[37] While minor adaptation and adjustment of their views on the basis of their experience and new information is endemic to the policy process and is a component of lesson-drawing, subsystems' understanding of public problems and solutions to them are remarkably durable. The common understanding obtaining in a policy subsystem can at times break down, however, setting the stage for the emergence of a new approach to the problem which may in turn lead to the establishment of a new paradigm.

NOTES

1   Margaret Weir, 'Ideas and the Politics of Bounded Innovation' in S. Steinmo, K. Thelen, and F. Longstreth (eds), *Structuring Politics: Historical Institutionalism in Comparative Analysis* (Cambridge: Cambridge University Press, 1992): 188-216.

2   Jenny Stewart, 'Corporatism, Pluralism and Political Learning: A Systems Approach', *Journal of Public Policy* 12, 3 (1992): 243-56.

3   Nelson W. Polsby, *Political Innovation in America: The Politics of Policy Initiation* (New Haven: Yale University Press, 1984).

4   Michael T. Hayes, *Incrementalism and Public Policy* (New York: Longmans, 1992).

5   Frank R. Baumgartner and Bryan D. Jones, *Agendas and Instability in American Politics* (Chicago: University of Chicago Press, 1993).

6   Gary P. Freeman, 'National Styles and Policy Sectors: Explaining Structured Variation', *Journal of Public Policy* 5, 4 (1985): 467-96; William D. Coleman, 'Policy Convergence in Banking: A Comparative Study', *Political Studies* 42 (1994): 274-92.

7   Vogel, *National Styles of Regulation* (Ithaca: Cornell University Press, 1986).

8   Carolyn Tuohy, *Policy and Politics in Canada: Institutionalized Ambivalence* (Philadelphia: Temple University Press, 1992); David Vogel, *National Styles of Regulation: Environment Policy in Great Britain and the United States* (Ithaca: Cornell University Press, 1986).

9   Jeremy Richardson, Gunnel Gustafsson, and Grant Jordan, 'The Concept of Policy Style' in Jeremy J. Richardson (ed.), *Policy Styles in Western Europe* (London: George Allen and Unwin, 1982): 13.

10   Freeman, 'National Styles and Policy Sectors', *Journal of Public Policy* 5, 4 (1985): 467-96.

11   In this sense, the concept of a paradigm owes its modern origin to Thomas Kuhn's work on the nature of scientific learning and the development of scientific theories. In Kuhn's original formulation, the exact contours of a paradigm were unclear, extending from the limited sense of a specific scientific theory about a phenomenon to the more general sense of a pre-scientific inquisitive *weltanschauung* or 'world-view' which allowed science to be carried out at all. Margaret Masterman, 'The Nature of a Paradigm' in Imre Lakatos and Alan Musgrave (eds), *Criticism and the Growth of Knowledge* (London: Cambridge University Press, 1970). In his later works Kuhn was more specific, arguing that a paradigm was synonymous with the notion of a 'disciplinary matrix'. It was 'what the members of a scientific community, and they alone, share'. Thomas S. Kuhn, 'Second Thoughts on Paradigms' in Frederick Suppe (ed.), *The Structure of Scientific Theories* (Chicago: University of Chicago Press, 1974): 463.

12   Burkart Holzner and John H. Marx, *Knowledge Application: The Knowledge System in*

Society (Allyn and Bacon: Boston, 1979); Allen W. Imershein, 'The Epistemological Bases of Social Order: Toward Ethnoparadigm Analysis' in D.R. Heise (ed.), *Sociological Methodology* (San Francisco: Jossey-Bass, 1977).

13   Thomas S. Kuhn, *The Structure of Scientific Revolutions* (Chicago: University of Chicago Press, 1962): 110.

14   Derek L. Phillips, 'Paradigms and Incommensurability', *Theory and Society* 2, 1 (1975): 56.

15   This was not the first use of such a model of change, of course. It corresponds quite closely with the notion of dialectical change found in the works of Hegel and his followers, including, most obviously, Karl Marx. See Gudmund Hernes, 'Structural Change in Social Processes', *American Journal of Sociology* 82, 3 (1976): 513-47.

16   Connie J.G. Gersick, 'Revolutionary Change Theories: A Multilevel Exploration of the Punctuated Equilibrium Paradigm', *Academy of Management Review* 16, 1 (1991): 19.

17   Kuhn, *The Structure of Scientific Revolutions*: 52.

18   Jack L. Walker, 'The Diffusion of Knowledge and Policy Change: Toward A Theory of Agenda-Setting', Paper presented to the Annual Meeting of the American Political Science Association, Chicago, 1974: 8-9.

19   Hernes, 'Structural Change in Social Processes': 538.

20   Connie J.G. Gersick, 'Revolutionary Change Theories: 10-36; Jane Jenson, 'Paradigms and Political Discourse: Protective Legislation in France and the United States Before 1914', *Canadian Journal of Political Science* 22, 2 (1989): 235-58.

21   Michel Foucault, 'The Discourse on Language' in Michel Foucault (ed.), *The Archaeology of Knowledge* (New York: Pantheon, 1972): 215-35.

22   Jenson, 'Paradigms and Political Discourse': 238-9.

23   Murray J. Edelman, *Constructing the Political Spectacle* (Chicago: University of Chicago Press, 1988); Stephen Hilgartner and Charles L. Bosk, 'The Rise and Fall of Social Problems: A Public Arenas Model', *American Journal of Sociology* 94, 1 (1981): 53-78; Joseph W. Schneider, 'Social Problems Theory: The Constructionist View', *Annual Review of Sociology* 11 (1985): 209-29.

24   Gersick, 'Revolutionary Change Theories': 10-36; Hernes, 'Structural Change in Social Processes': 513-47; Thomas S. Kuhn, *The Structure of Scientific Revolutions*.

25   Peter A. Hall, 'Policy Paradigms, Experts, and the State: The Case of Macroeconomic Policy-Making in Britain' in Stephen Brooks and A.-G. Gagnon (eds), *Social Scientists, Policy, and the State* (New York: Praeger, 1990): 59.

26   Hall, 'Policy Paradigms, Experts, and the State': 61. Although Kuhn argued in his earlier work that a paradigm would change quickly from old to new paradigm, in his later works he suggested that there was a transitional period between the two phases. Kuhn, 'Second Thoughts on Paradigms' in Frederick Suppe (ed.), *The Structure of Scientific Theories* (Chicago: University of Chicago Press, 1974).

27   Hall, 'Policy Paradigms, Experts, and the State': 61.

28   Jenson, 'Paradigms and Political Discourse': 235-58.

29   Paul Sabatier, 'Knowledge, Policy-Oriented Learning, and Policy Change', *Knowledge: Creation, Diffusion, Utilization* 8, 4 (1987): 671. Sabatier does not clearly state what constitutes 'secondary' as opposed to 'core' aspects of the policy in question. This is made more complicated by his later references to 'Deep (normative) Core' beliefs, 'Near (policy) Core' beliefs, and 'Secondary' aspects. Paul A. Sabatier, 'An Advocacy Coalition Framework of Policy Change and the Role of Policy-Oriented Learning Therein', *Policy Sciences* 21, 2/3 (1988): 145.

30 Sabatier, 'Knowledge, Policy-Oriented Learning, and Policy Change': 657-8.
31 See also the modifications to this position contained in Paul Sabatier, 'Policy Change Over A Decade or More' and Paul Sabatier and Hank Jenkins-Smith, 'The Advocacy Coalition Framework: Assessment, Revisions, and Implications for Scholars and Practitioners' in *Policy Change and Learning: An Advocacy Coalition Approach*, eds P.A. Sabatier and H.C. Jenkins-Smith (Boulder: Westview, 1993).
32 Sabatier, 'Knowledge, Policy-Oriented Learning, and Policy Change': 664.
33 Hank C. Jenkins-Smith, Gilbert K. St Clair, and Brian Woods, 'Explaining Change in Policy Subsystems: Analysis of Coalition Stability and Defection over Time', *American Journal of Political Science* 35, 4 (1991): 851-80.
34 Frank R. Baumgartner and Bryan D. Jones, 'Agenda Dynamics and Policy Subsystems', *Journal of Politics* 53, 4 (1991): 1044-74.
35 Peter A. Hall, 'Introduction' in Peter A. Hall (ed.), *The Political Power of Economic Ideas: Keynesianism Across Nations* (Princeton: Princeton University Press, 1989): 3-26.
36 Wilfred L. David, *The IMF Policy Paradigm: The Macroeconomics of Stabilization, Structural Adjustment, and Economic Development* (New York: Praeger, 1985). It is possible to argue that paradigm changes have also occurred in many other areas of social life, such as the areas of social policy or transportation policy. Thus, for example, crime is being defined increasingly as an instance of lawlessness, rather than as a manifestation of lack of economic and education opportunities for certain sections of the society. Solutions are being sought in increased expenditures on policing and keeping criminals in prisons rather than alleviating poverty. See John Martin Gillroy and Maurice Wade (eds), *The Moral Dimensions of Public Policy Choice: Beyond the Market Paradigm* (Pittsburgh, PA: University of Pittsburgh Press, 1992). See also Ian Masser, Ove Sviden, and Michael Wegener, 'From Growth to Equity and Sustainability: Paradigm Shift in Transport Planning?' *Futures* 23, 6 (1992): 539-58.
37 Patrick Kenis, 'The Pre-Conditions for Policy Networks: Some Findings From a Three Country Study on Industrial Re-Structuring' in B. Marin and R. Mayntz (eds), *Policy Networks: Empirical Evidence and Theoretical Considerations* (Boulder: Westview Press, 1991): 297-330.

FURTHER READING

Baumgartner, Frank R. and Bryan D. Jones. 'Agenda Dynamics and Policy Subsystems', *Journal of Politics* 53, 4 (1991): 1044-74.

Castles, Francis G., 'The Dynamics of Policy Change: What Happened to the English-speaking Nations in the 1980s', *European Journal of Political Research* 18, 5 (1990): 491-513.

Gersick, Connie J.G., 'Revolutionary Change Theories: A Multilevel Exploration of the Punctuated Equilibrium Paradigm', *Academy of Management Review* 16, 1 (1991): 10-36.

Hall, Peter A., 'Policy Paradigms, Social Learning and the State: The Case of Economic Policy-making in Britain', *Comparative Politics* 25, 3 (1993): 275-96.

Hernes, Gudmund, 'Structural Change in Social Processes', *American Journal of Sociology* 82, 3 (1976): 513-47.

Howlett, Michael, 'Policy Paradigms and Policy Change: Lessons from the Old and New Canadian Policies Towards Aboriginal Peoples', *Policy Studies Journal* 22, 4 (1994): 631-51.

Jenkins-Smith, Hank C., Gilbert K. St Clair, and Brian Woods, 'Explaining Change in Policy Subsystems: Analysis of Coalition Stability and Defection over Time', *American Journal of Political Science* 35, 4 (1991): 851-80.

Jenson, Jane, 'Paradigms and Political Discourse: Protective Legislation in France and the United States Before 1914', *Canadian Journal of Political Science* 22, 2 (1989): 235-58.

Kuhn, Thomas S., *The Structure of Scientific Revolutions*, Chicago: University of Chicago Press, 1962.

Kuhn, Thomas S., 'Second Thoughts on Paradigms' in F. Suppe (ed.), *The Structure of Scientific Theories*, Urbana: University of Illinois Press, 1974.

Rochefort, David A. and Roger W. Cobb, 'Problem Definition, Agenda Access, and Policy Change', *Policy Studies Journal* 21, 1 (1993): 56-71.

Chapter 11

Afterword—Still Studying Public Policy

Public policy is a highly complex matter, consisting of a series of decisions, involving a large number of actors operating within the confines of an amorphous, yet inescapable, institutional set-up, and employing a variety of instruments. Its complexity poses grave difficulties for those seeking a comprehensive understanding of the subject.

One of the simplest and most effective ways to deal with this complexity has been to break down the public policy-making process into series of discrete but related sub-processes, together forming a continuing cycle. The stages in the cycle correspond to the five stages in applied problem-solving, whereby problems are recognized, solutions are proposed, a solution is chosen, the chosen solution is put into effect, and finally the outcomes are monitored and evaluated. In the policy process, these stages are manifested as agenda-setting, policy formulation, decision-making, policy implementation, and policy evaluation.

Of course, the public policy process is not nearly as tightly sequential or goal-driven as the cycle model makes it appear. Policy actors, it is justifiably argued, do not go about making and implementing policies in the systematic manner the model seems to suggest. While this is no doubt a legitimate complaint against the 'stages' conception of public policy, it is also true that the limitation can be mitigated to a large extent with caution and diligence in its application. The advantage of employing the cycle model is that it facilitates the understanding of the public policy process by breaking it into sub-processes, each of which can be investigated alone or in terms of its relationship to the other stages of the cycle. This allows study of individual cases, a comparative study of a series of cases, or study of one or many stages of one or several cases. The model's greatest virtue, however, is its empirical orientation which enables analysis of a wide range of different factors at work at the various stages. While abstract conceptualization is necessary for ascertaining a broad picture of the process, an analytical framework that takes into account the details of the sub-processes as well as the abstract schema for the whole process is needed. It was for this reason that we have discussed the stages of the policy cycle in terms of factors highlighted by many case studies of public policy-making.

The factors to be considered at each stage of the policy cycle are the actors, institutions, and ideas involved in the policy in question, and the instruments available to carry it out. The actors participating in the policy process include individuals and groups drawn from both within and without the government. We referred to these actors as constituting the policy subsystem. The government actors playing a critical role in the process are the executive, bureaucracy, and legislature. In most instances, the bureaucracy plays the main role, though high-profile issues or the talents and determination of individual ministers are likely to encourage a greater role for the executive. Only in a limited number of circumstances are legislatures able to influence the policy process and its outcomes.

The societal actors involved to a significant extent in the public policy process include interest groups, research organizations, and mass media. Depending on their internal resources and links with the government actors, they can be highly influential actors. Groups endowed with large and supportive membership, adequate funds, scarce information, and close links with relevant bureaucratic and executive actors can be expected to be influential players in the policy subsystem. All the actors involved in the process have interests, based on their materials, needs, or ideology, which they seek to achieve through participation in the policy process. How they go about their participation and the extent to which they are successful is affected by the broader institutional context in which they operate.

The institutions of most relevance to policy-making pertain to the state and the society, and the links between them. How they are organized internally and in relation to each other determines the nature of their capacity to affect the policy process and its outcomes. A state's fragmentation is reflected in its executive and bureaucratic officials' capabilities to dominate the policy subsystem. An internally divided state is often unable to resist the conflicting demands placed upon it by societal groups. Similarly, fragmentation among major societal groups make it difficult for them to devise coherent positions which they can present at the deliberations of policy subsystems. The organizational features that are particularly weakening are federalism, a presidential system, and an unprofessional bureaucracy. Federalism divides authority between two levels of government, whereas a presidential system divides authority among various branches of the government; the net effect of both is to reduce state capacity compared to unitary and parliamentary systems. An under-resourced, fragmented, or demoralized bureaucracy is similarly debilitating because of its inability to devise coherent policy and defend it against pressures from social groups and politicians.

The organization of societal groups is also an important factor in the policy process and its outcomes. It is often the society's problems that the state seeks to address through public policies, and it is therefore to be expected that those directly affected by the problem will organize into groups to influence policy-making. The societal actors active in the policy process vary across policy sectors, as each policy normally involves only the groups with direct interests in the issue in question. Only business's and labour's influences cut across policy sectors because of the crucial role they play in the production process, a fundamental activity in every society. However, what position they take and how they make the representation depends on their internal organization. Groups that are encompassing and cohesive are able to devise coherent positions that rise above narrow sectional interests and are therefore more likely to serve the interests of the society as a whole. The worst situation is when groups are individually so strong as to make it difficult for the state to ignore them, yet too disunited to develop cohesive proposals for addressing public problems.

The organization of the international system also plays an increasingly large role in shaping states' public policies. International regimes in the areas of production, finance, and security affect what policy actors can or cannot do, thus influencing the policy that is eventually chosen and how it is implemented.

In addition to the institutional context in which the state and societal actors operate, the overarching sets of policy ideas are also important. They shape the policy discourse by conditioning the policy subsystem members' perception of what is desirable and possible, thus affecting policy outcomes. The sources of these ideas are varied, not to mention contentious; they range from purely ideological constructs to manifestations of material conditions. What is beyond doubt, however, is that they affect the policy process. A critical component of this process is learning based on policy-makers' experiences with addressing problems within existing policy discourses.

Discussion of the relationship between policy subsystems, policy learning, and policy change offers an alternate way to view the operation of a policy cycle from that typically found in the literature. Chapters One through Four set out the basic intentions of the policy sciences, and discussed the manner in which the existing general theories failed to provide a satisfactory understanding of public policy-making and the relevant actors, institutions and instruments found in the policy process in liberal democratic states. Chapters Five to Nine discussed the various stages of the policy cycle but said little about how these stages fit together, or whether characteristic patterns of policy change exist in the public policy process. The discussion in Chapter Ten highlighted the manner in which actors, interests, and ideas combine to produce public policies in a process which results in not one but two interlinked patterns of policy change. One is a process of normal change in which the settings and instruments used to pursue policy goals change incrementally within an overall, well-established policy style. The other is a process of paradigmatic change in which there is a rapid transition in policy outcomes and styles.

The notion of fundamental policy change occurring as a result of changes in policy paradigms brings to the fore the notion that public policy-making is not simply a process of conflict resolution, as most economic and political science-based theories allege, but is also very much a process influenced by past experiences and by the development of new ideas.

More specifically, the book shows how public policies emerge from a complex interplay of forms of government, types of issues, and the organization of states and societies into particular types of policy subsystems. Each sectoral subsystem tends to develop a particular style of public policy-making, with a distinct set of pre-established preferences for particular types of instruments and sets of policy claims or problems, and these styles change in a particular fashion characterized by alternating periods of slow incremental change and periods of rapid, radical, transition.

The move away from a traditional linear interpretation of the policy cycle and towards a more nuanced position on the investigation and conceptualization of the public policy process reflects a general recent trend towards 'post-positivist' modes of analysis in the policy science as a whole. Scholars recognize that social phenomena are shaped by highly contingent and complex processes, which require an appropriate research methodology to accommodate the uncertainty and the complexity.[1] In this view, the mode of analysis itself becomes just as much a subject of analysis and reflection as the object of the analysis. Grand theories are eschewed and replaced by the recognition that social problems and the government's response to them are affected by a range of factors which cannot be assumed in advance.[2] The emphasis is on considering as many factors as possible. There is no pretence of claiming one solution to be better than others on scientific grounds. Studying public policy is complex because the subject and object of study, government decision-making, is complex.

NOTES

1   See Stephen Hilgartner and Charles L. Bosk, 'The Rise and Fall of Social Problems: A Public Arenas Model', *American Journal of Sociology* 94, 1 (1981): 53-78, and Burkhart Holzner and John H. Marx, *Knowledge Application: The Knowledge System in Society* (Allyn and Bacon: Boston, 1979).

2   See Thomas D. Cook, 'Postpositivist Critical Multiplism' in R. Lance Shotland and Melvin M. Mark (eds), *Social Science and Social Policy* (Beverly Hills: Sage, 1985): 21-63; Bruce Jennings, 'Interpretation and the Practice of Policy Analysis' in Frank Fischer and John Forester (eds), *Confronting Values in Policy Analysis: The Politics of Criteria* (Newbury Park: Sage, 1987): 128-52; Warren J. Samuels, ' "Truth" and "Discourse" in the Social Construction of Economic Reality: An Essay on Relation of Knowledge to Socioeconomic Policy', *Journal of Post-Keynesian Economics* 13, 4 (1991): 515.

Bibliography

Aaron, Henry J., 'Social Security: International Comparisons' in *Studies in the Economics of Income Maintenance*, ed. O. Eckstein. Washington, DC: Brookings Institution, 1967.

Aberbach, Joel D., Robert D. Putnam, and Bert A. Rockman, *Bureaucrats and Politicians in Western Democracies*. Cambridge: Harvard University Press, 1981.

Adie, R.F. and P.G. Thomas, *Canadian Public Administration: Problematical Perspectives*, 2nd ed. Scarborough: Prentice Hall, 1987.

Ahroni, Yair, *Evolution and Management of State Owned Enterprises*. Cambridge, MA: Ballinger, 1986: 6.

Aldrich, Howard E. and David A. Whetten, 'Organization-sets, Action-sets, and Networks: Making the Most of Simplicity' in *Handbook of Organizational Design*, eds P. Nystrom and W.H. Starbuck. Oxford: Oxford University Press, 1980.

Allison, Graham T. and Morton H. Halperin. 'Bureaucratic Politics: A Paradigm and Some Policy Implications'. *World Politics* 24 (Supplement, 1972): 40-79.

Almond, Gabriel A., 'The Return to the State', *American Political Science Review* 82, 3 (1988): 853-901.

Althusser, L. and E. Balibar, *Reading 'Capital'*. London: New Left Books, 1977.

Amariglio, Jack L., Stephen A. Resnick, and Richard D. Wolff, 'Class, Power, and Culture' in *Marxism and the Interpretation of Culture*, eds C. Nelson and L. Grossberg. Urbana: University of Illinois Press, 1988.

Anderson, Charles W., 'Comparative Policy Analysis: The Design of Measures', *Comparative Politics* 4, 1 (1971): 117-31.

Anderson, Charles W., 'The Place of Principles in Policy Analysis', *American Political Science Review* 73, 3 (1979): 711-23.

Anderson, James, ed., *Economic Regulatory Policies*. Lexington: Lexington Books, 1976.

Anderson, James E., *Public Policy-Making: An Introduction*, 3rd ed. Boston: Houghton Mifflin 1984.

Anderson, Paul A., 'Decision Making by Objection and the Cuban Missile Crisis', *Administrative Science Quarterly* 28 (1983): 201-22.

Angus, William H., 'Judicial Review: Do We Need It?' in *The Individual and the Bureaucracy*, ed. D.J. Baum. Toronto: Carswell, 1974.

Argyris, Chris and Donald A. Schon, *Organizational Learning: A Theory of Action Perspective*. Reading, PA: Addison-Wesley, 1978.

Arrow, Kenneth, *Social Choice and Individual Values*, 2nd ed. New York: Wiley, 1963.

Atkinson, Michael M., 'Public Policy and the New Institutionalism' in *Institutions and Public Policy*, ed. M.M. Atkinson. Toronto: Harcourt Brace Jovanovich, 1978.

Atkinson, M. and W. Coleman, *The State, Business, and Industrial Change in Canada*. Toronto: University of Toronto Press, 1989.

Atkinson, M. and W. Coleman, 'Strong States and Weak States: Sectoral Policy Networks in Advanced Capitalist Economies', *British Journal of Political Science* 19, 1 (1989): 47-67.

Atkinson, Michael M. and William D. Coleman, 'Policy Networks, Policy Communities and the Problems of Governance', *Governance* 5, 2 (1992): 154-80.

Atkinson, Michael M. and Robert A. Nigol, 'Selecting Policy Instruments:

Neo-Institutional and Rational Choice Interpretations of Automobile Insurance in Ontario', *Canadian Journal of Political Science* 22, 1 (1989): 107-35.

Bakvis, Herman and David MacDonald, 'The Canadian Cabinet: Organization, Decision-Rules, and Policy Impact' in *Governing Canada: Institutions and Public Policy*, ed. M. Michael Atkinson. Toronto: Harcourt Brace Jovanovich, 1993.

Balbus, Isaac D., 'The Concept of Interest in Pluralist and Marxian Analysis', *Politics and Society* 1, 2 (1971): 151-77.

Banting, Keith G., *The Welfare State and Canadian Federalism*. Kingston: Queen's University Institute of Intergovernmental Relations, 1982.

Bardach, Eugene, *The Implementation Game: What Happens After a Bill Becomes a Law*. Cambridge: MIT Press, 1977.

Bardach, Eugene, 'Social Regulation as a Generic Policy Instrument' in *Beyond Privatization: The Tools of Government Action*, ed. L.M. Salamon. Washington, DC: Urban Institute, 1989.

Barker, Anthony and B. Guy Peter, eds, *The Politics of Expert Advice: Creating, Using and Manipulating Scientific Knowledge for Public Policy*. Pittsburgh, PA: University of Pittsburgh Press, 1993.

Barr, Nicholas, *The Economics of the Welfare State*. London: Weidenfeld and Nicolson, 1987.

Barrett, Susan and Colin Fudge, *Policy and Action: Essays on the Implementation of Public Policy*. London: Methuen, 1981.

Bator, Francis M., 'The Anatomy of Market Failure', *Quarterly Journal of Economics* 72, 3 (1958): 351-79.

Baumgartner, Frank R. and Bryan D. Jones, 'Agenda Dynamics and Policy Subsystems', *Journal of Politics* 53, 4 (1991): 1044-74.

Baumgartner, Frank R. and Bryan D. Jones, *Agendas and Instability in American Politics*. Chicago: University of Chicago Press, 1993.

Baumgartner, Frank R. and Bryan D. Jones, 'Attention, Boundary Effects, and Large-Scale Policy Change in Air Transportation Policy' in *The Politics of Problem Definition: Shaping the Policy Agenda*, eds D.A. Rochefort and R.W. Cobb. Lawrence: University of Kansas Press, 1994.

Baxter-Moore, Nicolas, 'Policy Implementation and the Role of the State: A Revised Approach to the Study of Policy Instruments' in *Contemporary Canadian Politics: Readings and Notes*, eds R.J. Jackson, D. Jackson, and N. Baxter-Moore. Scarborough: Prentice-Hall, 1987.

Becker, Gary S. 'Competition and Democracy', *Journal of Law and Economics* 1 (1958): 105-9.

Becker, Gary S., 'Nobel Lecture: The Economic Way of Looking at Behavior', *Journal of Political Economy* 101, 3 (1993): 385-409.

Bennett, Colin J., 'What is Policy Convergence and What Causes It?', *British Journal of Political Science* 21, 2 (1991): 215-33.

Bennett, Colin J., 'The International Regulation of Personal Data: From Epistemic Community to Policy Sector'. Charlottetown, Prince Edward Island: Annual Meeting of the Canadian Political Science Association, (1992).

Bennett, Colin J., *Regulating Privacy: Data Protection and Public Policy in Europe and the United States*. Ithaca: Cornell University Press, 1992.

Bennett, Colin J. and Michael Howlett, 'The Lessons of Learning: Reconciling Theories of Policy Learning and Policy Change', *Policy Sciences* 25, 3 (1992): 275-94.

Benson, J. Kenneth. 'A Framework for Policy Analysis' in *Interorganizational Co-ordination:*

Theory, Research and Implementation, eds D.L. Rogers and D. A. Whetton. Ames: Iowa State University Press, 1982

Bentley, Arthur F., *The Process of Government*. Chicago: University of Chicago Press, 1908.

Berger, Peter L. and Thomas Luckmann, *The Social Construction of Reality: A Treatise in the Sociology of Knowledge*. New York: Doubleday, 1966.

Berger, Suzanne, ed., *Organizing Interests in Western Europe: Pluralism, Corporatism and the Transformation of Politics*. Cambridge: Cambridge University Press, 1981.

Berle, Adolf, *Power Without Property*. New York: Harcourt Brace, 1959.

Bernstein, Marver H., *Regulating Business by Independent Commission*. Princeton: Princeton University Press, 1955

Birnbaum, Pierre, 'The State versus Corporatism', *Politics and Society* 11, 4 (1982): 477-501.

Blankart, Charles, 'Market and Non-Market Alternatives in the Supply of Public Goods: General Issues' in *Public Expenditure and Government Growth*, eds F. Forte and A. Peacock. Oxford: Basil Blackwell, 1985.

Block, Fred, 'Beyond Relative Autonomy: State Managers as Historical Subjects', *Socialist Register* (1980): 227-42.

Bobrow, Davis B. and John S. Dryzek, *Policy Analysis by Design*. Pittsburgh: University of Pittsburgh Press, 1987.

Boddy, Raford and James Crotty, 'Class Conflict and Macro-Policy: The Political Business Cycle', *Review of Radical Political Economics* 7, 1 (1975): 1-19.

Braybrooke, David and Charles Lindblom, *A Strategy of Decision: Policy Evaluation as a Social Process*. New York: Free Press of Glencoe, 1963.

Bressers, Hans and Pieter-Jan Klok, 'Fundamentals for a Theory of Policy Instruments', *International Journal of Social Economics* 15, 3/4 (1988): 22-41.

Brewer, Garry and Peter DeLeon, *The Foundations of Policy Analysis*. Homewood: Dorsey, 1983.

Brewer, Garry D., 'The Policy Sciences Emerge: To Nurture and Structure a Discipline', *Policy Sciences* 5, 3 (1974): 239-44.

Breyer, Stephen, 'Analyzing Regulatory Failure: Mismatches, Less Restrictive Alternatives, and Reform', *Harvard Law Review* 92, 3 (1979): 549-609.

Breyer, Stephen, *Regulation and Its Reform*. Cambridge: Harvard University Press, 1982.

Brooks, Stephen, *Public Policy in Canada: An Introduction*. Toronto: McClelland and Stewart, 1989.

Brooks, Stephen and Alain-G. Gagnon, eds, *Social Scientists, Policy, and the State*. New York: Praeger, 1990.

Bruce, Neil, ed., *Tax Expenditures and Government Policy: Proceedings of a Conference held at Queen's University 17-18 November 1988*. Kingston: John Deutsch Institute for the Study of Economic Policy, 1988.

Bruton, Jim and Michael Howlett, 'Differences of Opinion: Round Tables, Policy Networks and the Failure of Canadian Environmental Strategy', *Alternatives* 19, 1 (1992): 25.

Bryman, Alan, *Quantity and Quality in Social Research*. London: Unwin Hyman, 1988.

Buchanan, James, *The Limits of Liberty*. Chicago: University of Chicago Press, 1975.

Buchanan, James M., 'Rent Seeking and Profit Seeking' in *Toward a Theory of the Rent-Seeking Society*, eds J.M. Buchanan, R.D. Tollison, and G. Tullock. College Station: Texas A&M University Press, 1980.

Buchanan, James M. et al., *The Economics of Politics*. London: Institute of Economic Affairs, 1978.

Buchanan, James M., R.D. Tollison, and G. Tullock, eds, *Toward a Theory of the Rent-Seeking Society*. College Station: Texas A&M Press, 1980.

Buchanan, James M. and Gordon Tullock, *The Calculus of Consent: Logical Foundations of Constitutional Democracy*. Ann Arbor: University of Michigan Press, 1962.

Burt, Sandra, 'Canadian Women's Groups in the 1980s: Organizational Development and Policy Influence', *Canadian Public Policy* 16, 1 (1990): 17-28.

Cahill, Anthony G. and E. Sam Overman, 'The Evolution of Rationality in Policy Analysis' in *Policy Theory and Policy Evaluation: Concepts, Knowledge, Causes, and Norms*, ed. S.S. Nagel. New York: Greenwood Press, 1990.

Cairns, Alan C., 'Alternative Styles in the Styles of Canadian Politics', *Canadian Journal of Political Science* 7 (1974): 101-34.

Cairns, Alan, 'The Past and Future of Canadian Administrative State', *University of Toronto Law Journal* 40 (1990): 310-61.

Cameron, David R., 'The Expansion of the Public Economy: A Comparative Analysis', *American Political Science Review* 72, 4 (1978): 1243-61.

Cameron, David R., 'Social Democracy, Corporatism, Labour Quiescence and the Representation of Economic Interest in Advanced Capitalist Society' in *Order and Conflict in Contemporary Capitalism*, ed. J.H. Goldthorpe. Oxford: Clarendon Press, 1984.

Cammack, Paul, 'Bringing the State Back In?' *British Journal of Political Science* 19, 2 (1989): 261-90.

Cammack, Paul, 'The New Institutionalism: Predatory Rule, Institutional Persistence, and Macro-Social Change', *Economy and Society* 21, 4 (1992): 397-429.

Campbell, John Creighton, 'Afterword on Policy Communities: A Framework for Comparative Research', *Governance* 2, 1 (1989): 86-94.

Canada, *Account of the Costs of Selective Tax Measures*. Ottawa: Department of Finance, 1985.

Canada, Auditor General of, *Annual Report of the Auditor General*. Ottawa: Parliament of Canada, 1983.

Canada, Auditor General of, *Report of the Auditor General to the House of Commons*. Ottawa: Supply and Services Canada, 1993.

Canada, Department of Finance, *The Canada-U.S. Free Trade Agreement: An Economic Assessment*. Ottawa: Fiscal Policy and Economic Analysis Branch, Dept. of Finance, 1988.

Canada, Economic Council of, *Responsible Regulation: An Interim Report*. Ottawa: Supply and Services Canada, 1979.

Canada, Treasury Board, *A Manager's Guide to Performance Measurement*. Ottawa: Treasury Board of Canada, 1976.

Canada, Treasury Board, *The Policy and Expenditure Management System*. Ottawa: Treasury Board of Canada, 1981.

Carley, Michael, *Rational Techniques in Policy Analysis*. London: Heinemann Educational Books, 1980.

Castles, Francis et al., eds, *The Future of Party Government: Vol. 3: Managing Mixed Economies*. New York: DeGruyter, 1987.

Castles, Francis and Robert D. McKinlay, 'Does Politics Matter: An Analysis of the Public Welfare Commitment in Advanced Democratic States', *European Journal of Political Research* 7, 2 (1979): 169-86.

Castles, Francis G., 'The Impact of Parties on Public Expenditure' in *The Impact of Parties: Politics and Policies in Democratic Capitalist States*, ed. Francis G. Castles. London: Sage Publications, 1982.

Castles, Francis G., 'The Dynamics of Policy Change: What Happened to the English-speaking Nations in the 1980s', *European Journal of Political Research* 18, 5 (1990): 491-513.

Castles, Francis G. and Vance Merrill, 'Towards a General Model of Public Policy Outcomes', *Journal of Theoretical Politics* 1, 2 (1989): 177-212.

Cater, Douglas, *Power in Washington: A Critical Look at Today's Struggle in the Nation's Capital.* New York: Random House, 1964.

Cawson, Alan, 'Pluralism, Corporatism and the Role of the State', *Government and Opposition* 13, 2 (1978): 178-98.

Cawson, Alan, *Corporatism and Political Theory.* Oxford: Basil Blackwell, 1986.

Chase-Dunn, Christopher K., *Global Formation: Structures of the World-Economy.* Cambridge, MA: Basil Blackwell, 1989.

Clarke, Michael, 'Implementation' in *Power and Policy in Liberal Democracies*, ed. M. Harrop. Cambridge: Cambridge University Press, 1992.

Coase, R.H., 'The Problem of Social Cost', *The Journal of Law and Economics* 3 (1960): 1-44.

Cobb, R., J.K. Ross, and M.H. Ross, 'Agenda Building as a Comparative Political Process', *American Political Science Review* 70, 1 (1976): 126-38.

Cobb, Roger W. and Charles D. Elder, *Participation in American Politics: The Dynamics of Agenda-Building.* Boston: Allyn and Bacon, 1972.

Cohen, G.A., *Karl Marx's Theory of History: A Defense.* Oxford: Clarendon Press, 1978.

Cohen, M., J. March, and J. Olsen, 'A Garbage Can Model of Organizational Choice', *Administrative Science Quarterly* 17, 1 (1972): 1-25.

Cohen, Michael D., James G. March, and Johan P. Olsen. 'People, Problems, Solutions and the Ambiguity of Relevance' in *Ambiguity and Choice in Organizations*, eds J.G. March and J.P. Olsen. Bergen: Universitetsforlaget, 1979.

Cohen, Wesley M. and Daniel A. Levinthal, 'Absorptive Capacity: A New Perspective on Learning and Innovation', *Administrative Science Quarterly* 35 (1990): 128-52.

Coleman, William D., 'Analyzing the Associative Action of Business: Policy Advocacy and Policy Participation', *Canadian Public Administration.* 28, 3 (1985): 413-33.

Coleman, William D., 'Canadian Business and the State' in *The State and Economic Interests*, ed. K. Banting. Toronto: University of Toronto Press, 1986.

Coleman, William D., *Business and Politics: A Study of Collective Action.* Kingston: McGill-Queen's University Press, 1988.

Coleman, William D., 'Policy Convergence in Banking: A Comparative Study', *Political Studies* 42 (1994): 274-92.

Coleman, William D. and Grace Skogstad, eds, *Policy Communities and Public Policy in Canada: A Structural Approach.* Mississauga, ON: Copp Clark Pitman, 1990.

Connolly, Michael E.H. and Andrew W. Stark, 'Policy Making and the Demonstration Effect: Privatization in a Deprived Region', *Public Administration* 70, 3 (1992): 369-85.

Connolly, William E., 'The Challenge to Pluralist Theory' in *The Bias of Pluralism*, ed. W.E. Connolly. New York: Atherton Press, 1969.

Connolly, William E., 'On "Interests" in Politics', *Politics and Society* 2, 4 (1972): 459-77.

Cook, F.L. et al., 'Media and Agenda Setting: Effects on the Public, Interest Group Leaders, Policy Makers, and Policy', *Public Opinion Quarterly* 47, 1 (1983): 16-35.

Cook, Thomas D., 'Postpositivist Critical Multiplism' in *Social Science and Social Policy*, eds R.L. Shotland and M. M. Mark. Beverly Hills: Sage, 1985.

Cox, Robert W., *Production, Power and World Order: Social Forces in the Making of History*. New York: Columbia University Press, 1987.

Cushman, Robert E., *The Independent Regulatory Commissions*. London: Oxford University Press, 1941.

Cutright, P., 'Political Structure, Economic Development, and National Security Programs', *American Journal of Sociology* 70, 5 (1965): 537-50.

Dahl, Robert A. and Charles E. Lindblom, *Politics, Economics and Welfare: Planning and Politico-economic Systems Resolved into Basic Social Processes*. New York: Harper and Row, 1953.

Dahl, Robert, *A Preface to Democratic Theory*. Chicago: University of Chicago Press, 1956.

Dahl, Robert A., *Who Governs?: Democracy and Power in an American City*. New Haven: Yale University Press, 1961.

Dahl, Robert A., *Pluralist Democracy in the United States: Conflict and Consent*. Chicago: Rand McNally, 1967.

David, Wilfred L., *The IMF Policy Paradigm: The Macroeconomics of Stabilization, Structural Adjustment, and Economic Development*. New York: Praeger, 1985.

Davis, Sandra and Charles Davis, 'Analyzing Change in Public Lands Policymaking: From Subsystems to Advocacy Coalitions', *Policy Studies Journal* 17, 1 (1988): 3-24.

de Smith, S.A., *Judicial Review of Administrative Action*. London: Stevens and Son, 1973.

de Tocqueville, Alexis, *Democracy in America*. New York: New American Library, 1956.

deHaven-Smith, Lance and Carl E. Van Horn, 'Subgovernment Conflict in Public Policy', *Policy Studies Journal* 12, 4 (1984): 627-42.

DeLeon, Peter, 'A Theory of Policy Termination' in *The Policy Cycle*, eds J.V. May and A.B. Wildavsky. Beverly Hills: Sage, 1978.

DeLeon, Peter, 'Policy Evaluation and Program Termination', *Policy Studies Review* 2, 4 (1983): 631-47.

DeLeon, Peter, 'Trends in Policy Sciences Research: Determinants and Developments', *European Journal of Political Research* 14, 1/2 (1986): 3-22.

DeLeon, Peter, *Advice and Consent: The Development of the Policy Sciences*. New York: Russell Sage Foundation, 1988.

DeLeon, Peter, 'Reinventing the Policy Sciences: Three Steps Back to the Future', *Policy Sciences* 27 (1994): 77-95.

Dery, David, *Problem Definition in Policy Analysis*. Lawrence: University of Kansas, 1984.

DeSario, Jack and Stuart Langton, *Citizen Participation in Public Decision-Making*. Westport: Greenwood, 1987.

Desveaux, James A., Evert Lindquist, and Glen Toner, 'Organizing for Innovation in Public Bureaucracy: AIDS, Energy and Environment Policy in Canada', *Canadian Journal of Political Science* 27, 3 (1994): 493-528.

Dobell, Rodney and David Zussman, 'An Evaluation System for Government: If Politics is Theatre, then Evaluation is (mostly) Art', *Canadian Public Administration* 24, 3 (1981): 404-27

Dobuzinskis, Laurent, 'Modernist and Postmodernist Metephors of the Policy Process: Control and Stability vs Chaos and Reflexive Understanding', *Policy Sciences* 25 (1992): 355-80.

Dodgson, Mark, 'Organizational Learning: A Review of Some Literatures', *Organization Studies* 14, 3 (1993): 375-94.

Doern, G.B., 'The Role of Royal Commissions in the General Policy Process and in Federal-Provincial Relations', *Canadian Public Administration* 10, 4 (1967): 417-33.

Doern, G. Bruce, 'The Concept of Regulation and Regulatory Reform' in *Issues in Canadian Public Policy*, eds G.B. Doern and V.S. Wilson. Toronto: Macmillan, 1974.

Doern, G.B., *The Nature of Scientific and Technological Controversy in Federal Policy Formation*. Ottawa: Science Council of Canada, 1981.

Doern, G. Bruce and Richard W. Phidd, *Canadian Public Policy: Ideas, Structure, Process*, 2nd ed. Toronto: Nelson Canada, 1992.

Doern, G.B. and V.S. Wilson, 'Conclusions and Observations' in *Issues in Canadian Public Policy*, eds G.B. Doern and V.S. Wilson. Toronto: Macmillan, 1974.

Downs, Anthony, *An Economic Theory of Democracy*. New York: Harper, 1957.

Downs, Anthony, *Inside Bureaucracy*. New York: Harper and Row, 1967.

Dror, Yehezkel, 'Muddling Through–"Science" or Inertia', Public *Administration Review* 24, 3 (1964): 154-7.

Dror, Yehezkel, *Public Policymaking Re-examined*. San Francisco: Chandler Publishing Co., 1968.

Dryzek, John S., *Discursive Democracy: Politics, Policy, and Political Science*. Cambridge: Cambridge University Press, 1990.

Dryzek, John S., 'How Far Is It From Virginia and Rochester to Frankfurt? Public Choice as Global Theory', *British Journal of Political Science* 22, 4 (1992); 397-418.

Dryzek, John S. and Brian Ripley, 'The Ambitions of Policy Design', *Policy Studies Review* 7, 4 (1988): 705-19.

Dunleavy, Patrick, 'Explaining the Privatization Boom: Public Choice versus Radical Approaches', *Public Administration* 64, 1 (1986): 13-34.

Dunn, William N., 'Methods of the Second Type: Coping with the Wilderness of Conventional Policy Analysis', *Policy Studies Review* 7, 4 (1988): 720-37.

Dussault, R. and L. Borgeat, *Administrative Law: A Treatise*. Toronto: Carswell, 1990.

Dye, Thomas R., *Politics, Economics, and the Public: Policy Outcomes in the American States*. Chicago: Rand McNally, 1966.

Dye, Thomas R., *Understanding Public Policy*. Englewood Cliffs, NJ: Prentice-Hall, 1972.

Dye, Thomas R., 'Politics Versus Economics: The Development of the Literature on Policy Determination', *Policy Studies Journal* 7, 4 (1979): 652-62.

Dyerson, Romano and Frank Mueller, 'Intervention by Outsiders: A Strategic Perspective on Government Industrial Policy', *Journal of Public Policy* 13, 1 (1993): 69-88.

Dyson, Kenneth H.F., *The State Tradition in Western Europe: A Study of an Idea and Institution*. Oxford: Martin Robertson, 1980.

Economic Council of Canada, *Minding the Public's Business*. Ottawa: Economic Council of Canada, 1986.

Economist, The, Special Survey of Multinationals (27 March 1993): 6.

Edelman, Murray J., *Constructing the Political Spectacle*. Chicago: University of Chicago Press, 1988.

Edwards, George C. and Ira Sharkansky, *The Policy Predicament: Making and Implementing Public Policy*. San Francisco: Freeman, 1978.

Edwards, Ward, 'The Theory of Decision Making', *Psychological Bulletin* 51, 4 (1954): 380-417.

Elkin, Stephen L., 'Regulation and Regime: A Comparative Analysis', *Journal of Public Policy*, 6, 1 (1986): 49-72.

Elmore, Richard F., 'Organizational Models of Social Program Implementation', *Public Policy* 26, 2 (1978): 185-228.

Elmore, Richard F., 'Instruments and Strategy in Public Policy', *Policy Studies Review* 7, 1 (1987): 174-86.

Elster, Jon, 'The Possibility of Rational Politics' in *Political Theory Today*, ed. D. Held. Oxford: Polity, 1991.

Englehart, Kenneth G. and Michael J. Trebilcock, *Public Participation in the Regulatory Process: The Issue of Funding*. Ottawa: Economic Council of Canada, 1981.

Esping-Andersen, Gosta, 'From Welfare State to Democratic Socialism: The Politics of Economic Democracy in Denmark and Sweden' in *Political Power and Social Theory*, ed. M. Zeitlin. 1981.

Esping-Andersen, Gosta, *Politics Against Markets: The Social Democratic Road to Power*. Princeton: Princeton University Press, 1985.

Esping-Andersen, Gosta, *The Three Worlds of Welfare Capitalism*. Cambridge, UK: Polity, 1990.

Esping-Andersen, Gosta and Walter Korpi, 'Social Policy as Class Politics in Post-War Capitalism: Scandinavia, Austria, and Germany' in *Order and Conflict in Contemporary Capitalism*, ed. J.H. Goldthorpe. Oxford: Clarendon Press, 1984.

Etheredge, Lloyd S., 'Government Learning: An Overview' in *The Handbook of Political Behavior*, ed. S.L. Long. New York: Plenum, 1981.

Etheredge, Lloyd S. and James Short, 'Thinking About Government Learning', *Journal of Management Studies* 20, 1 (1983): 41-58.

Etzioni, Amitai. 'Mixed-Scanning: A "Third" Approach to Decision-Making', *Public Administration Review* 27, 5 (1967): 385-92.

Evans, P.B., D. Rueschemeyer, and T. Skocpol, eds, *Bringing the State Back In*. Cambridge: Cambridge University Press, 1985.

Evans, Peter, 'State as Problem and Solution: Predation, Embedded Autonomy, and Structural Change' in *The Politics of Economic Adjustment: International Constraints, Distributive Conflicts, and the State*, eds Stephen Haggard and Robert R. Kaufman. Princeton: Princeton University Press, 1992: 139-81.

Fayol, Henri, *Studies in the Science of Administration*, 1895.

Feick, Jurgen, 'Comparing Comparative Policy Studies—A Path Towards Integration?', *Journal of Public Policy* 12, 3 (1992): 257-86.

Feldman, Elliot J., 'An Antidote for Apology, Service and Witchcraft in Policy Analysis' in *Problems of Theory in Policy Analysis*, ed. P.M. Gregg. Lexington, MA: Lexington Books, 1976.

Finkelstein, Neil and Brian M. Rogers, eds, *Recent Developments in Administrative Law*. Agincourt, ON: Carswell, 1987.

Finlayson, Jock A. and Mark W. Zacher, 'The GATT and the Regulation of Trade Barriers: Regime Dynamics and Functions', *International Organization* 35, 4 (1981): 561-602.

Fischer, Frank and John Forester, eds, *Confronting Values in Policy Analysis: The Politics of Criteria*. Beverly Hills, CA: Sage, 1987.

Fischer, Frank and John Forester, eds, *The Argumentative Turn in Policy Analysis and Planning*. Durham: Duke University Press, 1993.

Fischhoff, Baruch, 'Cost Benefit Analysis and the Art of Motorcycle Maintenance', *Policy Sciences* 8, 2 (1977): 177-202

Flathman, Richard E., *The Public Interest: An Essay Concerning the Normative Discourse of Politics*. Chicago: University of Chicago Press, 1979.

Flora, Peter and Arnold J. Heidenheimer, eds, *The Development of Welfare States in Europe and America*. New Brunswick, NJ: Transaction Books, 1981.

Foley, Duncan K., 'State Expenditure From a Marxist Perspective', *Journal of Public Economics* 9, 2 (1978): 221-38.

Foot, David K., 'Political Cycles, Economic Cycles and the Trend in Public Employment in Canada' in *Studies in Public Employment and Compensation in Canada*, ed. M.W. Bucovetsky. Toronto: Butterworths for Institute for Research on Public Policy, 1979.

Forester, John, 'Bounded Rationality and the Politics of Muddling Through', *Public Administration Review* 44, 1 (1984): 23-31.

Forester, John, *Planning in the Face of Power*. Berkeley: University of California Press, 1989.

Formaini, Robert, *The Myth of Scientific Public Policy*. New Brunswick, NJ: Transaction Publishers, 1990.

Foucault, Michel, 'The Discourse on Language' in *The Archaeology of Knowledge*, ed. Michel Foucault. New York: Pantheon, 1972.

Fox, Charles J., 'Implementation Research: Why and How to Transcend Positivist Methodology' in *Implementation and the Policy Process: Opening up the Black Box*, eds D.J. Palumbo and D.J. Calista. New York: Greenwood Press, 1990.

Frankel, Boris, 'On the State of the State: Marxist Theories of the State After Leninism' in *Classes, Power and Conflict: Classical and Contemporary Debates*, eds A. Giddens and D. Held. Berkeley: University of California Press, 1982.

Freeman, Gary P., 'National Styles and Policy Sectors: Explaining Structured Variation', *Journal of Public Policy* 5, 4 (1985): 467-96.

Freeman, John Leiper, *The Political Process: Executive Bureau-Legislative Committee Relations*. New York: Random House, 1955.

Freeman, John R., *Democracy and Markets: The Politics of Mixed Economies*. Ithaca: Cornell University Press, 1989.

French, Richard, *How Ottawa Decides: Planning and Industrial Policy-Making*, 1968-1980. Toronto: James Lorimer, 1980.

Frey, Bruno S., 'Politico-Economic Models and Cycles', *Journal of Public Economics* 9, 2 (1978): 203-20.

Frieden, Jeffry, 'Invested Interests: the Politics of National Economic Policies in a World of Global Finance', *International Organisation* 45, 4 (1991): 425-51.

Gall, Gerald L., *The Canadian Legal System*, 2nd ed. Toronto: Carswell, 1983.

Gamble, Andrew et al., *Ideas, Interests and Consequences*. London: Institute of Economic Affairs, 1989.

Garant, Patrice, 'Crown Corporations: Instruments of Economic Intervention—Legal Aspects' in *Regulations, Crown Corporations, and Administrative Tribunals*, eds I. Bernier and A. Lajoie. Toronto: University of Toronto Press, 1985.

Garrett, Geoffrey and Peter Lange, 'Political Responses to Interdependence: What's "Left" for the Left?', *International Organization* 45, 4 (1991): 539, 564.

Garson, G. David, *Group Theories of Politics*. Beverly Hills: Sage, 1978.

Garson, G. David, 'From Policy Science to Policy Analysis: A Quarter Century of Progress' in *Policy Analysis: Perspectives, Concepts, and Methods*, ed. W.N. Dunn. Greenwich, CT: JAI Press, 1986.

Gawthrop, Louis C., *Administrative Politics and Social Change*. New York: St Martin's Press, 1971.

Gersick, Connie J.G., 'Revolutionary Change Theories: A Multilevel Exploration of the Punctuated Equilibrium Paradigm', *Academy of Management Review* 16, 1 (1991): 10-36.

Gierke, Otto von, *Natural Law and the Theory of Society, 1500-1800*. Cambridge: Cambridge University Press, 1958.

Gierke, Otto von, *Political Theories of the Middle Age*. Cambridge: Cambridge University Press, 1958.

Gilbert, Neil and Barbara Gilbert, *The Enabling State: Modern Welfare Capitalism in America*. New York: Oxford University Press, 1989.

Gillroy, John Martin, 'The Ethical Poverty of Cost-Benefit Methods: Autonomy, Efficiency and Public Policy Choice', *Policy Sciences* 25, 2 (1992): 83-102.

Gillroy, John Martin and Maurice Wade, eds, *The Moral Dimensions of Public Policy Choice: Beyond the Market Paradigm*. Pittsburgh, PA: University of Pittsburgh Press, 1992.

Gilpin, Robert, *The Political Economy of International Relations*. Princeton: Princeton University Press, 1987.

Goldthorpe, John H. and Gordon Marshall, 'The Promising Future of Class Analysis: A Response to Recent Critiques', *Sociology* 26, 3 (1992): 381-400.

Golembiewski, R.T., '"The Group Basis of Politics": Notes on Analysis and Development', *American Political Science Review* 54, 4 (1960): 962-71.

Gordon, I., J. Lewis, and K. Young, 'Perspectives on Policy Analysis', *Public Administration Bulletin* 25 (1977): 26-30.

Gortner, Harold, Julianne Mahler, and Jeanne Bell Nicholson, *Organization Theory: A Public Perspective*. Chicago: Dorsey Press, 1987.

Gough, Ian, 'State Expenditure in Advanced Capitalism', *New Left Review* 92 (1975): 53-92.

Gough, Ian, *The Political Economy of the Welfare State*. London: Macmillan, 1979.

Gourevitch, Peter, *Politics in Hard Times: Comparative Responses to International Economic Crises*. Ithaca: Cornell University Press, 1986.

Graber, Doris Appel, *Mass Media and American Politics*. Washington: Congressional Quarterly Press, 1989.

Grafstein, Robert, 'The Problem of Institutional Constraint', *Journal of Politics* 50 (1988): 577-99.

Gramlich, Edward M., *Benefit-Cost Analysis of Government Programs*. Englewood: Prentice-Hall, 1981.

Gramsci, A., *Selections from the Prison Notebooks*. NY: International Publishers, 1972.

Grant, Wyn, 'Models of Interest Intermediation and Policy Formation Applied to an Internationally Comparative Study of the Dairy Industry', *European Journal of Political Research* 21, 1/2 (1992): 53-68.

Greenberg, Edward S., 'State Change: Approaches and Concepts' in *Changes in the State: Causes and Consequences*, eds E.S. Greenberg and T.F. Mayer. Newbury Park: Sage Publications, 1990.

Greenberg, George D. et al., 'Developing Public Policy Theory: Perspectives from Empirical Research', *American Political Science Review* 71 (1977): 1532-43

Gulick, Luther and Lyndal Urwick, eds, *Papers on the Science of Administration*. New York: Institute of Public Administration, 1937.

Gulick, Luther H., 'Notes on the Theory of Organization' in *Papers on the Science of Administration*, eds L. Gulick and L. Urwick. New York: Institute of Public Administration, 1937.

Gunderson, Morley et al., *Taxes as Instruments of Public Policy*. Toronto: University of Toronto Press, 1993.

Haas, Ernst B., 'Is there a Hole in the Whole? Knowledge, Technology, Interdependence, and the Construction of International Regimes', *International Organization* 29, 3 (1975): 827-76.

Haas, Ernst B., *When Knowledge is Power: Three Models of Change in International Organizations*. Berkeley: University of California Press, 1990.

Haas, Peter M., 'Introduction: Epistemic Communities and International Policy Coordination', *International Organization* 46, 1 (1992): 1-36.

Habermas, Jurgen, *Legitimation Crisis*. Boston: Beacon Press, 1975.

Haggard, Stephen and Chung-In Moon, 'Institutions and Economic Policy: Theory and a Korean Case Study', *World Politics* 42, 2 (1990): 210-37.

Haggard, Stephen and Beth A. Simmons, 'Theories of International Regimes', *International Organization* 41, 3 (1987): 491-517.

Haider, Donald, 'Grants as a Tool of Public Policy' in *Beyond Privatization: The Tools of Government Action*, ed. L.M. Salamon. Washington, DC: Urban Institute, 1989.

Hale, M.Q., 'The Cosmology of Arthur F. Bentley', *American Political Science Review* 54, 4 (1960): 955-61.

Hall, John A. and G. John Ikenberry, *The State*. Minneapolis: University of Minnesota Press, 1989.

Hall, Peter A., 'Policy Innovation and the Structure of the State: The Politics-Administration Nexus in France and Britain', *The Annals of the American Academy of Political and Social Science* 466 (1983): 43-59.

Hall, Peter A., *Governing the Economy: the Politics of State Intervention in Britain and France*. Cambridge: Polity Press, 1986.

Hall, Peter A., ed., *The Political Power of Economic Ideas: Keynesianism Across Nations*. Princeton: Princeton University Press, 1989.

Hall, Peter A., 'Policy Paradigms, Experts, and the State: The Case of Macroeconomic Policy-Making in Britain' in *Social Scientists, Policy, and the State*, eds S. Brooks and A.-G. Gagnon. New York: Praeger, 1990.

Hall, Peter A., 'Policy Paradigms, Social Learning and the State: The Case of Economic Policy Making in Britain', *Comparative Politics* 25, 3 (1993): 275-96.

Hamm, Keith E., 'Patterns of Influence Among Committees, Agencies, and Interest Groups', *Legislative Studies Quarterly* 8, 3 (1983): 379-426.

Hansen, Susan B., 'Public Policy Analysis: Some Recent Developments and Current Problems', *Policy Studies Journal* 12 (1983): 14-42.

Harrison, Kathryn and George Hoberg, 'Setting the Environmental Agenda in Canada and the United States: The Cases of Dioxin and Radon', *Canadian Journal of Political Science* 24, 1 (1991): 3-27.

Hayes, Michael T., 'The Semi-Sovereign Pressure Groups: A Critique of Current Theory and an Alternative Typology', *Journal of Politics* 40, 1 (1978): 134-61.

Hayes, Michael T., *Incrementalism and Public Policy*. New York: Longmans, 1992.

Heclo, Hugh, *Modern Social Politics in Britain and Sweden: From Relief to Income Maintenance*. New Haven: Yale University Press, 1974.

Heclo, Hugh, 'Issue Networks and the Executive Establishment' in *The New American Political System*, ed. A. King. Washington, DC: American Enterprise Institute for Public Policy Research, 1978.

Hedberg, Bo, 'How Organizations Learn and Unlearn' in *Handbook of Organizational Design, Vol.1 Adapting Organizations to their Elements*, eds P.C. Nystrom and W.H. Starbuck. Oxford: Oxford University Press, 1981.

Heidenheimer, Arnold J., Hugh Heclo, and Carolyn Teich Adams, eds, *Comparative Public*

Policy: The Politics of Social Choice in Europe and America. New York: St Martin's Press, 1975.

Heineman, Robert A. et al., *The World of the Policy Analyst: Rationality, Values and Politics.* Chatham, NJ: Chatham House, 1990.

Heinz, John P. et al., *The Hollow Core: Private Interests in National Policy Making.* Cambridge: Harvard University Press, 1993.

Heinz, John P. et al., 'Inner Circles or Hollow Cores', *Journal of Politics* 52, 2 (1990): 356-90.

Held, David, 'The Relevance of Privatization to Developing Economies', *Public Administration and Development* 10, 1 (1990).

Held, David, 'Democracy, the Nation-State and the Global System' in *Political Theory Today*, ed. D. Held. Oxford: Polity, 1991.

Held, David and Anthony McGrew, 'Globalization and the Liberal Democratic State', *Government and Opposition* 28, 2 (1993): 261-85.

Henderson, Edith G., *Foundations of English Administrative Law.* Cambridge: Harvard University Press, 1963.

Herman, Edward S. and Noam Chomsky, *Manufacturing Consent: The Political Economy of the Mass Media.* New York: Pantheon Books, 1988.

Hernes, Gudmund, 'Structural Change in Social Processes', *American Journal of Sociology* 82, 3 (1976): 513-47.

Hibbs, Douglas A. Jr, 'Political Parties and Macroeconomic Policy', *American Political Science Review* 71, 4 (1977): 1467-87.

Hibbs, Douglas A. Jr, 'On the Political Economy of Long-run Trends in Strike Activity', *British Journal of Political Science* 8, 2 (1978): 153-75.

Hibbs, Douglas A. Jr, *The Political Economy of Industrial Democracies.* Cambridge, MA: Harvard University Press, 1987.

Hilgartner, Stephen and Charles L. Bosk, 'The Rise and Fall of Social Problems: A Public Arenas Model', *American Journal of Sociology* 94, 1 (1988): 53-78.

Hill, Larry B., ed., *The State of Public Bureaucracy.* Armonk, NY: M.E. Sharpe, 1992.

Hill, Michael, ed., *The Policy Process: A Reader.* New York: Harvester-Wheatsheaf, 1993.

Hill, Michael J. and Glen Bramley, *Analyzing Social Policy.* Oxford: Basil Blackwell, 1986.

Hintze, Otto, *The Historical Essays of Otto Hintze.* New York: Oxford University Press, 1975.

Hjern, Benny, 'Implementation Research—The Link Gone Missing', *Journal of Public Policy* 2, 3 (1982): 301-8.

Hjern, Benny and David O. Porter, 'Implementation Structures: A New Unit of Administrative Analysis' in *The Policy Process: A Reader*, ed. M. Hill. London: Harvester Wheatsheaf, 1993

Hoberg, George Jr, 'Technology, Political Structure, and Social Regulation: A Cross-National Analysis', *Comparative Politics* 18, 3 (1986): 357-76.

Hofferbert, Richard I., *The Study of Public Policy.* Indianapolis, IN: Bobbs-Merrill, 1974.

Hogg, P.W., 'The Supreme Court of Canada and Administrative Law, 1949-1971', *Osgoode Hall Law Journal* 11, 2 (1973): 187-223.

Hogwood, Brian W., *Trends in British Public Policy: Do Governments Make Any Difference.* Buckingham: Open University Press, 1992.

Hogwood, Brian W. and Lewis A. Gunn, *Policy Analysis for the Real World.* New York: Oxford University Press, 1984.

Hogwood, Brian W. and B. Guy Peters, *Policy Dynamics.* Brighton: Wheatsheaf, 1983.

Holzner, Burkart and John H. Marx, *Knowledge Application: The Knowledge System in Society*. Wellesley, MA: Allyn and Bacon, 1979.

Hood, Christopher, 'Using Bureaucracy Sparingly', *Public Administration* 61, 2 (1983): 197-208.

Hood, Christopher C., *Administrative Analysis: An Introduction to Rules, Enforcement, and Organizations*. Sussex: Wheatsheaf, 1986.

Hood, Christopher C., *The Tools of Government*. Chatham: Chatham House, 1986.

Hough, Jerry F., 'The Soviet System: Petrification or Pluralism', *Problems of Communism* 21, (March-April 1972): 25-45.

Howard, John L. and W. T. Stanbury, 'Measuring Leviathan: The Size, Scope and Growth of Governments in Canada' in *Probing Leviathan: An Investigation of Government in the Economy*, ed. G. Lermer. Vancouver: Fraser Institute, 1984.

Howard, S. Kenneth, 'Analysis, Rationality, and Administrative Decision-Making' in *Toward a New Public Administration: The Minnowbrook Perspective*, ed. F. Marini. Scranton: Chandler, 1971.

Howlett, Michael, 'Acts of Commission and Acts of Omission: Legal-Historical Research and the Intentions of government in a Federal State', *Canadian Journal of Political Science* 19 (1986): 363-71.

Howlett, Michael, 'Policy Instruments, Policy Styles, and Policy Implementation: National Approaches to Theories of Instrument Choice', *Policy Studies Journal* 19, 2 (1991): 1-21.

Howlett, Michael, 'Policy Paradigms and Policy Change: Lessons from the Old and New Canadian Policies towards Aboriginal Peoples', *Policy Studies Journal* 22, 4 (1994): 631-51.

Howlett, Michael and M. Ramesh, *The Political Economy of Canada: An Introduction*. Toronto: McClelland and Stewart, 1992.

Howlett, M. and M. Ramesh. 'Patterns of Policy Instrument Choice: Policy Styles, Policy Learning and the Privatization Experience', *Policy Studies Review* 12, 1 (1993).

Huber, George P. 'Organization Learning: The Contributing Processes and the Literatures', *Organization Science* 2, 1 (1991): 88-115.

Hudson, Joe, John Mayne and Ray Thomlinson (eds), *Action-Oriented Evaluation in Organizations*. Toronto: Wall and Emerson, 1992.

Huitt, Ralph K., 'Political Feasibility' in *Political Science and Public Policy*, ed. A. Rannay. Chicago: Markham Publishing Co., 1968.

Hula, Richard C., 'Using Markets to Implement Public Policy' in *Market-Based Public Policy*, ed. R.C. Hula. New York: St Martin's, 1988.

Hult, Karen M. and Charles Walcott, *Governing Public Organizations: Politics, Structures and Institutional Design*. Pacific Grove: Brooks/Cole, 1990.

Huntington, Samuel P., 'The Marasmus of the ICC: The Commissions, the Railroads and the Public Interest', *Yale Law Review* 61, 4 (1952): 467-509.

Ikenberry, G. John, 'Conclusion: An Institutional Approach to American Foreign Economic Policy', *International Organization* 42, 1 (1988): 219-43.

Ikenberry, G. John, 'The International Spread of Privatization Policies: Inducements, Learning, and "Policy Bandwagoning"' in *The Political Economy of Public Sector Reform and Privatization*, eds E.N. Suleiman and J. Waterbury. Boulder: Westview Press, 1990.

Ikenberry, G. John and Charles A. Kupchan, 'Socialization and Hegemonic Power', *International Organization* 44, 3 (1990): 283-515.

Imershein, Allen W., 'Organizational Change as a Paradigm Shift', *The Sociological Quarterly* 18, 1 (1977): 33-43.

Ingram, Helen and Anne Schneider, 'Improving Implementation Through Framing Smarter Statutes', *Journal of Public Policy* 10, 1 (1990): 67-88.

Ingram, Helen M. and Dean E. Mann, 'Policy Failure: An Issue Deserving Analysis' in *Why Policies Succeed or Fail*, eds H.M. Ingram and D.E. Mann. Beverly Hills: Sage, 1980.

Ingram, Helen M. and Dean E. Mann, *Why Policies Succeed or Fail*. Beverly Hills: Sage, 1980.

Jacek, Henry J., 'Pluralist and Corporatist Intermediation, Activities of Business Interest Associations, and Corporate Profits: Some Evidence from Canada', *Comparative Politics* 18, 4 (1986): 419-37.

Jaffe, Louis L., *Judicial Control of Administrative Action*. Boston: Little Brown, 1965.

Jaffe, Louis L., *English and American Judges as Lawmakers*. Oxford: Clarendon Press, 1969.

James, Simon, 'The Idea Brokers: The Impact of Think Tanks on British Government', *Public Administration* 71 (1993): 491-506.

Jenkins, William I., *Policy Analysis: A Political and Organizational Perspective*. London: Martin Robertson, 1978.

Jenkins-Smith, Hank, 'Continuing Controversies in Policy Analysis' in *Policy Analysis and Economics: Developments, Tensions, Prospects*, ed. D.L. Weimer. Boston: Kluwer, 1991.

Jenkins-Smith, Hank C., *Democratic Politics and Policy Analysis*. Pacific Grove: Brooks/Cole, 1990.

Jenkins-Smith, Hank C., Gilbert K. St Clair, and Brian Woods, 'Explaining Change in Policy Subsystems: Analysis of Coalition Stability and Defection over Time', *American Journal of Political Science* 35, 4 (1991): 851-80.

Jenkins-Smith, Hank C. and Paul A. Sabatier, 'The Study of the Public Policy Processes' in *Policy Change and Learning: An Advocacy Coalition Approach*, eds Paul A. Sabatier and Hank C. Jenkins-Smith. Boulder: Westview, 1993.

Jennings, Bruce, 'Interpretation and the Practice of Policy Analysis' in *Confronting Values in Policy Analysis: The Politics of Criteria*, eds F. Fischer and J. Forester. Newbury Park: Sage, 1987.

Jenson, Jane, 'Paradigms and Political Discourse: Protective Legislation in France and the United States Before 1914', *Canadian Journal of Political Science* 22, 2 (1989): 235-58.

Jenson, Jane, 'All the World's a Stage: Ideas About Political Space and Time', *Studies in Political Economy* 36 (1991): 43-72.

Johnson, David B., *Public Choice: An Introduction to the New Political Economy*. Mountain View, CA: Mayfield Publishing, 1991.

Johnson, Norman, *The Welfare State in Transition: The Theory and Practice of Welfare Pluralism*. Brighton, Sussex: Wheatsheaf Books, 1987.

Johnston, Richard, *Public Opinion and Public Policy in Canada: Questions of Confidence*. Toronto: University of Toronto Press, 1986.

Jones, Charles O., *An Introduction to the Study of Public Policy*, 3rd ed. Monterey, CA: Brooks/Cole, 1984.

Jordan, A. Grant, 'Iron Triangles, Woolly Corporatism and Elastic Nets: Images of the Policy Process', *Journal of Public Policy* 1, 1 (1981): 95-123.

Jordan, Grant, 'Policy Community Realism versus "New" Institutionalist Ambiguity', *Political Studies* 38, 3 (1990): 470-84.

Jordan, Grant, 'Sub-governments, Policy Communities and Networks: Refilling the Old Bottles?', *Journal of Theoretical Politics* 2, 3 (1990): 319-38.

Jordan, Grant and Jeremy Richardson, 'The British Policy Style or the Logic of Negotiation?' in *Policy Styles in Western Europe*, ed. J. Richardson. London: Allen and Unwin, 1982.

Jordan, Grant and Klaus Schubert, 'A Preliminary Ordering of Policy Network Labels', *European Journal of Political Research* 21, 1/2 (1992): 7-27.

Jordan, J.M. and S.L. Sutherland, 'Assessing the Results of Public Expenditure: Program Evaluation in the Federal Government', *Canadian Public Administration* 22, 4 (1979): 581-609.

Katzenstein, Peter J., 'Conclusion: Domestic Structures and Strategies of Foreign Economic Policy', *International Organization* 31, 4 (1977): 879-920.

Katzenstein, Peter J., *Between Power and Plenty: Foreign Economic Policies of Advanced Industrial States*. Madison: University of Wisconsin Press, 1978.

Katzenstein, Peter J., *Small States in World Markets: Industrial Policy in Europe*. Ithaca: Cornell University Press, 1985.

Keeler, John T.S., 'Opening the Window for Reform: Mandates, Crises and Extra-ordinary Policy-Making', *Comparative Political Studies* 25, 4 (1993): 433-86.

Kelman, Steven, '"Public Choice" and Public Spirit', *Public Interest* 87 (Spring 1987): 80-94.

Kenis, Patrick and Volker Schneider, 'Policy Networks and Policy Analysis: Scrutinizing a New Analytical Toolbox' in *Policy Networks: Empirical Evidence and Theoretical Considerations*, eds B. Marin and R. Mayntz. Boulder: Westview, 1991.

Kennamer, J. David, ed., *Public Opinion, the Press, and Public Policy*. Westport, CT: Praeger, 1992.

Keohan, Robert O., *International Institutions and State Powers: Essays in International Relations Theory*. Boulder: Westview Press, 1989: 163.

Keohane, Robert O., 'Multilateralism: An Agenda for Research', *International Journal* 45, 4 (1990): 731-64.

Keohane, Robert O. and Joseph S. Nye, *Power and Interdependence*. Glenview, IL: Scott, Foresman, 1989.

Kernaghan, K., 'Power, Parliament and Public Servants in Canada: Ministerial Responsibility Reexamined', *Canadian Public Policy* 5, 3 (1979): 383-96.

Kernaghan, Kenneth, 'Judicial Review of Administration Action' in *Public Administration in Canada: Selected Readings*, ed. K. Kernaghan. Toronto: Methuen, 1985.

Kernaghan, Kenneth, 'The Public and Public Servants in Canada' in *Public Administration in Canada: Selected Readings*, ed. K. Kernaghan. Toronto: Methuen, 1985.

Kerr, Clark, *The Future of Industrial Societies: Convergence or Continuing Diversity?* Cambridge: Harvard University Press, 1983.

Kerr, Donna H., 'The Logic of "Policy" and Successful Policies', *Policy Sciences* 7, 3 (1976): 351-63.

King, Anthony, 'Ideas, Institutions and the Policies of Governments: A Comparative Analysis: Part III', *British Journal of Political Science* 3, 4 (1973): 409-23.

King, Anthony, 'What Do Elections Decide?' in *Democracy at the Polls: A Comparative Study of Competitive National Elections*, eds D. Butler, H.R. Penniman, and A. Ranney. Washington, DC: American Enterprise Institute for Public Policy Research, 1981.

Kingdon, John W., *Agendas, Alternatives and Public Policies*. Boston: Little, Brown and Company, 1984.

Kiser, Larry and Elinor Ostrom, 'The Three Worlds of Action' in *Strategies of Political Inquiry*, ed. Elinor Ostrom. Beverly Hills: Sage, 1982.

Kirschen, E.S. et al., *Economic Policy in Our Time. Vol. I—General Theory*. Chicago: Rand McNally, 1964.

Korpi, Walter, *The Democratic Class Struggle*. London: Routledge and Kegan Paul, 1983.

Krasner, S.D., 'Structural Causes and Regime Consequences: Regimes as Intervening Variables', *International Organization* 36, 2 (1982): 185-205.

Krasner, Stephen D., ed., *International Regimes*. Ithaca: Cornell University Press, 1983.

Krasner, Stephen D., 'Approaches to the State: Alternative Conceptions and Historical Dynamics', *Comparative Politics* 16, 2 (1984): 223-46.

Krasner, Stephen D., 'Sovereignty: An Institutional Perspective', *Comparative Political Studies* 21, 1 (1988): 66-94.

Kreuger, Anne O., 'The Political Economy of the Rent-Seeking Society', *American Economic Review* 64, 3 (1974): 291-303.

Kuhn, Thomas S., *The Structure of Scientific Revolutions*. Chicago: University of Chicago Press, 1962.

Kuhn, Thomas S., 'Second Thoughts on Paradigms' in *The Structure of Scientific Theories*, ed. F. Suppe. Urbana: University of Illinois Press, 1974.

Lacroix, L., 'Strike Activity in Canada' in *Canadian Labour Relations*, ed. W.C. Riddell. Toronto: University of Toronto Press, 1986.

Lange, Peter and Hudson Meadwell, 'Typologies of Democratic Systems: From Political Inputs to Political Economy' in *New Directions in Comparative Politics*, ed. H.J. Wiarda. Boulder, CO: Westview Press, 1991.

Larson, James S., *Why Government Programs Fail: Improving Policy Implementations*. New York: Praeger, 1980.

Lasswell, Harold D., 'The Policy Orientation' in *The Policy Sciences: Recent Developments in Scope and Method*, ed. D. Lerner and H.D. Lasswell. Stanford: Stanford University Press, 1951.

Lasswell, Harold D., *The Decision Process: Seven Categories of Functional Analysis*. College Park: University of Maryland, 1956.

Lasswell, Harold D., *A Pre-View of Policy Sciences*. New York: American Elsevier, 1971.

Latham, Earl, 'The Group Basis of Politics: Notes for a Theory', *American Political Science Review* 46, 2 (1952): 376-97.

Le Grand, Julian, 'The Theory of Government Failure', *British Journal of Political Science* 21, 4 (1991): 423-42

Le Grand, Julian and Ray Robinson, eds, *Privatization and the Welfare State*. London: George, Allen and Unwin, 1984.

Le Pan, Nick, 'Tax Expenditure Analysis: Some Conceptual Problems', *Canadian Taxation* 1, 2 (1979): 15-18.

Leeuw, Frans L., 'Policy Theories, Knowledge Utilization, and Evaluation', *Knowledge and Policy* 4, 3 (1991): 73-91.

Lehmbruch, Gerhard, 'Consociational Democracy, Class Conflict and the New Corporatism' in *Trends Towards Corporatist Intermediation*, eds P.C. Schmitter and G. Lehmbruch. Beverly Hills: Sage, 1979.

Lehmbruch, G., 'Introduction: Neo-Corporatism in Comparative Perspective' in *Patterns of Corporatist Policy-Making*, eds G. Lehmbruch and P.C. Schmitter. Beverly Hills: Sage, 1982.

Leman, Chistopher K., 'The Forgotten Fundamental: Successes and Excesses of Direct Government' in *Beyond Privatization: The Tools of Government Action*, ed. L.M. Salamon. Washington D.C.: Urban Institute, 1989.

Lerner, Daniel and Harold D. Lasswell, eds, *The Policy Sciences: Recent Developments in Scope and Method.* Stanford: Stanford University Press, 1951.

Levi, M., *Of Rule and Revenue.* Berkeley: University of California Press, 1988.

Lewis, David and Helen Wallace, eds, *Policies into Practice: National and International Case Studies in Implementation.* London: Heinemann Educational, 1984.

Lindblom, Charles E., *Bargaining: The Hidden Hand in Government.* Los Angeles: Rand Corporation, 1955.

Lindblom, Charles E., 'Policy Analysis', *American Economic Review* 48, 3 (1958): 298-312.

Lindblom, Charles E., 'The Science of Muddling Through', *Public Administration Review* 19, 2 (1959): 79-88.

Lindblom, Charles E., 'Decision-Making in Taxation and Expenditures' in *Public Finances: Needs, Sources, and Utilization, ed. by Universities-National Bureau Committee for Economic Research.* Princeton: Princeton University Press, 1961.

Lindblom, Charles E., 'Contexts for Change and Strategy: A Reply', *Public Administration Review* 24, 3 (1964): 157-58.

Lindblom, Charles E., *The Policy-Making Process.* Englewood Cliffs: Prentice-Hall, 1968.

Lindblom, Charles E., 'The Sociology of Planning: Thought and Social Interaction' in *Economic Planning, East and West, ed. M. Bernstein.* Cambridge: Ballinger, 1975.

Lindblom, Charles E., *The Policy-Making Process.* New Haven: Yale University Press, 1977.

Lindblom, Charles E., *Politics and Markets: The World's Political Economic Systems.* New York: Basic Books, 1977.

Lindblom, Charles E., 'Still Muddling, Not Yet Through', *Public Administration Review* 39, 6 (1979): 517-26.

Lindblom, Charles E., 'The Market as Prison' in *The Political Economy, eds T. Ferguson and J. Rogers.* Armonk, NY: M.E. Sharpe, 1984.

Lindblom, Charles E. and D.K. Cohen, *Usable Knowledge: Social Science and Social Problem Solving.* New Haven: Yale University Press, 1979.

Linder, Stephen and B. Guy Peters, 'The Design of Instruments for Public Policy' in *Policy Theory and Policy Evaluation: Concepts, Knowledge, Causes, and Norms, ed. S.S. Nagel.* New York: Greenwood Press, 1990.

Linder, Stephen H. and B. Guy Peters, 'From Social Theory to Policy Design', *Journal of Public Policy* 4, 3 (1984): 237-59.

Linder, Stephen H. and B. Guy Peters, 'The Analysis of Design or the Design of Analysis?' *Policy Studies Review* 7, 4 (1988): 738-50.

Linder, Stephen H. and B. Guy Peters, 'Instruments of Government: Perceptions and Contexts', *Journal of Public Policy* 9, 1 (1989): 35-58.

Linder, Stephen H. and B. Guy Peters, 'Research Perspectives on the Design of Public Policy: Implementation, Formulation, and Design' in *Implementation and the Policy Process: Opening up the Black Box, ed. D.J. Palumbo and D.J. Calista.* New York: Greenwood Press, 1990.

Linder, Stephen H. and B. Guy Peters, 'The Logic of Public Policy Design: Linking Policy Actors and Plausible Instruments', *Knowledge in Society* 4 (1991): 125-51.

Lindquist, Evert, 'Tax Expenditures, Competitiveness and Accountability' in *Policy Making and Competitiveness, ed. Bryne Purchase.* Kingston: Queen's University School of Political Studies, 1994.

Lindquist, Evert A., 'What do Decision Models Tell Us about Information Use?', *Knowledge in Society* 1, 2 (1988): 86-111.

Lindquist, Evert A., 'Public Managers and Policy Communities: Learning to Meet New Challenges', *Canadian Public Administration* 35, 2 (1992): 127-59.

Lindquist, Evert A., 'Think Tanks or Clubs? Assessing the Influence and Roles of Canadian Policy Institutes', *Canadian Public Administration* 36, 4 (1993): 547-79.

Lipsky, Michael, *Street-Level Bureaucracy: Dilemmas of the Individual in Public Services*. New York: Russell Sage Foundation, 1980.

Livingston, Steven G., 'Knowledge Hierarchies and the Politics of Ideas in American International Commodity Production', *Journal of Public Policy* 12, 3 (1992): 223-42.

Locksley, Gareth, 'The Political Business Cycle: Alternative Interpretations' in *Models of Political Economy*, ed. P. Whiteley. London: Sage Publications, 1980.

Lowi, Theodore J., 'Distribution, Regulation, Redistribution: The Functions of Government' in *Public Policies and Their Politics: Techniques of Government Control*, ed. R.B. Ripley. New York: W.W. Norton, 1966.

Lowi, Theodore J., *The End of Liberalism: Ideology, Policy and the Crisis of Public Authority*. New York: Norton, 1969.

Lowi, Theodore J., 'Four Systems of Policy, Politics and Choice', *Public Administration Review* 32, 4 (1972): 298-310.

Lund, Michael S., 'Between Welfare and the Market: Loan Guarantees as a Policy Tool' in *Beyond Privatization: The Tools of Government Action*, ed. L.M. Salamon. Washington, DC: Urban Institute, 1989.

Lundqvist, Lennart J., 'Explaining Privatization: Notes Towards a Predictive Theory', *Scandinavian Political Studies* 12, 2 (1989): 129-45.

Lustick, Ian, 'Explaining the Variable Utility of Disjointed Incrementalism: Four Propositions', *American Political Science Review* 74, 2 (1980): 342-53.

Lynn, Laurence Jr, ed., *Knowledge and Policy: The Uncertain Connection*. Washington, DC: National Academy of Sciences, 1978.

Macdonald, R.A., 'Understanding Regulation by Regulations' in *Regulations, Crown Corporations, and Administrative Tribunals*, eds I. Bernier and A. Lajoie. Toronto: University of Toronto Press, 1985.

MacRae, Duncan, 'Policy Analysis and Knowledge Use', *Knowledge and Policy* 4, 3 (1991): 27-40.

MacRae, Duncan Jr and James A. Wilde, *Policy Analysis for Public Decisions*. Lanham, MD: University Press of America, 1985.

Madison, James and Jay Hamilton, *The Federalist Papers: A Collection of Essays Written in Support of the Constitution of the United States*. Garden City, NY: Anchor Books, 1961.

Majone, Giandomenico, *Evidence, Argument, and Persuasion in the Policy Process*. New Haven: Yale University Press, 1989

Malloy, James M., 'Statecraft, Social Policy, and Governance in Latin America', *Governance* 6, 2 (1993): 220-74.

Mann, Michael, 'The Autonomous Power of the State: Its Origins, Mechanisms and Results', *European Journal of Sociology* 25, 2 (1984): 185-213.

Manning, Nick, 'What is a Social Problem?' in *The State or the Market: Politics and Welfare in Contemporary Britian*, eds Martin Loney et al. London: Sage, 1987.

Manzer, Ronald, 'Policy Rationality and Policy Analysis: The Problem of the Choice of Criteria for Decision-making' in *Public Policy and Administrative Studies*, ed. O.P. Dwivedi. Guelph: University of Guelph, 1984.

March, James G. and Johan P. Olsen, 'Organizational Choice Under Ambiguity' in

Ambiguity and Choice in Organizations, eds J.G. March and J.P. Olsen. Bergen: Universitetsforlaget, 1979.

March, James G. and Johan P. Olsen, 'The New Institutionalism: Organizational Factors in Political Life', *American Political Science Review* 78, 3 (1984): 734-49.

March, James G. and Johan P. Olsen, 'Institutional Perspectives on Political Institutions', Paper presented at the Meeting of the International Political Science Association, Berlin: (1994).

Marin, Bernd and Renate Mayntz, eds, *Policy Networks: Empirical Evidence and Theoretical Considerations*. Boulder: Westview Press, 1991.

Markoff, John, 'Governmental Bureaucratization: General Processes and an Anomalous Case', *Comparative Studies in Society and History* 17, 4 (1975): 479-503.

Markoff, John and Veronica Montecinos, 'The Ubiquitous Rise of Economists', *Journal of Public Policy* 13, 1 (1993): 37-68.

Marsh, David and R.A.W. Rhodes, eds, *Policy Networks in British Government*. Oxford: Clarendon Press, 1992.

Maslove, Allan, ed., *Taxing and Spending: Issues of Process*. Toronto: University of Toronto Press, 1994.

Masser, Ian, Ove Sviden, and Michael Wegener, 'From Growth to Equity and Sustainability: Paradigm Shift in Transport Planning?' *Futures* 24, 6 (1992): 539-58.

Masterman, Margaret, 'The Nature of a Paradigm' in *Criticism and the Growth of Knowledge*, eds. I. Lakatos and A. Musgrave. Cambridge: Cambridge University Press, 1970.

May, Peter J., 'Politics and Policy Analysis', *Political Science Quarterly* 101, 1 (1986): 109-25.

May, Peter J., 'Reconsidering Policy Design: Policies and Publics', *Journal of Public Policy* 11, 2 (1991): 187-206.

May, Peter J., 'Policy Learning And Failure', *Journal of Public Policy* 12, 4 (1992): 331-54.

Mayne, John and Robert S. Mayne, 'Will Program Evaluation be Used in Formulating Policy?' in *The Politics of Canadian Public Policy*, eds M.M. Atkinson and M.A. Chandler. Toronto: University of Toronto Press, 1983.

Mayntz, Renate, 'Governing Failure and the Problem of Governability: Some Comments on a Theoretical Peradigm' in *Modern Governance: New Government-Society Interactions*, ed. J. Kooiman. London: Sage, 1993.

Mayntz, Renate, 'Legitimacy and the Directive Capacity of the Political System' in *Stress and Contradiction in Modern Capitalism: Public Policy and the Theory of the State*, ed. L.N. Lindberg. Lexington: Lexington Press, 1975.

Mazmanian, Daniel A. and Paul A. Sabatier, *Implementation and Public Policy*. Glenview: Scott, Foresman, 1983.

McConnell, Grant, *Private Power and American Democracy*. New York: Knopf, 1966.

McCool, Daniel, 'Subgovernments and the Impact of Policy Fragmentation and Accommodation', *Policy Studies Review* 8, 2 (1989): 264-87.

McDaniel, Paul R., 'Tax Expenditures as Tools of Government Action' in *Beyond Privatization: The Tools of Government Action*, ed. L.M. Salamon. Washington, DC: Urban Institute, 1989.

McDonnell, Lorraine M. and Richard F. Elmore, *Alternative Policy Instruments*. Santa Monica, CA: Center for Policy Research in Education, Publications Dept, Rand Corp [distributor], 1987.

McFarland, Andrew S., 'Interest Groups and Theories of Power in America', *British Journal of Political Science* 17, 2 (1987): 129-47.

McLaughlin, Milbrey W., 'Implementation Realities and Evaluation Design' in *Social Science and Social Policy*, eds R.L. Shotland and M.M. Mark. Beverly Hills: Sage, 1985.

McLean, Iain, *Public Choice: An Introduction*. Oxford: Basil Blackwell, 1987.

McLennan, Gregor, *Marxism, Pluralism and Beyond: Classic Debates and New Departures*. Cambridge: Polity Press, 1989.

McRoberts, Kenneth, 'Federal Structures and the Policy Process' in *Governing Canada: Institutions and Public Policy*, ed. M. Michael Atkinson. Toronto: Harcourt Brace Jovanovich, 1993.

Mead, Lawrence M., 'Policy Studies and Political Science', *Policy Studies Review* 5, 2 (1985): 319-35.

Miller, Leonard S., 'The Structural Determinants of the Welfare Effort: A Critique and a Contribution', *Social Service Review* 50, 1 (1976): 57-79.

Milward, H. Brinton and Ronald A. Francisco, 'Subsystem Politics and Corporatism in the United States', *Policy and Politics* 11, 3 (1983).

Milward, H. Brinton and Gary L. Walmsley, 'Policy Subsystems, Networks and the Tools of Public Management' in *Public Policy Formation*, ed. R. Eyestone. Greenwich: JAI Press, 1984.

Minogue, Martin, 'Theory and Practice in Public Policy and Administration', *Policy and Politics* 1, 1 (1983): 1.

Mitchell, Timothy, 'The Limits of the State: Beyond Statist Approaches and Their Critics', *American Political Science Review* 85, 1 (1991): 77-96.

Mitnick, B.M., *The Political Economy of Regulation: Creating, Designing, and Removing Regulatory Forms*. New York: Columbia University Press, 1980.

Moe, Terry M., *The Organization of Interests: Incentives and the Internal Dynamics of Political Interest Groups*. Chicago: The University of Chicago Press, 1980.

Moore, Mark H., 'What Sort of Ideas Become Public Ideas?' in *The Power of Public Ideas*, ed. R.B. Reich. Cambridge: Ballinger, 1988.

Morell, Jonathan A., *Program Evaluation in Social Research*. New York: Pergamon Press, 1979.

Mueller, Dennis C., *Public Choice*. Cambridge: Cambridge University Press, 1989.

Munns, Joyce M., 'The Environment, Politics, and Policy Literature: A Critique and Reformulation', *Western Political Quarterly* 28, 4 (1975): 646-67.

Muskin, Selma J. and Charles L. Vehorn, 'User Fees and Charges' in *Managing Fiscal Stress: The Crisis in the Public Sector*, ed. C.H. Levine. Chatham, NJ: Chatham House, 1980.

Musolf, Lloyd D., 'The Government Corporation Tool: Permutations and Possibilities' in *Beyond Privatization: The Tools of Government Action*, ed. L.M. Salamon. Washington, DC: Urban Institute, 1989.

Muzzio, Douglas and Gerald De Maio, 'Formal Theory and the Prospects of a Policy Science' in *Handbook of Political Theory and Policy Science*, eds E.B. Portis, M.B. Levy, and M. Landau. New York: Greenwood Press, 1988.

Nachmias, David, *Public Policy Evaluation: Approaches and Methods*. New York: St Martin's Press, 1979.

Nagel, Stuart S., 'Introduction: Bridging Theory and Practice in Policy/Program Evaluation' in *Policy Theory and Policy Evaluation: Concepts, Knowledge, Causes, and Norms*, ed. S.S. Nagel. New York: Greenwood Press, 1990.

Nakamura, Robert T. and Frank Smallwood, *The Politics of Policy Implementation*. New York: St Martin's Press, 1980.

Nelson, Richard R. and Sidney G. Winter, *An Evolutionary Theory of Economic Change*. Cambridge: Harvard University Press, 1982.

Nettl, J.P., 'The State as a Conceptual Variable', *World Politics* 20, 4 (1968): 559-92.

Nice, D.C., 'Incremental and Nonincremental Policy Responses: The States and the Railroads', *Polity* 20 (1987): 145-56.

Nicolaus, Martin, 'Proletariat and Middle Class in Marx: Hegelian Choreography and the Capitalist Dialectic', *Studies on the Left* 7, 1 (1967): 22-49.

Niskanen, William A., *Bureaucracy and Representative Government*. Chicago: University of Chicago Press, 1971.

Nordlinger, Eric A., *On the Autonomy of the Democratic State*. Cambridge: Harvard University Press, 1981.

Nordlinger, Eric A., 'Taking the State Seriously' in *Understanding Political Development*, eds M. Weiner and S.P. Huntington. Boston: Little, Brown and Company, 1987.

Nordlinger, Eric A., 'The Return to the State: Critiques', *American Political Science Review* 82, 3 (1988): 875-85.

North, Douglas C., *Institutions, Institutional Change and Economic Performance*. Cambridge: Cambridge University Press, 1990.

O'Connor, James R., *The Fiscal Crisis of the State*. New York: St Martin's Press, 1973.

Offe, Claus, 'Political Authority and Class Structures–An Analysis of Late Capitalist Societies', *International Journal of Sociology* 2, 1 (1972): 73-108.

Offe, Claus, 'Social Policy and the Theory of the State' in *Contradictions of the Welfare State*, ed. J. Keane. London: Hutchinson, 1984.

Offe, Claus, 'Challenging the Boundaries of Institutional Politics: Social Movements since the 1960s' in *Changing Boundaries of the Political: Essays on the Evolving Balance Between the State and Society, Public and Private in Europe*, ed. C.S. Maier. Cambridge: Cambridge University Press, 1987.

Offe, Claus, 'Competitive Party Democracy and the Keynesian Welfare State: Factors of Stability and Disorganization', *Policy Sciences* 15 (1983): 225-46.

Olson, David M. and Michael L. Mezey, eds, *Legislatures in the Policy Process: The Dilemmas of Economic Policy*. Cambridge: Cambridge University Press, 1991.

Olson, Mancur, *The Logic of Collective Action: Public Goods and the Theory of Groups*. Cambridge: Harvard University Press, 1965.

Olson, Mancur, *The Rise and Decline of Nations: Economic Growth, Stagflation, and Social Rigidities*. New Haven: Yale University Press, 1982.

Olson, Mancur, 'A Theory of the Incentives Facing Political Organizations: Neo-Corporatism and the Hegemonic State', *International Political Science Review* 7, 2 (1986): 165-89.

Ossowski, Stanislaw, *Class Structure in the Social Consciousness*, trans. Sheila Patterson. New York: Free Press of Glencoe, 1963.

Ostrander, Susan A. and Stuart Langton, eds, *Shifting the Debate: Public/Private Sector Relations in the Modern Welfare State*. New Brunswick: Transaction Books, 1987: 31.

Ostrom, Elinor, 'An Agenda for the Study of Institutions', *Public Choice* 48 (1986): 3-25.

Ostrom, Elinor, 'A Method of Institutional Analysis' in *Guidance, Control and Evaluation in the Public Sector*, eds F.X. Kaufman, G. Majone and V. Ostrom. Berlin: deGruyter, 1986.

Ozawa, Connie P., *Recasting Science: Consensual Procedures in Public Policy Making*. Boulder: Westview Press, 1991.

Padgett, Stephen, 'Policy Style and Issue Environment: The Electricity Supply Sector in West Germany', *Journal of Public Policy* 10, 2 (1990): 165-93.

Page, Edward, 'Laws as an Instrument of Policy: A Study in Central-Local Government Relations', *Journal of Public Policy* 5, 2 (1985): 241-65.

Page, Edward C., *Political Authority and Bureaucratic Power: A Comparative Analysis*. Brighton, Sussex: Wheatsheaf, 1985.

Pal, Leslie A., *Public Policy Analysis: An Introduction*. Toronto: Methuen, 1987.

Pal, Leslie A., *Public Policy Analysis: An Introduction*, 2nd ed. Scarborough: Nelson, 1992.

Palumbo, Dennis J., *The Politics of Program Evaluation*. Beverly Hills: Sage, 1987.

Palumbo, Dennis J. and Donald J. Calista, 'Opening Up the Black Box: Implementation and the Policy Process' in *Implementation and the Policy Process: Opening Up the Black Box*, eds D.J. Palumbo and D.J. Calista. New York: Greenwood Press, 1990.

Palumbo, Dennis J. and D.J. Calista, *Implementation and the Policy Process: Opening Up the Black Box*. New York: Greenwood Press, 1990.

Panitch, Leo, 'The Development of Corporatism in Liberal Democracies', *Comparative Political Studies* 10, 1 (1977): 61-90.

Panitch, Leo, 'Corporatism in Canada', *Studies in Political Economy* 1, 1 (1979): 43-92.

Panitch, Leo, 'Recent Theorizations of Corporatism: Reflections on a Growth Industry', *British Journal of Sociology* 31, 2 (1980): 159-87.

Parenti, Michael, *Inventing Reality: The Politics of the Mass Media*. New York: St Martin's Press, 1986.

Partridge, P.H., 'An Evaluation of Bureaucratic Power', *Public Administration (Australia)* 33, (Sept. 1974): 99-124.

Pateman, Carole, *Participation and Democratic Theory*. Cambridge: Cambridge University Press, 1970.

Peters, B. Guy, 'The Structure and Organization of Government: Concepts and Issues', *Journal of Public Policy* 5, 1 (1985): 107-20.

Peters, B. Guy, 'The Policy Process: An Institutionalist Perspective', *Canadian Public Administration* 35, 2 (1992): 160-80.

Peters, B. Guy, *The Politics of Bureaucracy: A Comparative Perspective*. New York: Longman, 1984.

Peters, B. Guy, John C. Doughtie, and M. Kathleen McCulloch, 'Types of Democratic Systems and Types of Public Policy', *Comparative Politics* 9 (1977): 327-55.

Peters, B.G., J.C. Doughtie, and M.K. McCulloch, 'Do Public Policies Vary in Different Types of Democratic System?' in *The Practice of Comparative Politics: A Reader*, eds P.G. Lewis, D.C. Potter and F.G. Castles. London: Longman, 1978.

Peters, B. Guy and Brian W. Hogwood, 'Policy Succession: The Dynamics of Policy Change.' *Studies in Public Policy*. 69 (1980).

Peters, B. Guy and Brian W. Hogwood, *The Pathology of Public Policy*. New York: Oxford University Press, 1985.

Phidd, Richard and G. Bruce Doern, *Canadian Public Policy: Ideas, Structures, Process*. Toronto: Methuen, 1983.

Phillips, Derek L., 'Paradigms and Incommensurability', *Theory and Society* 2, 1 (1975): 37-61.

Phillips, Susan, 'Meaning and Structure in Social Movements: Mapping the Network of National Canadian Women's Organizations', *Canadian Journal of Political Science* 24, 4 (1991): 755-82.

Pigou, A.C., *The Economics of Welfare*, 4th ed. London: Macmillan, 1932.

Pollock, Phillip H. III, Stuart A. Lilie, and M. Elliot Vittes, 'Hard Issues, Core Values and Vertical Constraint: The Case of Nuclear Power', *British Journal of Political Science* 23, 1 (1993): 29-50.

Polsby, Nelson W., *Community Power and Political Theory*. New Haven: Yale University Press, 1963.

Polsby, Nelson W., *Political Innovation in America: The Politics of Policy Initiation*. New Haven: Yale University Press, 1984.

Portis, Edward Bryan, Michael B. Levy, and Martin Landau, eds, *Handbook of Political Theory and Policy Science*. New York: Greenwood Press, 1988.

Posner, Richard A., 'Theories of Economic Regulation', *Bell Journal of Economics and Management Science* 5, 2 (1974): 335-58.

Poulantzas, Nicos, 'The Problem of the Capitalist State', *New Left Review* 58 (1969): 67-78.

Poulantzas, Nicos, 'On Social Classes', *New Left Review* 78 (1973): 27-54.

Poulantzas, Nicos, *Political Power and Social Classes*. London: New Left Books, 1973.

Poulantzas, Nicos, 'Internationalization of Capitalist Relations and the Nation-State', *Economy and Society* 3, 2 (1974): 145-79.

Poulantzas, Nicos A., *State, Power, Socialism*. London: New Left Books, 1978.

Powell, Walter W. and Paul J. DiMaggio, eds, *The New Institutionalism in Organizational Analysis*. Chicago: University of Chicago Press, 1991.

Pressman, Jeffrey L. and Aaron B. Wildavsky, *Implementation: How Great Expectations in Washington are Dashed in Oakland*, 3rd ed. Berkeley: University of California Press, 1984 (first published 1973).

Presthus, Robert V., *Elite Accommodation in Canadian Politics*. Cambridge: Cambridge University Press, 1973.

Prichard, J. Robert S., ed., *Crown Corporations in Canada: The Calculus of Instrument Choice*. Toronto: Butterworths, 1983.

Priest, Margot and Aron Wohl, 'The Growth of Federal and Provincial Regulation of Economic Activity 1867-1978' in *Government Regulation: Scope, Growth, Process*, ed. W.T. Stanbury. Montreal: Institute for Research on Public Policy, 1980.

Pritchard, David, 'The News Media and Public Policy Agendas' in *Public Opinion, the Press, and Public Policy*, ed. J.D. Kennamer. Westport: Praeger, 1992.

Pross, A. Paul, *Group Politics and Public Policy*, 2nd ed. Toronto: Oxford University Press, 1992.

Pross, A.P. and Susan McCorquodale, 'The State, Interests, and Policy-Making in the East Coast Fishery' in *Policy Communities and Public Policy in Canada: A Structural Approach*, eds W. Coleman and G. Skogstad. Mississauga, ON: Copp Clark Pitman, 1990.

Pryor, F.L., *Public Expenditures in Communist and Capitalist Nations*. Homewood, IL: R.D. Irwin, 1968.

Przeworski, Adam, 'Proletariat into a Class: The Process of Class Formation' in *Capitalism and Social Democracy*, ed. A. Przeworski. Cambridge: Cambridge University Press, 1985.

Przeworski, Adam, *The State and the Economy Under Capitalism*. Chur, Switzerland: Harwood Academic Publishers, 1990.

Rakoff, Stuart H. and Guenther F. Schaefer, 'Politics, Policy, and Political Science: Theoretical Alternatives', *Politics and Society* 1, 1 (1970): 51-77.

Ramesh, M., 'Economic Globalization and Policy Choices: Singapore', *Governance* 10, 2 (1995): 243-60.

Reagan, Michael D., *Regulation: The Politics of Policy*. Boston: Little Brown, 1987.

Reich, Robert B., ed., *The Power of Public Ideas*. Cambridge, MA: Ballinger, 1987.

Reid, Timothy E., 'The Failure of PPBS: Real Incentives for the 1980s', *Optimum* 10, 4 (1979): 23-37.

Rein, Martin and Lee Rainwater, eds, *Public/Private Interplay in Social Protection: A Comparative Study*. Armonk, NY: M.E. Sharpe, 1986.

Reynolds, Harry W. Jr, 'Public Administration and Policy: Older Perspectives, New Direction', *International Journal of Public Administration* 16, 8 (1993): 1079-103.

Rhodes, R.A.W., 'Power-Dependence, Policy Communities and Intergovernmental Networks', *Public Administration Bulletin* 49 (1984): 4-31.

Richardson, Jeremy, Gunnel Gustafsson, and Grant Jordan, 'The Concept of Policy Style' in *Policy Styles in Western Europe*, ed. J.J. Richardson. London: George Allen and Unwin, 1982.

Richardson, J.J., ed., *Privatisation and Deregulation in Canada and Britain*. Aldershot: Dartmouth Pub. Co., 1990.

Richardson, J.J. and A. G. Jordan, *Governing Under Pressure: The Policy Process in a Post-Parliamentary Democracy*. Oxford: Martin Robertson, 1979.

Richardson, Jeremy J., William A. Maloney, and Wolfgang Rudig, 'The Dynamics of Policy Change: Lobbying and Water Privatization', *Public Administration* 70, 2 (1992): 157-75.

Riker, William H., *The Theory of Political Coalitions*. New Haven: Yale University Press, 1962.

Ripley, Randall B., *Policy Analysis in Political Science*. Chicago: Nelson-Hall, 1985.

Ripley, Randall B. and Grace A. Franklin, *Congress, the Bureaucracy, and Public Policy*, 3rd ed. Homewood, IL: Dorsey Press, 1980.

Rist, Ray C., 'The Preconditions for Learning: Lessons from the Public Sector' in *Can Governments Learn: Comparative Perspectives on Evaluation and Organizational Learning*, eds F.L. Leeuw, R.C. Rist, and R.C. Sonnischen. New Brunswick: Transaction Publishers, 1994.

Rittberger, Volker and Peter Mayer, eds, *Regime Theory and International Relations*. Oxford: Clarendon Press, 1993

Rochefort, David A. and Roger W. Cobb, 'Problem Definition, Agenda Access, and Policy Choice', *Policy Studies Journal* 21, 1 (1993): 56-71.

Rockman, Bert A., 'Minding the State—Or a State of Mind? Issues in the Comparative Conceptualization of the State', *Comparative Political Studies* 23, 1 (1990): 25-55.

Roemer, John, ed., *Analytical Marxism*. Cambridge: Cambridge University Press, 1986

Rogers, Harry, 'Management Control in the Public Service', *Optimum* 9, 3 (1978): 14-28.

Rogers, H.G., M.A. Ulrick, and K.L. Traversy, 'Evaluation in Practice: The State of the Art in Canadian Governments', *Canadian Public Administration* 24, 3 (1981): 371-86.

Rose, Richard, 'Comparative Policy Analysis: The Program Approach' in *Comparing Pluralist Democracies: Strains on Legitimacy*, ed. M. Dogan. Boulder: Westview Press, 1988.

Rose, Richard, 'What is Lesson-Drawing?', *Journal of Public Policy* 11, 1 (1991): 3-30.

Rose, Richard, *Lesson-Drawing in Public Policy: A Guide to Learning Across Time and Space*. Chatham: Chatham House, 1993.

Rowley, C.K., 'The Political Economy of the Public Sector' in *Perspectives on Political Economy*, ed. R.J.B. Jones. London: Pinter, 1983.

Ruggie, John Gerard, 'International Responses to Technology: Concepts and Trends', *International Organization* 29, 3 (1975): 557-83.

Russell, Peter H., 'The Effect of a Charter of Rights on the Policy-Making Role of Canadian Courts', *Canadian Public Administration* 25 (1982): 1-33.

Sabatier, Paul A., 'Social Movements and Regulatory Agencies: Toward a More Adequate—and Less Pessimistic—Theory of "Clientele Capture"', *Policy Sciences* 6 (1975): 301-42.

Sabatier, Paul A., 'The Acquisition and Utilization of Technical Information by Administrative Agencies', *Administrative Science Quarterly* 23, 3 (1978): 396-417.

Sabatier, Paul A., 'Knowledge, Policy-Oriented Learning, and Policy Change', *Knowledge: Creation, Diffusion, Utilization* 8, 4 (1987): 649-92.

Sabatier, Paul A., 'An Advocacy Coalition Framework of Policy Change and the Role of Policy-Oriented Learning Therein', *Policy Sciences* 21, 2/3 (1988): 129-68.

Sabatier, Paul A., 'Toward Better Theories of the Policy Process', *PS: Political Science and Politics* 24, 2 (1991): 144-56.

Sabatier, Paul A., 'Top-down and Bottom-up Approaches to Implementation Research' in *The Policy Process: A Reader*, ed. M. Hill. London: Harvester Wheatsheaf, 1993.

Sabatier, Paul A. and Hank C. Jenkins-Smith, 'The Advocacy Coalition Framework: Assessment, Revisions, and Implications for Scholars and Practitioners' in *Policy Change and Learning: An Advocacy Coalition Approach*, eds. P.A. Sabatier and H.C. Jenkins-Smith. Boulder: Westview, 1993.

Sabatier, Paul A. and Hank C. Jenkins-Smith, eds, *Policy Change and Learning: An Advocacy Coalition Approach*. Boulder: Westview, 1993.

Sabatier, Paul A. and D.A. Mazmanian, *Effective Policy Implementation*. Lexington: Lexington Books, 1981.

Salamon, Lester M., 'Rethinking Public Management: Third-Party Government and the Changing Forms of Government Action', *Public Policy* 29, 3 (1981): 255-75.

Salamon, Lester M., 'Of Market Failure, Voluntary Failure, and Third-Party Government' in *Shifting the Debate: Public/Private Sector Relations in the Modern Welfare State*, eds Susan A. Ostrander and Stuart Langhorn. New Brunswick, NJ: Transaction Books, 1989: 31.

Salamon, Lester M., ed., *Beyond Privatization: The Tools of Government Action*. Washington, DC: Urban Institute, 1989.

Salamon, Lester M., 'The Changing Tools of Government Action: An Overview' in *Beyond Privatization: The Tools of Government Action*, ed. L.M. Salamon. Washington, DC: Urban Institute, 1989.

Salamon, Lester M., 'Conclusion: Beyond Privatization' in *Beyond Privatization: The Tools of Government Action*, ed. L.M. Salamon. Washington, DC: Urban Institute, 1989.

Salamon, Lester M. and Michael S. Lund, 'The Tools Approach: Basic Analytics' in *Beyond Privatization: The Tools of Government Action*, ed. L.S. Salamon. Washington, DC: Urban Institute, 1989.

Salisbury, Robert H., 'An Exchange Theory of Interest Groups', *Midwest Journal of Political Science* 13, 1 (1969): 1-32.

Salisbury, Robert H. et al., 'Who Works with Whom? Interest Group Alliances and Opposition', *American Political Science Review* 81, 4 (1987): 1217-34.

Salter, Liora, *Public Inquiries in Canada*. Ottawa: Science Council of Canada, 1981.

Samuels, Warren J., '"Truth" and "Discourse" in the Social Construction of Economic Reality: An Essay on the Relation of Knowledge to Socioeconomic Policy', *Journal of Post-Keynesian Economics* 13, 4 (1991): 511-24.

Sartori, Giovanni, 'Concept Misformation in Comparative Politics', *American Political Science Review* 64, 4 (1970): 1033-53.

Savas, E.S., *Alternatives for Delivering Public Services: Toward Improved Performance*. Boulder: Westview, 1977.

Savas, E.S., *Privatization: The Key to Better Government*. Chatham: Chatham House Publishers, 1987.

Savoie, Donald J., *The Politics of Public Spending in Canada*. Toronto: University of Toronto Press, 1990.

Savoie, Donald J. and Gerard Veilleux, 'Kafka's Castle: The Treasury Board of Canada Revisited', *Canadian Public Administration* 31, 4 (1988): 517-38.

Schattschnieder, E.E., *The Semisovereign People: A Realist's View of Democracy in America*. New York: Holt, Rinehart and Winston, 1960.

Schmitter, Phillipe C., 'Modes of Interest Intermediation and Models of Societal Change in Western Europe', *Comparative Political Studies* 10, 1 (1977): 7-38.

Schmitter, P.C., 'Reflections on Where the Theory of Neo-Corporatism Has Gone and Where the Praxis of Neo-Corporatism May be Going' in *Patterns of Corporatist Policy-Making*, eds G. Lehmbruch and P.C. Schmitter. London: Sage, 1982.

Schmitter, Phillipe C., 'Neo-corporatism and the State' in *The Political Economy of Corporatism*, ed. W. Grant. London: Macmillan, 1985.

Schneider, Anne L. and Helen Ingram, 'Policy Design: Elements, Premises, and Strategies' in *Policy Theory and Policy Evaluation: Concepts, Knowledge, Causes, and Norms*, ed. S.S. Nagel. New York: Greenwood Press, 1990.

Schneider, Anne and Helen Ingram, 'Behavioural Assumptions of Policy Tools', *Journal of Politics* 52, 2 (1990): 510-29.

Schneider, Joseph W., 'Social Problems Theory: The Constructionist View', *Annual Review of Sociology* 11 (1985): 209-29.

Schultz, Richard and Alan Alexandroff, *Economic Regulation and the Federal System*. Toronto: University of Toronto Press, 1985.

Schultze, Charles L., *The Public Use of Private Interests*. Washington: Brookings Institution, 1977.

Searing, Donald D., 'Roles, Rules, and Rationality in the New Institutionalism', *American Political Science Review* 85, 4 (1991): 1239-60.

Sechrest, Lee, 'Social Science and Social Policy: Will Our Numbers Ever be Good Enough?' in *Social Science and Social Policy*, eds R.L. Shotland and M.M. Mark. Beverly Hills: Sage, 1985.

Self, Peter, *Political Theories of Modern Government: Its Role and Reform*. London: Allen and Unwin, 1985.

Shapiro, Michael J., *Language and Political Understanding: The Politics of Discursive Practices*. New Haven: Yale University Press, 1981.

Sharkansky, Ira, 'Constraints on Innovation in Policy Making: Economic Development and Political Routines' in *Toward a New Public Administration: The Minnowbrook Perspective*, ed. F. Marini. Scranton: Chandler, 1971.

Sharpe, L.J., 'Central Coordination and the Policy Network', *Political Studies* 33, 3 (1985): 361-81.

Shotland, R. Lance and Melvin M. Mark, *Social Science and Social Policy*. Beverly Hills: Sage, 1985.

Shrivastava, Paul, 'A Typology of Organizational Learning Systems', *Journal of Management Studies* 20, 1 (1983): 7-28.

Simeon, Richard, 'Studying Public Policy', *Canadian Journal of Political Science* 9, 4 (1976): 548-80.

Simon, Herbert A., 'The Proverbs of Administration', *Public Administration Review* 6, 1 (1946): 53-67.

Simon, Herbert A., 'A Behavioral Model of Rational Choice', *Quarterly Journal of Economics* 69, 1 (1955): 99-118.

Simon, Herbert A., *Administrative Behavior: A Study of Decision-Making Processes in Administrative Organization*, 2nd ed. New York: Macmillan, 1957.

Simon, Herbert A., *Models of Man, Social and Rational: Mathematical Essays on Rational Human Behavior in a Social Setting*. New York: Wiley, 1957.

Simon, Herbert A., *Reason in Human Affairs*. Stanford: Stanford University Press, 1983.

Simon, Herbert A., 'Bounded Rationality and Organizational Learning', *Organization Science* 2, 1 (1991): 125.

Sjoblom, Gunnar, 'Some Critical Remarks on March and Olsen's Rediscovering Institutions', *Journal of Theoretical Politics* 5, 3 (1993): 397-407.

Skilling, H.G., 'Interest Groups and Communist Politics', *World Politics* 18, 3 (1966): 435-51.

Skocpol, Theda, 'Bringing the State Back In: Strategies of Analysis in Current Research', in *Bringing the State Back In*, eds P.B. Evans, D. Rueschemeyer and T. Skocpol. New York: Cambridge University Press, 1985.

Smith, Gilbert and David May, 'The Artificial Debate Between Rationalist and Incrementalist Models of Decision-Making', *Policy and Politics* 8, 2 (1980): 147-61.

Smith, Martin J., 'Pluralism, Reformed Pluralism and Neopluralism: The Role of Pressure Groups in Policy-Making', *Political Studies* 38 (June 1990): 302-22.

Smith, Martin J., 'Policy Networks and State Autonomy' in *The Political Influence of Ideas: Policy Communities and the Social Sciences*, eds S. Brooks and A.-G. Gagnon. New York: Praeger, 1994.

Smith, Martin J., David Marsh, and David Richards, 'Central Government Departments and the Policy Process', *Public Administration* 71 (Winter 1993): 567-94.

Smith, Roger S., *Tax Expenditures: An Examination of Tax Incentives and Tax Preferences in the Canadian Federal Income Tax System*. Toronto: Canadian Tax Foundation, 1979.

Smith, Thomas B., 'The Policy Implementation Process', *Policy Sciences* 4 (1973): 197-209.

Smith, Thomas B., 'Evaluating Development Policies and Programmes in the Third World', *Public Administration and Development* 5, 2 (1985): 129-44.

Spector, Malcolm and John I. Kitsuse, *Constructing Social Problems*. New York: Aldine de Gruyter, 1987.

Spitzer, Robert J., ed., *Media and Public Policy*. Westport, CT: Praeger, 1993.

Sproule-Jones, M., 'Institutions, Constitutions, and Public Policies: A Public-Choice Overview' in *The Politics of Canadian Public Policy*, eds M. Atkinson and M. Chandler. Toronto: University of Toronto Press, 1983.

Sproule-Jones, Mark, 'Multiple Rules and the "Nesting" of Public Policies', *Journal of Theoretical Politics* 1, 4 (1989): 459-77.

Stanbury, W.T., *Business-Government Relations in Canada: Grappling with Leviathan*. Toronto: Methuen, 1986.

Stanbury, W.T. and Jane Fulton, 'Suasion as a Governing Instrument' in *How Ottawa Spends 1984: The New Agenda*, ed. A. Maslove. Toronto: Lorimer, 1984.

Stark, Andrew, '"Political-Discourse" Analysis and the Debate Over Canada's Lobbying Legislation', *Canadian Journal of Political Science* 25, 3 (1992): 513-34.

Starr, Paul, 'The Meaning of Privatization' in *Privatization and the Welfare State*, eds S.B. Kamerman and A.J. Kahn. Princeton: Princeton University Press, 1989.

Starr, Paul, 'The Limits of Privatization' in *Privatization and Deregulation in Global Perspective*, eds D.J. Gayle and J.N. Goodrich. New York: Quorum Books, 1990.

Starr, Paul, 'The New Life of the Liberal State: Privatization and the Restructuring of State-Society Relations' in *The Political Economy of Public Sector Reform and Privatization*, eds E.N. Suleiman and J. Waterbury. Boulder: Westview Press, 1990.

Stewart, Jenny, 'Corporatism, Pluralism and Political Learning: A Systems Approach', *Journal of Public Policy* 12, 3 (1992): 243-56.

Stigler, George J., *The Citizen and the State: Essays on Regulation*. Chicago: University of Chicago Press, 1975.

Stokey, Edith and Richard Zeckhauser, *A Primer for Policy Analysis*. New York: W.W. Norton, 1978.

Stone, Deborah A., *Policy Paradox and Political Reason*. Glenview: Scott, Foresman, 1988.

Stone, Deborah A., 'Causal Stories and the Formation of Policy Agendas', *Political Science Quarterly* 104, 2 (1989): 281-300.

Suchman, Edward A., *Evaluative Research: Principles and Practices in Public Service and Social Action Programs*. New York: Russell Sage Foundation, 1967.

Suchman, E.A, *Social Sciences in Policy-Making*. Paris: Organization for Economic Co-operation and Development, 1979.

Suleiman, Ezra N. and John Waterbury, eds, *Political Economy of Public Sector Reform and Privatization*. Boulder, CO: Westview Press, 1990.

Surrey, Stanley S., 'Tax Expenditure Analysis: The Concept and Its Uses', *Canadian Taxation* 1, 2 (1979): 3-14.

Surrey, Stanley S. and Paul R. McDaniel, *Tax Expenditures*. Cambridge: Harvard University Press, 1985.

Sutherland, Sharon L., 'The Public Service and Policy Development' in *Governing Canada: Institutions and Public Policy*, ed. M. Michael Atkinson. Toronto: Harcourt Brace Jovanovich, 1993.

Swain, J.W., 'Public Administrators and Policy Analysis: Beyond Political Science', *International Journal of Public Administration* 16, 8 (1993): 1153-75.

Taylor, Andrew J., *Trade Unions and Politics: A Comparative Introduction*. Basingstoke: Macmillan, 1989.

Thelan, Kathleen and Sven Steinmo, 'Historical Institutionalism in Comparative Perspective' in *Structuring Politics: Historical Institutionalism in Comparative Analysis*, eds S. Steinmo, K. Thelen, and F. Longstreth. Cambridge: Cambridge University Press, 1992.

Therborn, Goran, 'The Rule of Capital and the Rise of Democracy', *New Left Review* 103 (1977): 3-41.

Therborn, Goran, 'Neo-Marxist, Pluralist, Corporatist, Statist Theories and the Welfare State' in *The State in Global Perspective*, ed. A. Kazancigil. UK: Gower, 1986.

Therborn, Goran, 'Welfare States and Capitalist Markets', *Acta Sociologica* 30, 3-4 (1987): 237-54.

Thomas, Paul, 'Public Administration and Expenditure Management', *Canadian Public Administration* 25, 4 (1982): 674-95.

Thompson, E.P., *The Poverty of Theory and Other Essays*. London: Merlin Press, 1978.

Thompson, John B., *Ideology and Modern Culture: Critical Social Theory in the Era of Mass Communication*. Cambridge: Polity, 1990.

Tinbergen, J., *Economic Policy: Principles and Design*. Chicago: Rand McNally, 1967.

Torgerson, Douglas, 'Between Knowledge and Politics: Three Faces Of Policy Analysis', *Policy Sciences* 19, 1 (1986): 33-59.

Trebilcock, Michael J., 'Regulating Service Quality in Professional Markets' in *The Regulation of Quality: Products, Services, Workplaces, and the Environment*, ed. D.N. Dewees. Toronto: Butterworths, 1983.

Trebilcock, M.J. et al., *The Choice of Governing Instrument*. Ottawa: Canadian Government Publication Centre, 1982.

Trebilcock, M.J. and J.R.S. Prichard, 'Crown Corporations in Canada: The Calculus of Instrument Choice' in *Crown Corporations in Canada: The Calculus of Instrument Choice*, ed. J.R.S. Prichard. Toronto: Butterworths, 1983.

Trebilcock, M.J., C.J. Tuohy, and A.D. Wolfson, *Professional Regulation: A Staff Study of Accountancy, Architecture, Engineering, and Law in Ontario Prepared for the Professional Organizations Committee*. Toronto: Ministry of the Attorney General, 1979.

Tribe, Laurence H., 'Policy Science: Analysis or Ideology?' *Philosophy and Public Affairs* 2, 1 (1972): 66-110.

Trigg, Roger, *Understanding Social Science*. Oxford: Basil Blackwell, 1985.

Truman, David R., *The Governmental Process: Political Interests and Public Opinion*. New York: Knopf, 1964.

Tufte, Edward R., *Political Control of the Economy*. Princeton, New Jersey: Princeton University Press, 1978.

Tullock, Gordon, *Private Wants, Public Means: An Economic Analysis of the Desirable Scope of Government*. New York: Basic Books, 1970.

Tullock, Gordon, *The Vote Motive: An Essay in the Economics of Politics, with Applications to the British Economy*. London: IEA, 1976.

Tuohy, Caroline, *Policy and Politics in Canada: Institutionalized Ambivalence*. Philadelphia: Temple University Press, 1992.

Tuohy, C.J. and A.D. Wolfson, 'Self-Regulation: Who Qualifies?' in *The Professions and Public Policy*, eds P. Slayton and M.J. Trebilcock. Toronto: University of Toronto Press, 1978.

Tupper, Allan, 'The State in Business', *Canadian Public Administration* 22, 1 (1979): 124-50.

Tupper, A. and G.B. Doern, 'Public Corporations and Public Policy in Canada' in *Public Corporations and Public Policy in Canada*, eds A. Tupper and G.B. Doern. Montreal: Institute for Research on Public Policy, 1981.

Ulen, Thomas S., 'The Theory of Rational Choice, Its Shortcomings, and the Implications for Public Policy Decision Making', *Knowledge: Creation, Diffusion, Utilization* 12, 2 (1990): 170-98.

Utton, M.A., *The Economics of Regulating Industry*. Oxford: Basil Blackwell, 1986.

Uusitalo, Hannu, 'Comparative Research on the Determinants of the Welfare State: The State of the Art', *European Journal of Political Research* 12, 4 (1984): 403-22.

Van Meerhaeghe, M.A.G., *International Economic Institutions*. Dordrecht: Kluwer, 1992.

van Meter, D. and C. van Horn, 'The Policy Implementation Process: A Conceptual Framework', *Administration and Society* 6, 4 (1975): 445-88.

Van Waarden, Frans, 'Dimensions and Types of Policy Networks', *European Journal of Political Research* 21, 1/2 (1992): 29-52.

Ventriss, Curtis and Jeff Luke, 'Organizational Learning and Public Policy: Towards a Substantive Perspective', *American Review of Public Administration* 18, 4 (1988): 337-58.

Vining, Aidan R. and David L. Weimer, 'Government Supply and Government Production Failure: A Framework Based on Contestability', *Journal of Public Policy* 10, 1 (1990): 1-22.

Vogel, David, *National Styles of Regulation: Environmental Policy in Great Britain and the United States*. Ithaca: Cornell University Press, 1986.

von Beyme, Klaus, 'Neo-Corporatism: A New Nut in an Old Shell?' *International Political Science Review* 4, 2 (1983): 173-96.

von Beyme, Klaus, 'Do Parties Matter? The Impact of Parties on the Key Decisions in the Political System', *Government and Opposition* 19, 1 (1984): 5-29.

Wade, H.W.R., 'Anglo-American Administrative Law: Some Reflections', *Law Quarterly Review* 81 (1965): 357-79.

Wade, H.W.R., 'Anglo-American Administrative Law: More Reflections', *Law Quarterly Review* 82 (1966): 226-52.

Wagner, Peter et al., 'The Policy Orientation: Legacy and Promise' in *Social Sciences and Modern States: National Experiences and Theoretical Crossroads*, eds P. Wagner, C. Weiss, B. Wittrock, and H. Wollmann. Cambridge: Cambridge University Press, 1991.

Walker, Jack, 'Introduction: Policy Communities as Global Phenomena', *Governance* 2, 1 (1989): 1-4.

Walker, Jack L., 'The Diffusion of Knowledge and Policy Change: Toward A Theory of Agenda Setting', Chicago: Paper Presented to the Annual Meeting of the American Political Science Association, 1974.

Walker, Jack L., 'The Origins and Maintenance of Interest Groups in America', *American Political Science Review* 77, 2 (1983): 390-406.

Walsh, James E., 'International Constraints and Domestic Choices: Economic Convergence and Exchange Rate Policy in France and Italy', *Political Studies* XLII (1994): 243-58.

Weaver, R. Kent, 'The Politics of Blame Avoidance', *Journal of Public Policy* 6, 4 (1986): 371-98.

Weaver, R. Kent and Bert A. Rockman. 'Assessing the Effects of Institutions' in *Do Institutions Matter? Government Capabilities in the United States and Abroad*, eds R.K. Weaver and B.A. Rockman. Washington, DC: Brookings Institution, 1993.

Weaver, R. Kent and Bert A. Rockman, 'When and How do Institutions Matter?' in *Do Institutions Matter? Government Capabilities in the United States and Abroad*, eds R.K. Weaver and B.A. Rockman. Washington, DC: Brookings Institution, 1993.

Webber, David J., 'The Distribution and Use of Policy Knowledge in the Policy Process' in *Advances in Policy Studies Since 1950*, eds W.N. Dunn and R.M. Kelly. New Brunswick, NJ: Transaction Publishers, 1992.

Weber, Max, *Economy and Society: An Outline of Interpretive Sociology*. Berkeley: University of California Press, 1978.

Weimer, David L. and Aidan R. Vining, *Policy Analysis: Concepts and Practice*, 2nd ed. Englewood Cliffs: Prentice Hall, 1992.

Weir, Margaret, 'Ideas and the Politics of Bounded Innovation,' in *Structuring Politics: Historical Institutionalism in Comparative Analysis*, eds S. Steinmo, K. Thelen, and F. Longstreth. Cambridge: Cambridge University Press, 1992.

Weiss, Andrew and Edward Woodhouse, 'Reframing Incrementalism: A Constructive Response to Critics', *Policy Sciences* 25, 3 (1992): 255-73.

Weiss, Carol H., 'Research for Policy's Sake: The Enlightenment Function of Social Science Research', *Policy Analysis* 3, 4 (1977): 531-45.

Weiss, Carol H., *Using Social Research in Public Policy Making*. Lexington: Lexington Books, 1977.

Weiss, Janet A. and Mary Tschirhart, 'Public Information Campaigns as Policy Instruments', *Journal of Policy Analysis and Management* 13, 1 (1994): 82-119.

Wendt, Alexander E., 'The Agent-Structure Problem in International Relations Theory', *International Organization* 41, 3 (1987): 335-70.

Wengert, N., 'Citizen Participation: Practice in Search of a Theory' in *Natural Resources for a Democratic Society: Public Participation in Decision-Making*, ed. A.E. Utton. Boulder: Westview, 1976.

Wildavsky, Aaron, 'Rescuing Policy Analysis From PPBS', *Public Administration Review* March-April (1969): 189-202.

Wildavsky, Aaron B., *Speaking Truth to Power: The Art and Craft of Policy Analysis*. Boston: Little-Brown, 1979.

Wilensky, H.L., *The Welfare State and Equality: Structural and Ideological Roots of Public Expenditures*. Berkeley: University of California Press, 1975.

Wilensky, Harold L. et al., *Comparative Social Policy: Theories, Methods, Findings*. Berkeley: Institute of International Studies, 1985.

Wilensky, Harold L. and Lowell Turner, *Democratic Corporatism and Policy Linkages: The Interdependence of Industrial, Labor-Market, Incomes, and Social Policies in Eight Countries*. Berkeley: University of California International & Area Studies, 1987.

Wilks, Stephen and Maurice Wright, 'Conclusion: Comparing Government-Industry Relations: States, Sectors, and Networks' in *Comparative Government-Industry Relations: Western Europe, the United States, and Japan*, eds S. Wilks and M. Wright. Oxford: Clarendon Press, 1987.

Williams, Gwyn, 'The Concept of "Egemonia" in the Thought of Antonio Gramsci: Some Notes on Interpretation', *Journal of the History of Ideas* 21 (1960): 586-99.

Williamson, Oliver E., *The Economic Institutions of Capitalism: Firms, Markets, Relational Contracting*. New York: Free Press, 1985.

Williamson, Peter J., *Corporatism in Perspective: An Introductory Guide to Corporatist Theory*. London: Sage, 1989.

Wilson, Graham K., *Business And Politics: A Comparative Introduction* 2nd ed. London: Macmillan, 1990.

Wilson, Graham K., *Interest Groups*. Oxford: Basil Blackwell, 1990.

Wilson, James Q., 'The Politics of Regulation' in *Social Responsibility and the Business Predicament*, ed. J.W. McKie. Washington: Brookings Institution, 1974.

Wilson, V. Seymour 'The Role of Royal Commissions and Task Forces' in *The Structures of Policy-Making in Canada*, eds G.B. Doern and P. Aucoin. Toronto: Macmillan, 1971.

Winden, Frans A.A.M. Van, 'The Economic Theory of Political Decision-Making' in *Public Choice*, ed. J. van den Broeck. Dordrecht: Kluwer, 1988.

Winkler, J.T., 'Corporatism', *European Journal of Sociology* 17, 1 (1976): 100-36.

Winter, Soren, 'Integrating Implementation Research' in *Implementation and the Policy Process: Opening up the Black Box*, eds D.J. Palumbo and D.J. Calista. New York: Greenwood Press, 1990.

Wolf, Charles Jr, *Markets or Governments: Choosing Between Imperfect Alternatives*. Cambridge: MIT Press, 1988.

Wolf, Charles Jr, 'Markets and Non-Market Failures: Comparison and Assessment', *Journal of Public Policy* 7, 1 (1987): 43-70.

Wolf, Charles Jr, 'A Theory of Nonmarket Failure: Framework for Implementation Analysis', *Journal of Law and Economics* 22, 1 (1979): 107-39.

Wolfe, Joel D., 'Democracy and Economic Adjustment: A Comparative Analysis of Political Change' in *The Politics of Economic Adjustment*, eds R.E. Foglesong and J.D. Wolfe. New York: Greenwood Press, 1989.

Woodiwiss, Anthony, *Social Theory After Postmodernism: Rethinking Production, Law and Class*. London: Pluto Press, 1990.

Woodside, K., 'Tax Incentives vs. Subsidies: Political Considerations in Governmental Choice', *Canadian Public Policy* 5, 2 (1979): 248-56.

Woodside, K., 'The Political Economy of Policy Instruments: Tax Expenditures and Subsidies in Canada' in *The Politics of Canadian Public Policy*, eds M. Atkinson and M. Chandler. Toronto: University of Toronto Press, 1983.

Woodside, K., 'Policy Instruments and the Study of Public Policy', *Canadian Journal of Political Science* 19, 4 (1986): 775-93.

Wright, Erik Olin, *Classes*. London: Verso, 1985.

Wright, Erik Olin, ed., *The Debate on Classes*. London: Verso, 1989.

Wright, Maurice, 'Policy Community, Policy Network and Comparative Industrial Policies', *Political Studies* 36, 4 (1988): 593-612.

Wuthnow, Robert, ed., *Between States and Markets: The Voluntary Sector in Comparative Perspective*. Princeton: Princeton University Press, 1991.

Yanow, Dvoram, 'Tackling the Implementation Problem: Epistemological Issues in *Implementation Research'* in *Implementation and the Policy Process: Opening up the Black Box*, eds D.J. Palumbo and D.J. Calista. New York: Greenwood Press, 1990.

Yarbrough, Beth V. and Robert M. Yarbrough, 'International Institutions and the New Economics of Organization', *International Organization* 44, 2 (1990): 235-59.

Zeckhauser, Richard, 'Procedures for Valuing Lives', *Public Policy* 23, 4 (1975): 419-64.

Zeigler, L. Harmon, *Interest Groups in American Society*. Englewood Cliffs: Prentice Hall, 1964.

Index